ALSO BY PETER DUFFY

The Killing of Major Denis Mahon:
A Mystery of Old Ireland

The Bielski Brothers:
The True Story of Three Men Who Defied the Nazis,
Built a Village in the Forest, and Saved 1,200 Jews

DOUBLE AGENT

THE FIRST HERO OF WORLD WAR II
AND HOW THE FBI OUTWITTED
AND DESTROYED A NAZI SPY RING

PETER DUFFY

SCRIBNER

New York   London   Toronto   Sydney   New Delhi

SCRIBNER
A Division of Simon & Schuster, Inc.
1230 Avenue of the Americas
New York, NY 10020

First Scribner hardcover edition July 2014

SCRIBNER and design are registered trademarks of The Gale Group, Inc.,
used under license by Simon & Schuster, Inc., the publisher of this work.

For information about special discounts for bulk purchases,
please contact Simon & Schuster Special Sales at 1-866-506-1949
or business@simonandschuster.com.

The Simon & Schuster Speakers Bureau can bring authors to your live event.
For more information or to book an event, contact the Simon & Schuster Speakers Bureau
at 1-866-248-3049 or visit our website at www.simonspeakers.com.

Jacket design by Laurie Carkeet
Jacket photograph courtesy of the Library of Congress

Manufactured in the United States of America

1   3   5   7   9   10   8   6   4   2

Library of Congress Control Number: 2013050801

ISBN 978-1-4516-6795-0
ISBN 978-1-4516-6797-4 (ebook)

To Laura

CONTENTS

DOUBLE AGENT

PROLOGUE

I have everything I ever wished for, and Germany doesn't appeal to me a bit.

—Bill Sebold, in a letter to FBI special agent
Jim Ellsworth, August 9, 1946

In the early afternoon of December 11, 1941, Berlin time, Adolf Hitler mounted the rostrum in the Reichstag and delivered an eighty-eight-minute address that cataloged the sins of President Franklin Roosevelt (an "unsophisticated warmonger" who was "mentally unsound") and praised the Japanese attack on Pearl Harbor of four days earlier "as an act of deliverance" that "all of us, the German people and, I believe, all other decent people around the world as well," regard with "deep appreciation." The Führer took note of "the insulting attacks and rude statements by this so-called president against me personally," making particular mention of FDR's barb that he was a "gangster." "This term did not originate in Europe, where such characters are uncommon, but in America," he said to the delight of the deputies, assorted Nazi dignitaries, and honored Japanese guests. But the loudest cheers came when Hitler made clear that the purpose of his speech was to declare war on the United States, his voice suddenly drowned out by raucous applause that escalated into a standing ovation.

Late in the evening on the following day, Brooklyn time, a jury of nine men and three women filed into a packed courtroom in the old federal building on Washington Street. At a few minutes before midnight, the jury's foreman, Edward A. Logan, stood before the hushed assemblage and read guilty verdicts against the fourteen out of thirty-three Nazi spies who hadn't already confessed to their membership in what was known as the Duquesne Spy Ring, still to this day the largest espionage case in American history. The proceeding was unmarred by any disruption. "The defendants took the verdicts stoically, for the most part," wrote the *Times*. Judge Mortimer W. Byers then thanked Logan and his fellow jurors for their service. "It will readily appear," he said, "that you have rendered a very substantial contribution to the welfare of the country which you and I hold very dear." And so they had.

This, the first US victory of World War II, would've been impossible without one man whose contribution to the war effort has never been recognized, William G. Sebold. In a culture that has come to celebrate even the most tangential representation of the Greatest Generation, his identity has remained mysterious, his picture never published. By 1951, Sebold had "lapsed into an obscurity which has been protected ever since by the FBI," according to a magazine that used a pseudonym to describe him. "All we know is that somewhere in the U.S. today is a tall, gaunt, middle-aged man to whom each native-born American can well doff his hat in love and respect," neglecting to mention that the non-native-born citizen owed him a debt of gratitude, too. When Sebold died in February 1970, no obituary or death notice appeared in the newspapers. A pivotal figure in America's confrontation with Nazism had been forgotten.

■　■　■

PROLOGUE

In the years before the formal commencement of hostilities, Hitler's agents were active in New York. They were a collection of ideologues, opportunists, dupes, adventurers, thugs, sophisticates, poseurs, patriots, seductresses, lackeys, and sympathizers. Most (but not all) were German immigrants who would come to be associated in the public mind (not always unfairly) with a single neighborhood of upper Manhattan, the home base of a nationwide movement of uniform-wearing Nazis whose rallies and marches were a constant source of media fascination. Dwelling within this community of the like-minded were a handful of individuals with the genuine talent to provide meaningful assistance to the German war machine. Few today realize that a Bavarian-born immigrant living in Queens, Hermann W. Lang, succeeded in stealing the plans for America's greatest prewar secret, a precious instrument of mythic reputation designed to turn modern airplanes into bomb-dropping systems of unprecedented accuracy, a brazen act of thievery that represents the most significant intelligence coup of the Third Reich.

The spies of the thirties were initially able to conduct their work without worry of detection because the US government, focused on remedying economic misery in a period of rigid isolationism, hadn't assigned any agency to root them out. The story among the Soviet agents was that you could walk down Broadway wearing a sign identifying yourself as a spy and still not get caught. It took a botched investigation into a portion of the Nazi network in New York by an unprepared FBI to convince President Roosevelt that J. Edgar Hoover should be empowered to become the nation's first modern spymaster. Already a national celebrity for directing his "G-men" in a tommy-gun-assisted crusade against the John Dillingers and Pretty Boy Floyds of the early Depression, Hoover was given the authority to launch covert investigations against "those who reflect in their pernicious activities the desires of enemy modes of thought and action," as he said in a speech on October 24, 1939, less than two months after Nazi Germany's invasion of Poland marked the beginning of the war in Europe.

But Hoover's FBI couldn't rectify the failure to capture the most destructive Nazi agents in New York—and prove that it had the ability to construct a counterespionage operation of sufficient expertise—without Bill Sebold, a naturalized American of German birth who was both guileless and headstrong. In early 1939, he made the mistake of leaving Manhattan and returning to his mother's home in the Reich just as Hitler was stepping up his march to war. Through "a strange set of circumstances," as a US diplomat put it, Sebold was coerced into the German espionage service and sent to the United States, accepting the assignment "knowing that he would never go through with it, but knowing that he had to do something in order to get out of Germany alive," said the FBI. Upon his arrival in New York, he agreed to become the first double agent in Bureau history, the central figure in a pioneering undercover operation that steadily grew in size and sophistication, its expansion enabled by the Germans' willingness to allow him to reach into an ever-widening circle of Hitler's underground.

Under the guidance of the bespectacled special agent assigned to be his handler, Sebold proved to be a gifted improviser and tireless worker possessed of the fortitude to overcome his anxieties and face down some of the most ominous characters in the city. Since neutrality laws and political opposition prevented the Roosevelt administration from providing even limited military assistance to the Allied cause in Western Europe, the case represented our most consequential fight against Fascist aggression during the pivotal years of 1940 and 1941. The double agent, the skilled FBI men brought in from across the country to work with him, and even Hoover himself were among those honored few Americans who actually did something to stop Hitler at a time when national figures such as Charles Lindbergh were arguing for rapprochement. The thirty-three convictions ensured that the enemy could not call upon a small army of embedded loyalists once America joined the war and mobilized its full strength against the Axis. In February 1945, when the death of Nazi Germany was all but guaranteed, the *New York Times* said the "elimination of this organization, which had extensive ramifications, placed a decisive check on German espionage operations, from which it has found it difficult to recover." The Manhattan Project to create our greatest *wartime* secret, the atomic bomb, would be infiltrated by Soviet spies not Nazi ones.

Sebold became a particularly American kind of hero. He was an immigrant with a less-than-perfect grasp of English who stood in opposition to malignant beliefs from back home that were infecting his ethnic community. He was a brave man forced to endure the charge that he was a traitor to his own people because he regarded his oath of allegiance to the United States, taken when he became a citizen in 1936, as "a sacred thing," in his description. When one of the accused spies called him a "son of a bitch" in a voice loud enough to be heard throughout the Brooklyn courtroom, an assistant prosecutor approached the bench and confided to the judge, "This Sebold is the kind of a man that throws that kind of thing off like a duck throws water off." Judge Byers agreed. "Of course he has shown that he has taken his courage right in his hands in this whole thing," he said out of the hearing of the jury, press, and spectators. "Probably it is nothing new to him to hear people say those things, speak of him that way, but of course it is very distressing from the standpoint of decorum that that should be observed in the courtroom."

"As you know," FBI assistant director D. M. Ladd told Hoover in a memo on December 17, 1945, "Sebold gave us the most outstanding case in the Bureau's history."

CHAPTER ONE

THE OBJECT
OF THE BOMBARDMENT

It is only a question of moral steadfastness and boldness of spirit, imagination, and determination if we are to achieve the development of the air force into a weapon which will command the air.

—Lieutenant General Walter Wever,
chief of staff of the Luftwaffe,
November 1, 1935

During the early years of Adolf Hitler's dictatorship, the Nazi state had few greater priorities than its crash program of aerial rearmament that sought to build as many planes as the revived German aviation industry could churn out. The Führer wanted to throw a shield over the country so a more general war-preparation campaign could be completed, part of his goal to keep his enemies at bay as he prepared to lead a battle "not for an adjustment of boundaries" but to secure "so much land and ground that the future receives back many times the blood shed," as he said in 1928. Even though only about eight hundred aircraft were operationally ready for duty when the air force's existence was announced to the world in March 1935, a blatant violation of the terms of the Treaty of Versailles banning all but a nominal military force, Hitler boasted to visiting British officials that his Luftwaffe was already the equal of the Royal Air Force. His bluff played upon now-prevalent fears about the devastation that aerial bombardment would wreak in the modern era. Since "no power on earth" could protect the "man on the street" from "being bombed, whatever people may tell him," as former (and future) British prime minister Stanley Baldwin said in the House of Commons in 1932, the nation with both the ability and inclination to launch an all-out assault from the skies was one to be reckoned with on the world's stage. "The bomber will always get through," Baldwin warned, a comment that encapsulated the thinking of the era.

The emergent symbol of Nazi might went to war for the first time in July 1936, giving Air Marshal Hermann Göring "an opportunity to try out my young air force," as he said at the Nuremberg trials. The Nazi air fleet joined the Spanish Civil War on the side of the Nationalists led by General Francisco Franco in their violent uprising against the democratically elected Republican (or Loyalist) government that included Communists in its coalition of left-wing parties, a consequence of Moscow's decision to instruct its adherents throughout the world to participate in united or popular fronts with "fellow travelers" against the Fascist common enemy. From late July until October, the Germans played a central role in airlifting twenty thousand Nationalist soldiers from Spanish Morocco to the Spanish mainland, providing a lifeline to the struggling Fascist forces during the early months of the war. By September, the Luftwaffe was conducting its first low-level attacks in support of Nationalist troops and finding middling success in the Madrid region, where the Republican government was relying on the assistance of *its* most formidable foreign ally, the Soviet Union, which had sent enough aircraft and pilots to gain air superiority over the capital. During these days Nationalist general Emilio Mola announced that four columns would attack Madrid, but the initial blow would be struck by a "fifth column" within, "men now in hiding who will rise and support us the moment we march," a boast that guaranteed a vicious Republican campaign against those who were suspected to be "spies, scare-mongers, defeatists—those who, concealed in their hiding places, are awaiting the order to rush out into the streets . . . the *quinta columna facciosa.*" Over one month in late 1936, some two thousand Nationalist-supporting prisoners, including military officers, Catholic clergy, and white-collar professionals, were loaded onto buses, transported to the villages of Paracuellos del Jarama and Torrejón de Ardoz on Madrid's outskirts, and executed by Communists and their Anarchist auxiliaries, likely at the instigation of Soviet advisers, who were well practiced in the art of liquidating state enemies.

Frustrated by the stalemate, the German high command decided to send a larger force to carry out aerial assaults that would be lethal enough to help Franco but not so offensive as to spark a regional war that Germany wasn't yet equipped to fight. With five thousand personnel and a hundred planes, the Luftwaffe's Condor Legion deployed to northern Spain, where it was joined by a smaller number of Italian and Nationalist squadrons. Since the Republicans had mustered only a handful of aircraft to defend northern Spain, the Germans and their allies were given a chance to perform live-fire tests in close to optimal conditions. Beginning in March 1937, the combined air forces launched a vicious campaign against Republican strongholds in the Basque region, and they regarded Basque villages near the front lines as just as eligible for leveling as Basque Army positions, apparently in the belief that the world's first demonstration of carpet bombing wouldn't draw the French or British into the conflict.

Instead, the European powers were cowed, particularly after

word reached the front pages in late April 1937 about the near total destruction of Guernica, a market town of five thousand to seven thousand inhabitants with a resonant place in Basque political history. At about 4:40 p.m. on Monday, April 26, a lone German aircraft, a twin-engine, medium-range bomber designed to release its bombs while flying horizontally, appeared over the undefended town and flew toward its most important military asset, the Rentería Bridge. With explicit orders to knock out the bridge, the plane, likely a Heinkel He 111, dropped its payload wildly off target, striking in and around the plaza in front of the railway station, which, like the rest of the town at the end of that market day, was populated with civilians. Within several minutes, two or three additional medium bombers heading toward the same objective landed a direct blow on the nearby candy factory instead, igniting an inferno that quickly spread to other structures. By the time the next wave of bombers arrived—this time the lumbering trimotor Junkers Ju 52s—Guernica was so full of smoke that "nobody could recognize the streets, bridge, and suburb [on the other side of the bridge]," wrote Condor Legion commander Wolfram Freiherr von Richthofen in his diary. "We therefore dropped the bombs right into the midst of things."

Although some aspects of that day are still in dispute, over the next three hours wave after wave of bombers pummeled the center of the town with upward of fifty tons of highly explosive munitions. In addition, agile fighter planes—including the Heinkel He 51 and the brand-new Messerschmitt Me 109—used mounted machine guns and tossed hand grenades to slaughter civilians and animals (a detail integral to Pablo Picasso's masterpiece) that had fled into open areas outside of town. The total number of dead was likely around 300, less than the Basque government's official claim of 1,654, but the true figure will never be known. The sources agree that about 70 percent of the town's structures were destroyed, although the historic Casa de Juntas parliament building and the sacred tree of liberty in its court-yard, the Guernica Oak, were untouched.

In his famous dispatch that appeared on page 1 of both the *Times* of London and the *New York Times* on April 28, British war correspondent G. L. Steer wrote that the "object of the bombardment seemingly was demoralization of the civil population and destruction of the cradle of the Basque race," establishing the commonplace view that the Germans were conducting an experiment in terror bombing "to study the effects of those officially banned attacks on the civilian population," as a German historian later wrote. The world was aghast to discover that the Germans were not only willing to raze a population center from the air but able to conduct the mission with "scientific thoroughness" that made it a "model demonstration of Nazi efficiency," according to the editorials in the New York papers. "Rebels' Nazi Aces Destroy City, Kill 800" was the front-page headline in the *New York Daily News,* the city's great mass-market tabloid with the largest circulation of any newspaper in the country. "Guernica has taught us what to expect from the Germans," said an official in the British Foreign Office, which might tell us all we need know about the attack's persuasive power.

On April 30, von Richthofen arrived to inspect the carnage, noting in his diary what he apparently didn't know previously, that Guernica occupied an important place in Basque history. He described the "complete annihilation" of the townscape, marveled at the size of the bomb craters visible in the street ("just terrific"), and groused that the Nationalist Army didn't take better advantage of the fact that the "town was completely cut off for at least 24 hours." But the ruins of Guernica exposed a greater problem. The Luftwaffe had failed to eliminate the Republicans' most vital strategic installation, the bridge, because its level-flying bombers lacked an advanced "bombsight" able to guide their cargo, an analog computer with the ability to calculate the tug and countertug of gravity and air resistance that would play upon an explosive device of specific mass and shape as it was released from a particular altitude and velocity. "Germany did not possess a reliable bombsight that would allow a horizontal bomber to hit the target with any degree of accuracy," wrote aircraft manufacturer Ernst Heinkel. The Goerz Visier 219 was useful "only in closely limited areas and after a good deal of practice," according to a bomber group commander. The Air Ministry's Technical Office in Berlin had to devise a way for its warplanes to destroy "choke points" such as the old stone crossing over the Mundaca River, which had indeed allowed for the escape of Fascism's enemies. In the hours after the bombardment, G. L. Steer had watched their "long trek from Guernica to Bilbao in antique, solid-wheeled Basque farm carts drawn by oxen. The carts, piled high with such household possessions as could be saved from the conflagration, clogged the roads all night long."

While the attack on Guernica has come to be justly regarded as a prelude to the horrors that Nazi Germany would inflict upon innocents during World War II, the regime's technicians saw it as further evidence that the Luftwaffe needed to augment its airborne savagery with the ability to achieve basic military objectives. They weren't yet aware that a solution to "the bombsighting problem" could be found at a small plant in lower Manhattan that employed a high percentage of German immigrants.

CHAPTER TWO

THE HIGHEST HUMANITY

Having lived in the United States, subject thought to make use of some of his contacts there for the benefit of the Abwehr.
—FBI report on Nikolaus Ritter,
September 2, 1945

In early 1937, a Wehrmacht officer with a polished manner and a healthy girth was summoned to the Berlin headquarters of the Abwehr, the division of the German armed forces assigned to conduct spy missions on behalf of the army, navy, and air force. Founded in 1921 as a *counter*espionage service in accord with the strictures of Versailles, the Abwehr was undergoing an aggressive expansion, creating conflict and overlap with Nazi police-state institutions such as the SS, SD (its intelligence division), and Gestapo (secret state police), which were forever eager to expand their clandestine activities beyond German borders. Quite to his surprise, the officer, Nikolaus Adolf Fritz Ritter, then thirty-eight, was assigned to found and lead a new office of air intelligence at Abwehrstelle (or Ast) Hamburg, the post with primary authority for military espionage targeting Great Britain and the Americas. Ritter would be responsible for organizing a network of agents to supply the Luftwaffe with "everything that could be procured in terms of technical and military informa-tion . . . to make up for lost time," as he later wrote.

Nicknamed Fatty by at least one of his future spies, Ritter was the pampered scion of an aristocratic family from Lower Saxony, his father a severe college president who exemplified Prussian ideals of honor and duty, his mother a blue-blooded eminence never seen in anything but prim dresses with ankle-length petticoats. Yet the Ritters were a playful bunch, known for marching into the picturesque countryside around the Aller River for afternoon picnics and holding actual pissing contests among the males to see whose stream of urine could fly the farthest. Nikolaus, the oldest of six children, possessed an entitled air that prevented him from taking orders from anyone he regarded as his social inferior. He was schooled at a Prussian military academy, served as an officer during World War I, went to business college after the war, and wound up as a manager of a textile plant in Silesia with 250 employees.

But in the wake of a hyperinflation episode of such phantasmagorical severity that a single American dollar was worth 4.2 trillion marks before it crested, Ritter decided to leave behind the instability of the pre-Nazi Weimar Republic and move to the United States at age twenty-four in 1924. He claimed that after a period of youthful escapades (a cross-country trip with friends in an old Dodge included an extended visit to the Menominee Indian Reservation in Wisconsin) he knuckled down to a "steady, work-filled life" in New York, an assertion that would've been challenged by his wife, an auburn-haired schoolteacher from the backwoods of southeast Alabama whom he wed in 1926. Aurora Evans Ritter, who came from hardy, Bible-preaching stock, worked long hours as an English-language instructor in metropolitan-area schools and minded their two children of American citizenship (Klaus and Katharine) while he supped in private clubs in Manhattan with a circle of eccentric reactionaries who welcomed the rise of Nazism because they were "utterly convinced that Communism was the greatest threat to America and, on that score, they totally agreed with Hitler's policy," he wrote in his 1972 German-language memoir. Mrs. Ritter would recall to her children in later years how he "loved parties and glamour," never sat down to a meal in less than coat and vest, and positively reveled in the image of himself as a lead player in the center of a drama. "He simply could not resist the temptation of adventure," said his daughter, Katharine.

After twelve years during which he developed a near-perfect grasp of idiomatic American English, Ritter returned with his family to Germany, apparently at the invitation of Hitler's military attaché in Washington, Friedrich von Boetticher, who told him that the foreign office of the Armed Forces High Command was interested in his services. Ritter was impressed with Hitler's rise to power, believing that the German people were at last able "to breathe freely because, after so many horrible years of subjugation and unemployment, order and work had returned." By the autumn of 1936, he was living with his wife and children in Bremen and serving as a staff officer for the Wehrmacht. Soon after his surprise assignment to the Abwehr, he was promoted to captain and transferred from the army to the air force. On or about February 1, 1937, he entered the squat gray structure on Sophienterrasse that housed Ast Hamburg and was shown to an office that contained a desk, a chair, a typewriter, and "an empty cupboard," as he later said during a postwar interrogation with British intelligence. He was so disheartened that he immediately asked to be sent back to Bremen, only to be told "to stay and do my best, for I would find it most interesting and satisfying work," he said. A fellow spymaster took pity on him and dropped a gift into his lap. He told him about a man known as Pop, a New Yorker who had sent over technical documents that the Luftwaffe wasn't able to decipher. Pop's package included a note that "assured us that the blueprints were of the utmost importance and that it would be well worth our effort to send somebody over to establish personal contact," Ritter recalled in his memoir.

But any potential mission to America was put aside during the spring and summer of 1937 as Ritter immersed himself in the espionage trade. He was schooled in the latest micropho-tography techniques to create tiny reproductions of documents and in less cutting-edge "invisible ink" methods to disguise secret messages within ostensibly routine letters. He combed English-language newspapers and magazines for news on the air-craft industry (an often fruitful source of information) and took research trips to Luftwaffe installations to learn about the latest advancements. Posing as a glad-handing businessman with an international clientele, he began meeting with potential recruits, first in Germany and then (using fake passports for each coun-try) in Belgium, Holland, and Hungary, and succeeded in find-ing a handful of individuals to infiltrate England. Ritter sought "Germans or people of German origin, although here again we had to be cautious because they were not only a suitable target for us, they were also in the crosshairs of the counterintelligence service of the country in which they lived," he wrote. To his con-tacts, he was known variously as Dr. Rantzau, Dr. Renken, Dr. Weber, Dr. Rheinhardt, Dr. Leonhardt, or Dr. Jantzen. By the fall of 1937, Ritter was given a larger office and a second secretary to handle his increasing volume of work.

As he settled into his new routine, his eyes fell upon one of his clerical assistants, Irmgard von Klitzing, who was just twenty-four, from a prominent lineage that appealed to his grand sense of himself, and a member of the Nazi Party. She, too, was smitten. He "looked so American" as he "shook hands with everybody" and "raced through the hallway in his light-colored raincoat and frightfully bright-gray Stetson hat," she later recalled. Ritter often brought Ms. von Klitzing home for dinner at the family residence on the Alster Canal, and Mrs. Ritter found that she quite enjoyed the young lady's company, oblivious to the fact that she was hosting her successor. The marriage was doomed, not least because Ritter, who was coming to like his new life of glamorous subterfuge, knew he couldn't be comfortable in the military hierarchy while married to a foreigner. His explanation in his memoir was that "as an American" his wife had "no understanding for my kind of work nor for the extraordinary stress to which I was exposed as a result of my duties." When the divorce was "delivered" on November 11, 1937, according to court documentation, it was on the legal grounds of "sexual incompatibility."

On the same day the judgment was issued, Nikolaus Ritter strolled onto the deck of the SS *Bremen*, one of the thirteen ocean liners operated by the North German Lloyd and Hamburg America steamship companies that arrived every few days from Nazi Germany into the busiest port in the world, and "joined other passengers along the railing and admired the always breathtaking silhouette of New York," he wrote. He was gazing upon a truly international capital that was intimately connected to the great conflict between Fascism and Communism. On the far left of the political spectrum, New York was home to the headquarters of the Communist Party USA (35 East Twelfth Street), which boasted about thirty thousand local members who were the organizational energy behind emergent labor unions such as the Transport Workers Union and an endless list of Popular Front organizations (everything from the nationwide American League for Peace and Democracy to the local West Side Mothers for Peace), skillfully fashioning a broad-based coalition for progressivism at a time when the Soviet Union was a nightmare of show trials, purges, and mass shootings.

The streets of the city (or at least *some* of the streets) resonated with the sounds of the anti-Fascist message. Outraged by Mussolini's invasion of Ethiopia, Imperial Japan's continuing assault on China, and the proto-Axis onslaught against the Popular Front government in Spain, activists bellowed from soapboxes in Union Square and key intersections in several (usually Jewish) neighborhoods of Brooklyn and the Bronx and during parades, demonstrations, and picket lines that seemed to be organized anew every day. "The essential thing for a street corner speaker is to work the back-and-forth relationship, the give-and-take, because the audience in a street corner is not one that just stands quietly," said Irving Howe of his days as a young Socialist in the East Bronx. "It participates. It joins in. It heckles." About fifteen hundred volunteers from the city went to Spain to fight for the Abraham Lincoln Brigade at a time when the country was growing *more* isolationist in response to the instability abroad, leading the US Congress to pass, and President Roosevelt to reluctantly sign, neutrality legislation that forbade the sale of armaments to countries at war, which reflected the now-prevalent belief that America had been pulled into the World War by the greed of weapons manufacturers and international bankers. Yet broad support for the far left was hard to come by even in New York. The Irish working class, proud bearers of a revolutionary tradition that still had unfinished business in Northern Ireland, was generally repulsed by the idea of replicating a dictatorship that was murderously opposed to the Church, a position hammered home by steady coverage in the Irish and Catholic papers about atrocities committed by leftists against priests and nuns in Spain and Mexico. In the municipal elections held nine days before Ritter's arrival, the four Communist candidates for City Council were all defeated. When a teenage Joseph Papirofsky, later the theater director Joseph Papp, shook a can of coins seeking donations for radical causes on the subway, he was invariably told by impatient straphangers to "go back to Russia!"

On the farthest right, the picturesque activities of the pro-Nazi Amerikadeutscher Volksbund, or German American Bund, composed almost exclusively of German-born immigrants with less than two decades in the country and presided over by the burly figure of Bundesführer Fritz Kuhn, were on prominent display during the summer and fall of 1937. Reporters were dispatched to write up the "swastika waving, heiling and Hitler praising" engaged in by ever-larger assemblies at its local summer gathering spots, Camp Siegfried in Yaphank, Long Island, and Camp Nordland, at Andover, New Jersey, with Kuhn insisting that the camps were not "maintained for military training and the promotion of subversive aims," but for "the recreation of youngsters of German-American parents and to a lesser extent for the recreation of the parents themselves." In September, the *Chicago Daily Times* published a spectacular series of articles that sought to expose this statement as a lie, detailing how the Bund's true aim was to unite Germans and other Americans of Fascist sympathy into a militaristic front to prepare for the inevitable day when it would be necessary to take up arms against the Jewish-Communist revolutionaries intent on seizing America. The series claimed that the Bund had twenty thousand members in sixty chapters throughout the country, "at least" fifteen summer camps, about a hundred thousand fellow travelers willing to appear at Bund functions, a Nazi-centric indoctrination program for children, and a hard core of "former German army officers . . . expert machine-gunners, aviators and riflemen, some of whom wear on their shirts Iron Crosses awarded for bravery in the World War."

On the Saturday before Election Day in 1937, nine hundred Bundists paraded down East Eighty-Sixth Street, the bustling, neon-lit commercial strip running through the Yorkville neighborhood on the Upper East Side of Manhattan, the more prominent of the two large German enclaves in the city. Wearing steel gray shirts with black ties, Sam Browne belts, and black overseas caps, they goose-stepped past the European-style nightclubs, rowdy beer gardens with singing waiters clad in lederhosen, Viennese cafés, *Apfelstrudel*-dispensing bakeries, and German-language movie houses that made Yorkville a Germanic hub of sybaritic consumption and unrepentant capitalism that didn't seem to conform to the grim vision of National Socialism. The *New York Herald Tribune* reported that "thousands of spectators lifted their arms in the Nazi salute, a few raised clenched fists in Communist salute, and others saluted by raising the right hand with fingers outspread and placing the thumb to the nose." The *Times* said "the heils reached a loud crescendo" at the corner of Eighty-Sixth Street and Second Avenue, the geographical heart of the neighborhood, but "the boos were predominant" by the time the marchers reached Eighty-Sixth and Lexington at the western edge of the German colony.

The Bund officially claimed 17,000 members in the city, a small minority of the 237,588 German-born and 127,169 Austrian-born residents, but anti-Nazi sentiment in the wider German American community was hard to detect outside a small core of Socialists and Communists. A more typical viewpoint was expressed in an op-ed published in the Hitler-neutral *New Yorker Staats-Zeitung* in November, which took care to praise certain unnamed "Reich Germans" for seeking "to make German-Americans understand the new Germany better" before cautioning them to "not forget that they are guests in a foreign land, whose institutions and laws offer them protection as well as cultural and material advantages." A general "Nazi feeling" existed in outer-borough Ridgewood, which was home to a hundred thousand German Americans and straddled the unmarked Brooklyn-Queens border roughly along the path of the elevated subway lines. It "comes from pride in the way Germany has regained a dominant position in Europe," a neighborhood leader told the *New York Post*. "How many do I estimate are really Nazis? Five percent. Not more than 5 percent here are radicals—Nazis." The *Chicago Daily Times* reporter found that outspoken talk about Hitler was generally avoided in the tourist-friendly clubs along Eighty-Sixth Street in Yorkville because "bartenders want to avoid fights," but that in the shadowy *Bierstuben* under the el on Second Avenue, neighborhood joints with sawdust on the floor, a lone musician on the piano, and chopped-meat-and-Swiss-cheese sandwiches on the menu, locals were louder in their praise. "Oh, those Germans argue over Hitler every night," a waitress named Juliana who worked at St. Pauli's near Eighty-Seventh Street said. "You don't dare say anything against them, no matter what you think. When those guys get talking about Germany and drink toasts to Hitler and against the Jews, they're plenty tough. Nearly all of them that come in here are for Hitler."

Nikolaus Ritter had launched his great mission traveling under his real name and using his actual German passport. As far as the US government was concerned, he was a textile engineer with many years' experience in the country looking to tie up some business before returning back to Germany; this contained truth if not all of it. He was told by his Ast Hamburg overseers to stay away from Nazi diplomats at the embassy and/or consulates and avoid spies affiliated with the other Abwehr post conducting work in the city, Nebenstelle (or Nest) Bremen, which was based out of northern Germany's second city. But keeping Abwehr spy efforts on separate tracks was not easy, particularly since both Ast Hamburg and Nest Bremen relied on some of the same couriers, employees of the German passenger liners who spent their few-day stopovers involved in the whole range of pro-Nazi activity in New York, everything from transporting the latest propaganda publications to associating with secret-police organizations such as the Gestapo or SD, which were rumored to have a surreptitious presence in Yorkville and Ridgewood. "We called them undercover men, you see," said a Bundist of the mysterious figures seen lurking in the meeting halls and beer gardens. "They do a lot of work, but you do not know what they do." What was undoubtedly true was that a *single* German spy ring existed in New York, with several overlapping and mutating strands of official, pseudo-official, and unofficial provenance that together reached into the entirety of the Nazi-supporting community.

With the reluctant blessing of the Abwehr chief, Admiral Wilhelm Canaris, obtained during a face-to-face meeting in Berlin, Ritter was assigned to "build up an organization on the spot," a task he believed he could accomplish better than any other operative since American counterintelligence authorities were "not particularly active," he wrote. In this, he was right: The Office of Naval Intelligence (ONI) was so small it could barely complete routine work. The Military Intelligence Division (also known as G-2) had a single officer and two assistants protecting the entire Second Corps Area (New York, New Jersey, and Delaware) from spy infiltration. J. Edgar Hoover, then forty-two, had received verbal instructions from President Roosevelt to monitor Fascist and Communist groups to obtain "a broad picture of the general movement and its activities as may affect the economic and political life of the country as a whole," a pivotal step in restoring subversion-hunting powers that had been stripped from him after the lawless excesses of the Palmer or Red Raids of two decades earlier. But the FBI was rarely permitted to open up a *specific* counterespionage investigation in the absence of a request from the Army, Navy, or State Department, which meant that Hoover's special agents, celebrated as remorseless defenders of the nation's honor trained in the new science of forensic analysis and outfitted in the smartest of suits and snap-brim hats, had little incentive to develop expertise in the detection and apprehension of spies. In simple fact, the United States was doing next to nothing to protect itself from foreign espionage on the day Nikolaus Ritter arrived in the port of New York.

Yet in the seconds after he reached the two-story passenger terminal at Pier 86 at West Forty-Sixth Street on the Hudson River, Ritter thought his covert career had come to a premature end. As he was making his way through the entry process, he heard his name being shouted: "Ritter!" It was not an officer of the law preparing to haul him to the detention facility on Ellis Island, he was relieved to discover, but an acquaintance of his, a reporter for the *Staats* who was present to get a quote or two from disembarking notables. After an inspector spent many excruciating moments trying to determine whether a prescription drug found in his luggage could be carried into the US—it couldn't—he was asked to hand over his umbrella cane, which was of a type that was "not at all well-known in America at that time," he wrote. The inspector removed the casing, performed a careful examination, and announced that it would make "an excellent hiding place." Ritter joked, "I'm sorry that I have to disappoint you." Permitted to enter the United States of America at last, he hopped a cab bound for the Taft Hotel, the two-thousand-room behemoth at Seventh Avenue and Fifty-First Street, with the expectation that he would blend into its clientele of travelers from throughout the world.

Over the next few days, he acted the part of a legitimate businessman, constructing an alibi by loudly speaking to would-be clients over the lobby telephone. He reserved a room at the Wellington Hotel, four blocks to the north, under the name "Alfred Landing," and then mailed two postcards to his fictitious creation, one sent to the Wellington, the other to a nearby post office, general delivery, as he explained in his book. After checking out of the Taft as Ritter, he registered at the Wellington as Landing, where he was given the postmarked item that had earlier arrived for him and which he took to the post office and used as identification to receive the postcard waiting there. With his new identity given recognition by a branch of the US government, he gathered up all of his Ritter-related documents and stuffed them into a safe-deposit box, giving the key to a friend who would hold it until he was ready to return to Germany. Wearing a new felt hat he purchased on Broadway, his old gray overcoat from Hamburg, and an American pair of nickel eyeglasses, Ritter was now Alfred Landing, on the hunt for agents to work for Hitler.

His first stop was to see "Pop," Friederich Sohn, whom he described as a "stocky, middle-aged man in shirtsleeves." Sohn was an employee of Carl L. Norden Inc., the US military contractor in lower Manhattan that produced what Major General Benjamin D. Foulois, chief of staff of the US Army Air Corps, called "the most important military secret project under development." Known to the Navy as the Mark XV bombsight and to the Army as the M-9 or M-series bombsight, the "Norden bombsight," as it would eventually be known to the culture, was a mechanical-electrical-optical apparatus roughly the size of a watermelon. It weighed fifty pounds, boasted at least thirty-five patentable features, was interlaced with upward of two thousand minutely calibrated parts, had a single motor-driven, wide-angled telescope, and was stabilized with two servo-connected gyroscopes spinning at seventy-eight hundred revolutions per minute. Most significant, the bombardier wasn't required to hit the release button. When the axis of the sighting telescope and the pointer on the range bar clicked into alignment, the bombs fell automatically, sent along their path by the ingenious resolution to a problem of advanced mathematics, ballistics, electrical engineering, optics, and aeronautics.

The bombsight was the creation of Carl Lukas Norden, a Dutch citizen with a mechanical engineering degree from the prestigious Federal Polytechnic Institute in Zurich, who spent eight years in solitary experimentation (often in the sanctuary of his mother's home in Switzerland) before the Navy offered him a production contract in 1928, allowing for the formation of a corporation with his partner, Ted Barth, and the opening of a small production facility at 80 Lafayette Street. "Old Man Dynamite," as Norden was nicknamed for his feared explosions of temper, wouldn't countenance the production of any more than about a hundred bombsights a year between 1931 and 1938, ensuring that Norden Inc. was more a secret workshop of artisanal craftsmen than a war factory of low-skilled workers.

As a dedicated believer in the superiority of Northern European craftsmanship—he thought anyone too exposed to sunlight was mentally deficient—Norden favored German Americans who had been schooled in the apprentice system in Europe, which he felt gave them the necessary rigor to construct an instrument able to function in accord with his finely wrought mathematical formulas. According to an internal history, "Mr. Norden was so critical of each piece as it was turned out, that, when a part did not suit him, he had a habit of saying, 'That is not good—throw it out the window.'" Although several of the employees had arrived in New York during the Weimar years with an outward sympathy toward Nazism, the company's highly Germanic institutional culture was undisturbed by such ideological proclivities, especially at a time when few imagined the possibility of America's getting into another confrontation with Germany.

The Norden bombsight was designed to revolutionize armed conflict. It was the crown jewel of an American aerial doctrine that imagined the next war could be won by a few high-flying airplanes delivering a handful of precision strikes against the industrial and infrastructural hubs essential to the modern war-making effort. Carl Norden's handiwork would ensure that the American bombing campaign of the brave future would be so surgical that civilians wouldn't have to die, an attractive concept in a Depression-wracked nation uninterested in returning to the trenches and captivated by the increasingly fantastic feats achieved by contemporary aircraft. "My dear, we are a humane country," he later told a reporter. "We do not bomb women and children."

During their first meeting in the living room of his Queens apartment, Pop Sohn informed Ritter about a colleague of his whom he identified as "Paul," one of the select workers at 80 Lafayette Street working on the sixteenth floor, where the completed bombsights were assembled. Ritter knew that "our own bombsights did not meet expectations" and "everybody was feverishly working on improvements for the aiming instruments" but that "so far nobody had solved the problem successfully." He was electrified by the possibility of addressing a vital dilemma for the Luftwaffe. Attempting to conceal his excitement, Ritter expressed a wish to meet "Paul" in person, and Sohn offered to arrange a meeting at his place for a few days hence.

On a Sunday, Ritter wrote, he entered into the rarefied presence of a man he instantly recognized as a pure-hearted hero of the National Socialist movement, an embodiment of what Hitler called in *Mein Kampf* "the highest humanity." Hermann W. Lang, a native of a Bavarian mountain village who lived among his landsmen in an apartment building in Ridgewood, had "pleasant facial features and blue eyes that exuded so much openness that, when I shook his hand, I involuntarily felt well disposed toward him." A longtime Nazi who had been sanctified by his involvement in Hitler's failed Beer Hall Putsch in 1923, Lang arrived in New York in 1927 and found short-term employment here and there as a machinist. In February 1929, he was hired to work at Norden as a lowly benchhand. Over the next several years, he proved to be a respected member of the staff with a high mechanical intelligence and discreet manner, taking the subway in each day from the Forest Avenue stop and accruing the plaudits necessary to be promoted to be one of four assistant inspectors. Now thirty-six, he was unapologetic enough about his political beliefs to join the labor affiliate of the Bund, the German-American Vocational League or Deutsche Amerikanische Berufsgemeinschaft (DAB), which described itself as a "united workers' league of Germans abroad parallel with the league of German workers in the old homeland, which is united in a common front under the leadership of Adolf Hitler." The DAB included "technicians occupying responsible posts, many of them in defense plants," which made it "the most dangerous of Nazi organizations in the United States," the Justice Department would later say.

Speaking "rather modestly," Lang described how he secreted the bombsight plans out of the Norden plant at the end of the workday, made copies by hand on his kitchen table while his wife slept, and then returned the originals before anyone noticed the next morning. Asked by Ritter why he would take such a risk, Lang delivered a patriotic oration that could've been written by Joseph Goebbels: "I am a German, and I love Germany. I know that Germany is trying to be free and strong again. I know that Germany is diligent, and I also know that Germany is poor. . . . When I got my hands on these drawings, I said to myself, 'If you can bring this kind of instrument to Germany, then Germany will be able to save millions and lots of time. And then you have done something for the land of your forefathers.'" This was "an idealist," a man of "genuine conviction" with "strong nerves" whose unwavering loyalty was "simply incomprehensible," Ritter wrote.

When Ritter made the mistake of bringing up payment, Lang dismissed the suggestion as beneath his dignity. "I hope that was just a figure of speech," he said. All that mattered to him was that his materials be safely delivered to Germany, where "your experts will know what they're dealing with." Ritter had a plan for that. He left Pop Sohn's apartment with a sketch which, along with an additional one he received from Lang a week later, was slipped past US Customs at Pier 86 curled inside an umbrella cane carried by one of the Abwehr couriers working on a German liner. The courier wasn't using Ritter's cane but a cheap one purchased at the ship's store; Ritter got the idea from the inspector, he wrote. Yet the method was deemed too risky. Subsequent Norden copies would be cut up into numbered bands and inserted into the pages of a newspaper to make it past pier scrutiny. "Before I left New York for my own trip through a part of the United States, a second set of the bombsight drawings, subdivided into strips, was on the way to Hamburg and from there to Berlin," Ritter wrote.

He then traveled to Philadelphia, St. Louis, Detroit, and Chicago, meeting with two defense-plant technicians, a stamp collector who agreed to serve as a routing station (a *mail drop*, *live letter box*, or *cutout* in counterintelligence parlance) for other agents' letters, and an unnamed industrialist who wanted Hitler to know that he would "outfit an entire infantry division for Germany personally at my expense if he starts an open battle against Bolshevism." The idea never went anywhere but it proved to Ritter "what some of the powerful Americans were thinking." Back in New York, he made contact with the remarkable character later to be misidentified as the ringleader of his spies. He was a master yarn-spinner with an exotic accent and a monocle, a South African–born swashbuckler who had planted bombs for Imperial Germany during the Great War and whose claim to be the greatest covert agent to serve Kaiser Wilhelm had been given wide airing in a recent biography. "My old acquaintance," Ritter called him.

Frederick "Fritz" Joubert Duquesne was the grandest and most peculiar figure in the clique of self-appointed "colonels" and "commanders" who reclined in stodgy haunts such as the University Club on West Fifty-Fourth Street. Now sixty years old, he could go on for hours about how he took up arms on behalf of his people, the Boers, against the British Army during the Second Anglo-Boer War (1899–1902), becoming a guerrilla fighter with a claim to planting explosives at important junctures of the conflict that is unverified by South African history books. His life was given its great cause, he would tell his listeners, when troops commanded by Lord Horatio Herbert Kitchener destroyed the Duquesne farmstead at Nylstroom as part of a scorched-earth campaign that targeted civilian support for the Boer commandos, resulting in a horrible end for his sister, mother, and blind uncle Jan (who was hanged from a telephone pole with a cow rope). "I will wreck that bastard land, that bastard empire, to the last foul inch of its stolen possessions," he boasted of announcing to a British court that charged him with plotting with several others to set off bombs in Cape Town. He evaded the firing squad by agreeing to turn over (falsified) Boer secret codes and was transported to the penal colony on Burt's Island in Bermuda. There he escaped with the assistance of a pretty young woman of refinement who resided near the prison (said to be Alice Wortley, who later became his wife), swam across a mile and a half of shark-infested waters while dodging bullets from the guards' guns, survived in the wild for three weeks on little more than onions, obtained a seaman's uniform by drugging a tipsy sailor, and stowed away as a crew member on a yacht owned by Isaac Emerson, the "Bromo-Seltzer King," who was headed back to America. Some of which may even be true. Duquesne had the "superlative gift of oriental storytelling—a form of entertainment where the dividing line between fact and fiction is never confused by the native," according to an acquaintance.

Then he hit New York—ah, New York—where he was lavished with attention from newspaper and magazine editors eager to feed the public appetite for tales about the fantastical dangers of the African backcountry. Writing under the byline Captain Fritz Duquesne, he proved to be a hardworking redoubt of the yellow press, spending the next several years on staff at papers such as Joseph Pulitzer's *New York World* and writing commissioned pieces for an array of travel and adventure magazines. "Tracking the Man-Killer" was one of his contributions to *Everybody's Magazine*. He was respected enough as a purveyor of Africana to be invited to the White House on January 25, 1909, where he offered President Theodore Roosevelt advice on his upcoming postpresidential safari in east Africa. ("Suppose an elephant charges me, what should I do to distract its attention?"

the president asked.) The connection did such wonders for his career—when he expressed fears for Roosevelt's safety, the story made page 1 of the *Washington Post*—that Duquesne sought to capitalize on the ex-president's subsequent journey into the Brazilian jungle in 1913. Carrying film equipment to shoot motion pictures for an intended lecture series, Duquesne set out for the tropics a few days after becoming a US citizen in December 1913. But his plans apparently changed once the Great War broke out in the summer of 1914 and the Kaiser's representatives in port cities began recruiting "agents for arranging explosives [explosions] on ships bound for enemy countries, and for arranging delays, embroilments, and confusion during the loading, dispatch, and unloading of ships," according to a German government directive. Although Duquesne would boast of sinking twenty-two British ships, setting another hundred afire, and burning two waterfront towns, he was credibly accused of working with a gang of local conspirators to pack sixteen containers of timed explosives (probably encased within his film materials) on a British merchant steamer. Six days after the SS *Tennyson* left the Brazilian port of Bahia (now Salvador), a massive blast destroyed much of the commercial cargo and killed three British sailors but did not sink the ship. One of the conspirators admitted to Brazilian authorities that Duquesne "directed all operations connected with cases shipped by *Tennyson*," according to a British intelligence report. Whatever else we know about Fritz Duquesne and his grandiosity, we know this: he was entirely capable of murder.

Wanted by British authorities, he probably arranged for the *New York Times* to print a story ("Captain Duquesne Is Slain in Bolivia") on April 27, 1916, that reported how the "noted adventurer and soldier of fortune" had been killed in a battle with Indians on the Bolivian frontier. "His expedition was looted by the attacking band," it said, crediting the information to a "brief cablegram" sent to the paper. Duquesne resurrected himself on May 8, when the Associated Press printed a follow-up (under one of Duquesne's aliases) that detailed how he "has been found by troops at Rio Pilcomayo in a badly wounded state." The AP reported that the explorer was expected to recover. Why would Duquesne go to such lengths to concoct two contradictory stories? wondered a Duquesne biographer, Art Ronnie. "Speculation would suggest that he regretted the first story announcing his death even though its effect had been the desired one: to put a halt to the intensive manhunt for him," Ronnie wrote. "He might've feared that if he were 'dead,' he would never be able to return to America, Alice, and the good life."

Duquesne (pronounced "doo-cane" by Americans and "doo-cwez-nee" by South Africans) would then tell his boldest lie, how he traveled across the Atlantic Ocean, disguised himself as a Russian nobleman (Count Boris Zakrevsky), and somehow managed to be aboard the HMS *Hampshire* when it left the British naval base at Scapa Flow carrying the architect of Britain's war strategy and the brutal scourge of the Duquesne family, Lord Kitchener. At the decisive moment on June 5, 1916, Duquesne signaled a German U-boat, which launched a torpedo that sank the vessel, a more thrilling tale than the reality that Kitchener and some six hundred British seamen went to their deaths after the *Hampshire* struck a mine. Duquesne, who claimed he was plucked from the waters by the U-boat, was next heard from in New York, where he sought to capitalize on the US war effort by disguising himself as "Captain Claude Stoughton of the West Australia Lighthorse," a Croix de Guerre winner available for a fee to lecture on what it was *really* like to fight the Germans at the Somme, Flanders, etc. Soon discovered and arrested by the NYPD's bomb squad, which had been tipped off to his questionable loyalties, Duquesne was charged in connection with an insurance-fraud scheme that included an attempt to recoup the loss of his film that had been destroyed on the *Tennyson,* a nervy bit of gamesmanship. After pleading guilty to the fraud charges, he forestalled extradition to Great Britain on a charge of murder on the high seas (punishable by execution) in the deaths of the three sailors on the *Tennyson* by first feigning what the court called "hysterical insanity" and then pretending to be a hopeless paralytic, which was about the time that his wife, Alice, decided to file for divorce. He maintained the show long enough to escape from a second-story window at Bellevue on May 26, 1919, leaping onto First Avenue and disappearing from the public scene for more than a decade. The papers all said he fled to Mexico, but he probably never left the country. By 1930 at the latest, he was back in the city, working as a writer and critic for a publisher of theatrical and movie periodicals. Frank de Trafford Craven, as he was known, "wrote good copy and acted, in other respects, like the second son of an earl," said one of his coworkers.

Duquesne's cover story began to unravel in February 1932 when W. Faro Inc. released a 429-page biography called *The Man Who Killed Kitchener,* a tale so obviously fictionalized that its author, Clement Wood, wrote in the prologue that he employed an "interpretative" method, which was "infinitely truer than any bald statement of biographical facts can ever be." The book is a genuine achievement in romantic balderdash that inflates the outlines of Duquesne's life story into a glorious saga of world-historical import. "He was the champion swordsman of Europe before he was twenty," Wood writes. "He was the most adventurous man on earth in the nineteenth and twentieth centuries. He may have been the most adventurous man who ever lived. His prowess with sword and rifle, his many escapes from fortresses and jails regarded as impregnable, his amazing lone successful warfare against the widest and most powerful empire since Rome, his high-souled destruction of property and numberless lives in satisfaction of a vow he had made, these things read like ancient miracles or modern tabloid inventions. They are flat sober happenings of our own century."

Three months later, probably tipped off by the publishing house looking to boost lagging sales, police apprehended Frank Craven in his Broadway office, which resulted in a flurry of stories on the " 'cleverest and most dangerous' agent of the Central Powers in the World War" (the *New York Times*) who had "lost none of his dapperness and jaunty effrontery in his past thirteen years as a fugitive" (the *New York Sun*). The *New York Mirror* ran a splashy excerpt ("The True Story of Duquesne, Boer Soldier of Fortune, Arch Enemy of the British Empire") even as the *London Daily Express* quoted a British operative calling Duquesne "a good spy" who "certainly could not have had any hand in the loss of the *Hampshire*."

Confronted with a difficult case to prove so many years after the fact, His Majesty's government declined to pursue extradition on the murder warrant. Likewise, a city magistrate dismissed all charges stemming from the Bellevue escape. Duquesne, his self-advertised reputation for narrow escapes shown to have basis in fact, was free to assail the newspapers for participating in a "slanderous frame-up against me by Great Britain."

After Adolf Hitler assumed power in January of the following year, Duquesne became a picturesque member of a cabal of drawing-room habitués in Manhattan connected to Nazi diplomatic circles, the upper echelon of the Bund movement, and native-led Fascist groups. The entertaining monologist renowned for his charm was growing into a crank, offering his espionage services for pay to a Fifth Avenue real estate broker who founded a blue-blooded society (the Order of '76) that sought to save America from falling into the clutches of the Jews and the Communists. ("To this day the identity of this man has been withheld from most of the members," wrote John Spivak in an investigative report headlined "Plotting the American Pogroms" in the Communist magazine *New Masses* from October 1934. "They may know now. He is Col. Fritz Duquesne, war time German spy who claimed to have sunk the *Hampshire* with Lord Kitchener on board.") To Nikolaus Ritter, Duquesne was a prize recruit. They met in late 1937 at the midtown apartment that Duquesne shared, as was his wont, with a younger woman of means bewitched by his stories and willing to fund his comfortable existence. Ritter said that Duquesne agreed "at once" to serve a Nazi state that wasn't yet engaged in an open fight with his nemesis, Great Britain, but did represent the highest expression of the anti-Semitic belligerency he had been marinating in for the past half decade. With the Reich a long way from sponsoring violent acts on the American homeland, he wasn't yet recruited as a bomb-planting saboteur, his purported specialty. Instead, Duquesne would be assigned to procure "all information possible about the American aircraft industry" for a monthly payment and reimbursement of out-of-pocket expenses. Ritter furnished him with the services of a transatlantic courier, a mail-drop address in Coimbra, Portugal, and an advance of $100, a concession to the old guerrilla's perpetual need for cash.

On his last evening in town, Ritter took in a vaudeville performance in Times Square and had a cup of coffee at the Nedick's hot dog stand at the corner of Seventh Avenue and Forty-Second Street. Immigration documents report that he boarded the North German Lloyd liner *Europa* on December 16, 1937, a month and five days after arriving in New York for a mission that must be considered a major achievement of prewar Nazism. "I felt greatly relieved as the ship finally headed homeward," he wrote. Reaching Bremerhaven after the four-and-a-half-day journey, he was met at the dock by a driver, who transported him directly back to his office in Hamburg. "The entire landscape," he noticed, "was covered by a thick blanket of snow."

The nascent Duquesne Spy Ring was beginning its work without the least hindrance from American legal authority.

CHAPTER THREE

ALMOST SINGLE-HANDED

Only the wisest ruler can use spies; only the most benevolent and upright general can use spies; and only the most alert and observant person can get the truth using spies. It is subtle, subtle!

—Sun Tzu, *The Art of War*

It makes perfect sense that the Luftwaffe's Technical Office in Berlin took one look at the Norden blueprints that had been stolen from the United States and sent a message to Nikolaus Ritter at Ast Hamburg telling him they were the work of a charlatan. The idea that a humble machinist living in Queens could actually deliver an innovation able to address one of the air force's most pressing technological needs was not easily believable. Military bureaucracies are perhaps justly cautious of purported marvels gathered in the shadows by individuals of uncertain motivation. The Germans were so suspicious of a senior Polish officer who had recently offered his services to the Reich that he was hanged in the unfounded belief that he was a double agent. But the Luftwaffe was desperate to improve its ability to destroy targets on the ground and prove the much-feared fleet could actually conquer a foreign foe from the air. The Norden gift was too precious to go unrecognized for long.

Yet the Technical Office may have been less than receptive, at least initially, to the offering of a precision bombsight

for level-flying bombers for another reason. The unlikely figure appointed by Hermann Göring to lead the Technical Office,
Ernst Udet, was a World War I ace known throughout the world
for his individualistic feats of stunt flying and record breaking
who had decided that the bombsighting problem would be
solved by daredevil pilots in agile single-engine planes diving
in a near-vertical descent and releasing their bombs so close to
the target that they needed little more than a modified gunsight.
The regime's ideological leaders were attracted to the idea of a
Germanic knight of the sky plunging toward the earth in self-
less devotion to the cause of the Aryan war machine, striking
the target not because his plane was equipped with a newfan-
gled bomb-aimer (which they didn't have anyway) but because
he was a hurtling exemplar of the majesty of National Socialism.
Hitler himself was favorably impressed by the *Sturzkampfflug-
zeug* (dive-battle aircraft) or *Stuka* demonstrations he witnessed.
Further, the precise dive-bomber, the fast fighter with mounted
machine guns, and the imprecise level-flying medium bomber
(mostly responsible for the deliberate carnage at Guernica) were
believed sufficient to conduct the air attack against the regime's
presumed enemies, France, Poland, and Czechoslovakia, countries that Germany's military theorists had been plotting to fight
since the 1920s. During his meeting with military commanders
on November 5, 1937, Hitler announced that he was planning a
regional war that would achieve living space for the Aryan race
"in immediate proximity to the Reich." In an attempt to free up
valuable raw materials and production space to create the short-
range force, the Luftwaffe had downgraded plans to develop the
kind of four-engine heavy bomber (like America's newly introduced B-17 Flying Fortress) essential to fighting an aerial war far
from Germany's borders, in the belief that the project could be
resumed when the time was right. The Luftwaffe, then, felt it

had all the precision-bombing capability needed to serve *current* regime objectives.

But Nikolaus Ritter knew he had found a trophy that deserved immediate consideration. When he received the note from Berlin about the "completely worthless" plans that his source had provided in an attempt to "fraudulently get money," he slammed his fist on his desk so hard that his secretaries jumped. He was incensed by the suggestion that Hermann Lang, a patriotic Nazi with "open face" and "quiet and honest voice" would be out for anything other than the fatherland. After arguing on behalf of Lang's devotion with his Ast Hamburg superior, Ritter was permitted to fly to Berlin, where he pleaded his case to the officer who led the Abwehr division responsible for overall spying for the Luftwaffe, Friederich Grosskopf. He told Grosskopf that the plans represented "something entirely new, something revolutionary," which low-level staffers at the Technical Office couldn't be expected to understand. "In Germany we certainly have a specialist who is working on the problem of a bombsight," Ritter quoted himself as saying. "I would like to show these drawings to that man." Grosskopf agreed to allow him to see Wolfram Eisenlohr, the new director of the Department for Engines and Accessories within the Technical Office, which required Ritter to take a flight to Frankfurt. Once there, he told Eisenlohr the whole story and laid the drawings on his desk. The old professor studied them for several long minutes, taking out a pencil to sketch out some of the ideas. "You could hear a pin drop in the room," Ritter wrote. "Anxiously, I waited, my heart pounding." At last, Eisenlohr raised his head and pronounced them *etwas ganz Grosses*—something very great. He decreed that the deliveries must continue. "Bring me as many drawings as you can," Eisenlohr said, according to Ritter. "The more we have, the less we have to design ourselves."

Additional Norden plans were then smuggled out of the United States during the early months of 1938, just as the FBI's New York office suddenly received the necessary permissions from the bureaucratic hierarchy to investigate a Reich-sponsored spy operation of indefinite proportion. The catalyst had been the NYPD's apprehension of a low-level agent connected to Nest Bremen named Guenther Gustave Maria Rumrich.

"Arrest Bares Spy Ring Here" was the front-page headline in the *Daily News* when "Gus" Rumrich, a twenty-six-year-old grifter who was AWOL from the US Army, was taken into custody after telephoning the State Department's Passport Agency at 26 Wall Street, identifying himself as Secretary of State Cordell Hull (a sixty-seven-year-old Tennessean), and requesting that thirty-five blank US passports be delivered to the Abwehr's preferred hostelry, the Taft Hotel, for an "Edward Weston," whom he identified as an undersecretary of state. The supervisor answering the call knew instantly he was being hoaxed. In the single-spaced, ten-and-a-half-page confession he made to the State Department, Rumrich said he found work as a dishwasher at Meyer's Restaurant in downtown Brooklyn "much harder than the life I had been used to in the Army and quite a strain." So he volunteered his services to Nazi Germany, mostly mailing along reports of easily obtained info that he typed onto official-looking letterhead. Handed over to the FBI, Rumrich quickly implicated a Leipzig-born pal stationed at the US Army Air Corps' Mitchel Field on Long Island and a hairdresser/courier on the *Europa*, who, upon questioning following her arrival in port, spilled the beans on Dr. Ignatz Griebl, a Nazi theoretician and gynecologist who operated out of a fancy home/office on East Eighty-Seventh Street between Madison and Park in the Silk Stocking district.

During his second interrogation session, Griebl consented to provide information about Nazi spy activities just as long as he could remain free to continue his medical practice and not be required to affix his signature to a confession, a generous arrangement that was apparently approved by the US attorney in Manhattan, FBI headquarters in Washington, and, according to Griebl's later statement, President Roosevelt himself. "We handled him with gloves, for he was of more value to us as a willing witness than as an unwilling one," wrote Leon Turrou, the talented and egotistical special agent assigned to lead the Bureau investigation. "We did not arraign him, nor place him under bond, nor keep him under close surveillance after he began talking." Dr. Griebl showed his good faith by pointing out a German-born technician at Seversky (later Republic) Aircraft in Farmingdale, Long Island, an ideological Nazi who had spent the past three years in proximity with the designers transforming the now-obsolete P-35 single-engine fighter plane into the P-47 Thunderbolt, which, prized for its ability to endure heavy fighting in poor weather conditions, would be produced in greater numbers than any other US-made fighter during World War II.

Agent Turrou knew he was onto a blockbuster case. Dr. Griebl was filling his head with fantastical tales about a German spy apparatus that had penetrated all levels of the US defense establishment. Griebl described grand boasts he claimed were made to him by his superiors in Germany: "In every strategic point in your United States we have an operative," he quoted them as telling him. "In every armament factory in America we have a spy. In every shipyard we have an agent; in every key position. Your country cannot plan a warship, design a fighting plane, develop a new instrument or device, that we do not know of it at once!" Just at the point when he should've been chasing down leads, Turrou instead reached out to an ace reporter for the *New York Post,* with whom he began a secret project to write a series of articles, an exclusive view of the Nazi spy ring from the inside that would be published at an opportune time with an eye toward book and movie treatment. But Griebl was just stalling for time, offering "partly false, partly exaggerated remarks, in order to confuse the Federal agents by this mass of material and throw them off the right scent," according to the postwar revelations of his Nest Bremen spymaster. Asked to review statements attributed to him by Griebl about the expansiveness of the Abwehr operation in the United States, he told his British interrogators, "I only discussed with Griebl persons whom I was definitely sure he knew." The spymaster described Griebl's comments as a "rubbishy extravaganza."

According to Griebl's later statement, Agent Turrou told him "on May 9 or May 10" that he was about to be subpoenaed to appear before a federal grand jury. "I took that as a hint," Griebl said. On the evening of May 10 / May 11, he drove with his wife to Pier 86, boarded the *Bremen* alone without a ticket during prelaunch festivities, and ducked into a hiding place when the "all ashore that's going ashore" calls were heard. Agent Turrou was awakened at 6:00 a.m. the next morning by a hysterical phone call from Griebl's mistress, who had apparently heard from a taunting Mrs. Griebl that she would never again lay eyes on her Naz. "He has been kidnapped!" she shrieked. "They have taken him on a ship! They will kill him in Germany!" Turrou initially accepted this explanation of Griebl's flight, which became the commonplace view when the papers started reporting that Dr. Griebl was helping the FBI "break up" the spy ring. Frantic efforts were made to convince the *Bremen's* captain, contacted via radiophone, to relinquish him to a US Coast Guard seaplane ready to fly to international waters or to US diplomats who would meet the ship at the first stop in Cherbourg. Yet Dr. Griebl was delivered safely to Bremerhaven, where he boasted that "he had served Germany well to the last, surviving the most searching interrogations, 'the only rock on the shifting sands of German-American espionage.'" He wasn't interrogated about his actions nor was an attempt made to have him tried before the Volksgerichtshof (People's Court), the military-style tribunal established by Hitler to pronounce sentence on enemies of the state, with a reputation for its brutality against treasonous spies. The Western (and German) press regularly printed stories about the latest executions—"Nazis Behead Spy; Fifth in a Few Days" was a not-unrepresentative headline—with wide coverage given to the decapitation by ax of two German noblewomen caught cooperating with Polish intelligence. In fact, Griebl, a devoted evangelizer of the Nazi creed whose belief in Hitler had never been doubted, was sent to Berlin with "a recommendation that something be done for him." And so it was. When the Nuremberg Laws were amended to forbid Jews from practicing medicine, he was permitted to take over a successful Jewish practice at Reichsratstrasse 11 in Vienna's Old Town, which, following Hitler's forcible annexation (or *Anschluss*) of Austria, was now the heart of the new Ostmark (or Eastern March) of the Third Reich.

A few weeks after Griebl's flight, the New York papers reported that the FBI had lost *another* spy uncovered by the investigation, a German-born employee of the Curtiss-Wright aircraft factory in Buffalo who had twice testified before the grand jury. No one from the New York office was watching when Werner Georg Gudenberg boarded the Hamburg America liner *Hamburg* and escaped from American jurisdiction. J. Edgar Hoover was incensed, issuing a statement alleging that "the responsibility for the disappearance of Dr. Ignatz T. Griebl and the witness Werner G. Gudenberg is the responsibility of the United States Attorney and not the Federal Bureau of Investigation," using the word *responsibility* twice to ensure that his (unconvincing) message was clearly understood. Hoover was reported to be traveling to New York to take personal supervision of the foundering investigation.

In his memoir, Agent Turrou admitted that Dr. Griebl probably absconded of his own volition but wondered how long he could remain "free and alive" once the full extent of his cooperation was publicly known. Of Gudenberg, Turrou theorized that "Nazi *Gestapo* men saw him enter to testify before the grand jury and then followed him," he wrote. "I believe these *Gestapo* agents then prevailed upon him, by threats or force or other persuasion, or by a combination of methods, to flee." It was a stunning admission no matter what became of Gudenberg, who possessed specialized knowledge of the sort that the Luftwaffe was eager to exploit. Turrou was suggesting that the FBI's (and his) failure to provide a government witness with even a modicum of protection could well have resulted in his death. The amateurishness of the Bureau's operation was breathtaking to behold. The vaunted G-men had been exposed to the world as unprepared to confront a peril with a proven disregard for the sanctity of America's borders.

In the spring, the Abwehr arranged to bring Hermann Lang to Germany to meet with officials of the Technical Office, an indication, independent of Ritter's testimony, that the Luftwaffe understood the potential value of the Norden material. Hermann and his wife, Katherine (known as Betty), who had already been planning to spend vacation time back home, knew they would be traveling to a Nazi Germany that was on the brink of war.

Emboldened by the easy success of the *Anschluss,* Hitler had decided to deliver his lightning strike against Czechoslovakia, the multiethnic democracy of 15 million people that boasted large armed forces and an impressive armaments industry. He wanted to seize the country so quickly that France (a treaty-bound ally of the Czechs), Britain (France's ally), and the Soviet Union (which was bound by a mutual-assistance pact to aid Czechoslovakia if France did) wouldn't have a chance to intervene even if they wanted to—which they didn't—enabling the Nazi state to plunder natural and industrial resources needed for rearmament and prevent the Czech territory from being used by a future enemy as a base for an air attack on nearby Berlin.

Hitler's allies in this effort would be the ethnic Germans who had found themselves residents of Czechoslovakia when the nation was created following World War I. Two weeks after the annexation of Austria, Hitler met for three hours in Berlin with his chief agent in Czechoslovakia, Konrad Henlein, the führer of the Bund-like pro-Nazi organization that claimed to represent the 3.5 million Germans in the Sudetenland, the economically depressed region of western Czechoslovakia now surrounded on three sides by the Reich. A former gymnastics teacher who had risen to power through the sporting clubs that flourished wherever Germans settled, Henlein, or Little Hitler as he was sometimes called, had always sworn that his Sudeten German Party (SdP) was made up of loyal citizens of Czechoslovakia with no fealty whatsoever to the Nazi regime, which enabled him to gain significant power (including dozens of seats in the parliament) within the confines of the Czechs' tolerant democracy. Now he was free to be himself. Hitler instructed him to go public with calls for the Czech government to grant something like Nazi autonomy over the German-majority areas, which he did in a speech in Karlsbad on April 24. "We must always demand so much that we can never be satisfied," said Henlein in summarizing Hitler's order to him. During the weeks leading up to local elections in late May and June, Henlein's storm troopers, the Freiwilliger Deutscher Schutzdienst (Voluntary German Protective Service, or FS for short), launched a campaign of violence and intimidation to ensure that the Sudeten German population spoke with one voice at the ballot box. Nazi canvassers went door-to-door demanding everyone sign his or her name to the party list or face trouble "when Hitler comes," which helped push the SdP vote to 90 percent. "Not One Single Vote for the Enemies of Sudeten Germans" and "Every Decent German Must Vote for Henlein" were the slogans.

But the Czechs would not be as accommodating to Hitler's territorial ambitions as the Austrians. On the weekend of May 20 and 21, in response to (probably unfounded) rumors that German troops were maneuvering toward the border, the Czech government partially mobilized its army and ordered the occupation of frontier fortifications, which escalated the conflict into an international crisis with the potential of sparking a second World War. The French reaffirmed their commitment to defend ·Czechoslovakia, the British sent word (in less than Churchillian language) that they "could not guarantee they would not be forced by circumstances to become involved also," and the Nazi government was forced to tell the Czech ambassador in Berlin that Germany had no designs on his country. Humiliated by the Czechs' successful show of force, Hitler sputtered with rage. On May 28, he told his military leaders, "I am utterly determined that Czechoslovakia shall disappear from the map of Europe." On May 30, he ordered the armed forces to be ready by October 1, which caused his General Staff Chief Ludwig Beck (who would resign in August) to warn that "Germany, either alone or allied with Italy, is hardly in a position to meet France and England on the field of battle." Undeterred by such defeatism, Hitler decided he needed an "unbearable provocation" that "in the eyes of at least a part of the world opinion" would provide the "moral justification for military measures," as he told his generals. Konrad Henlein was ordered to send his thugs into the streets to cause so much trouble that the Czech militia would be required to initiate repressive counterstrikes. Joseph Goebbels filled the Nazi media with exaggerated and often fabricated stories ("Bloody Terror of Czech Bands," "Unleashed Mob Rages through Tortured Land") designed to prove that hateful Czechs were conducting race murder against peace-loving Germans. In a speech in Stettin, Rudolf Hess mocked Western expressions of concern about anti-Jewish measures that had been stepped up in the aftermath of the *Anschluss* by asking why the world stood by as "minorities have been deprived of rights, terrorized, and ill-treated," "struck, clubbed, or shot down repeatedly only because they are not Czechs." Hitler was building the case that he had to invade Czechoslovakia to prevent the extermination of ethnic Germans. It would be a humanitarian intervention, if you will.

The Langs were preferred travelers during their trip across the ocean on the Hamburg America liner *Hansa,* permitted to move from Room 312, a small inside room, to Room 310, a much larger outside room with a view of the water. After docking, they spent a few days in Hamburg. "I was at first surprised, then disappointed, and finally angry that I was not asked to go to Berlin with him," wrote Nikolaus Ritter. Exactly what happened in the Air Ministry building in the capital remains something of a mystery. In his later statements, given when he thought he was able to speak freely, Lang spoke of spending several days in conference with engineers and being granted the honor of meeting Ernst Udet. Ritter writes that Lang was presented with a bombsight that had already been constructed from the stolen plans, which would've meant that he was brought to Germany just to receive hearty congratulations.

Whatever the particulars of those sessions, Hermann Lang was in a position to provide the rapidly mobilizing Nazi state with a full understanding of America's most prized military device. The crusade to inspire German nationals living abroad into the service of the New Germany had scored a historic victory in the quiet action of a single devotee from the outer boroughs of New York City.

But in the middle of 1938, the Luftwaffe's Technical Office placed little priority in determining how Carl Norden's innovations could be incorporated into a Reich-constructed bombsight able to function within the confines of the Luftwaffe's twin-engine horizontal bombers, principally the Heinkel He 111 and Dornier Do 17 "Flying Pencil." For one, the "mammoth bureaucracy, composed of mediocrities," favored "increasingly sterile regimentation" over creative interplay with gifted designers, according to Ernst Heinkel, one of the most gifted. For another, Ernst Udet was becoming so obsessed with the dive-bomber concept that he was thinking of ending the production of horizontal bombers altogether. Third, the force had to be ready *now*. On July 8, Hermann Göring told German aircraft executives to increase production so exponentially that the bankruptcy of their companies might be the result. "If we win the fight, then Germany will be the greatest power on earth; the world's markets will belong to Germany, and the time will come for abundant prosperity in Germany," he said. "But we must venture something for this; we have to make the investment."

His service complete, Lang and his wife returned to Queens. They moved from the apartment building at the corner of Seventieth Avenue and Sixtieth Street in Ridgewood where they had been living to a nicer residence several blocks to the southeast, a single floor of a three-story structure on Sixty-Fourth Place in Glendale, around the corner from a young shortstop just out of high school who had signed with the Yankees, Phil Rizzuto. On his second day back, Lang resumed his work as an assistant inspector on the sixteenth floor of 80 Lafayette Street. Two weeks later, he submitted his petition for naturalization, his "second papers," affirming his desire to become an American citizen before a clerk of the federal court and two witnesses, both of them German American friends employed by Norden. He sought to blend back into the bustle of city life, just another immigrant striver hoping to achieve his share of the American dream. "I am sorry that I did not go back to Germany right away," he would later say.

Most Americans had few illusions about Hitler's motives. Although polls showed the public viewed the German and Soviet systems with about equal levels of disdain, 82 percent said they would support the Soviets over the Nazis if the two ever fought a war against each other. Hitler had "resurrected tribal instincts and the mystical sanctions of a savage society," which of necessity would lead to a fight against all inferior races on the ultimate stage of history, according to a writer for *Reader's Digest*, the voice of Middle America. The *Atlantic Monthly* said that Germany stood "in clattering armor before the world demanding vengeance," less interested in territory or raw materials than in fighting a war for the sake of victory to relieve the shame of Versailles. Yet while *Newsweek* detected an "increased backing for a sterner foreign policy" among the populace, the country was still resolutely isolationist, willing to support FDR's $1.1 billion naval expansion plan (which passed both houses of Congress in May 1938) for the purposes of self-defense but unwilling to consider joining a distant fight. The plight of the Jews would not bring a call to arms: according to Gallup, 65 percent of Americans thought anti-Jewish persecution in the Reich was either partly or completely the fault of the Jews themselves. In an editorial about the anti-Semitic violence committed by rampaging hordes of Nazis that followed the *Anschluss,* the *Daily News* mused that a respected statesman should avoid fanfare and "slip word" to Hitler "on the matter of calling off or toning down his vendetta against the Jewish race."

The new German ambassador in Washington, Hans Dieckhoff, was worried that the German American Bund would be just the thing to inflame the Americans from their isolationism and into a war on the side of France and England, the potentially devastating eventuality he was working so hard to prevent. He penned two long memos to Berlin suggesting that unambiguous action be taken to shutter the organization. "The tradition of the American nation, the American national ideology, is really built upon the concept of the amalgamation of races, the dissolving of racial segments into the great American whole," he wrote. "Anything which would give rise to the impression that this development was to be stopped or completely reversed would encounter strong antagonism on the part of the government and the people." The various functionaries in Berlin responsible for cultural outreach to Germans living in foreign countries fell in line, fully aware that the Reich *was* more interested at this point in keeping America out of Europe's affairs than in developing a public movement of German Americans to prepare for any eventuality.

In response to Dieckhoff's concerns, a directive of two sentences was released to the German news agency, DNB, which instructed Reich citizens who were members of the German American Bund to "immediately give up their membership."

Since German nationals represented the core of the organization, Bundesführer Fritz Kuhn saw the order as "tantamount to the destruction of the Bund." But Yorkville's Little Hitler had no intention of relinquishing his rightful place at the head of the Nazi movement in America. He had become a genuine celebrity, a boldfaced name in an era of tabloid excess who frequented non-Teutonic hot spots in midtown (Leon and Eddie's, El Morocco, Kelly's Stable) with pretty fräuleins while his loyal hausfrau minded the two children in their top-floor apartment in a brick-fronted row house in Jackson Heights, Queens. He was determined to remain the unchallenged proprietor of a handful of Bund entities that were collecting dues from members and allied businesses, selling newspapers and pamphlets, hosting celebrations in the city and in the pure air of the country, and soliciting donations to pay increasingly sizable lawyers' fees necessary to fight charges brought by municipalities looking for any legal pretext to take down those damn Nazis. To his followers, Kuhn delivered the fraudulent news that he had spoken with Göring and Goebbels and both had assured him that his rule was smiled upon favorably by the regime. In defiance of Berlin's directive, he established auxiliary divisions that were open to "any worthy Aryan" who expressed solidarity to the Bundist cause "by paying regular donations of money."

US congressman Martin Dies, a racist and xenophobic Democrat from the hill country of east Texas who had turned against Roosevelt and the New Deal, took advantage of the headlines about Hitler's bellicosity to introduce legislation to restart a tribunal (the Special Committee on Un-American Activities Authorized to Investigate Nazi Propaganda and Certain Other Propaganda Activities) that had examined mostly domestic Nazis for a few months in 1934–35. By a vote of 191 to 41, the House of Representatives removed the reference to Germany and set up the Special Committee to Investigate Un-American Activities and Propaganda in the United States. Although Martin Dies's committee would make its name with innuendo- and insinuation-laden expeditions to prove that the Roosevelt administration and its allies in labor unions, Popular Front groups, Hollywood, and New Deal agencies were serving the Communist agenda, it couldn't help but slip in testimony every once in a while against the German American Bund, which was seeking to establish "a powerful sabotage machine" and "a vast spy net," according to testimony. Two weeks after the creation of this early version of HUAC, Congress followed up by passing the Foreign Agents Registration Act (or FARA), which strengthened a 1917 law that required anyone engaged in political activities on behalf of a foreign power to register with the State Department. Congressman John McCormack said, "The spotlight of pitiless publicity will serve as a deterrent to the spread of pernicious propaganda."

With the explicit intention of rousing the American people to accept a more confrontational stance toward the Nazi danger, the US government announced its plan to salvage the espionage investigation that had been filling the papers for months now. With approval from the highest reaches of the Roosevelt administration, the US attorney in Manhattan decided to conduct a kind of democratic show trial, designed not solely to convict the four spies still in US custody but to lay before the public the full extent of the German government's efforts to infiltrate the US defense establishment as uncovered by Special Agent Leon Turrou's interrogations.

On Monday, June 20, 1938, a federal grand jury issued indictments against eighteen individuals, fourteen of whom were little more than names (or aliases) on a press release, which allowed all the papers to write front-page headlines focusing on "Nazi Spy Chiefs" while devoting less attention to the fact that only one agent of real significance would actually be in the dock (the Seversky technician). "The important point is that the American public must be made aware of the existence of this spy plot and impressed with the dangers," US Attorney Lamar Hardy said. Duly shaken, the country would then lend its support to the creation of "an efficient counterespionage service to protect us against such vicious spy rings as this," he said.

To spread the message to the widest possible audience, the indictments were announced two days before the Aryan superman Max Schmeling was to enter a Yankee Stadium ring against the pride of (a racially segregated) America, Joe Louis, in a feverishly anticipated bout that was already being seen as a symbolic clash between two antagonistic ideologies. It was a telling fact, wrote a young Richard Wright in the *Daily Worker*, that the fight was occurring in New York, "where a foul nest of Nazi spies has just been routed."

But Agent Turrou was not through making a mess of the case. On the same day as the indictments were issued, and months before the trial was expected to begin, he quit the FBI, announcing he was exhausted from his duties and wanted to devote his full energies to writing "fully and without restriction" about the dangers of German espionage to America, a decision that was reported to cause "confusion in the local FBI office and in federal circles," wrote one paper. The central witness for the prosecution in a major espionage trial would now be identified to jurors as an *ex*-FBI agent with a budding literary career and perhaps a pecuniary motive in hyping the threat. Then on June 22, just hours before the ringside bell was to sound in the Bronx, the *Post* hit the streets with the sensational news that it was preparing to run a multipart series authored by Turrou and reporter David A. Wittels, which would deliver "the most astounding revelation ever published by any newspaper." Across a two-page advertisement on facing pages was the announcement "G-Man Bares German Conspiracy to Paralyze United States! The Man Who Cracked the Spy Ring Reveals How Nazi Spies and Traitors Sold Out the United States Army and Navy." Beginning next day, the *Post* promised "amazing inside facts" would be delivered by "the ONE MAN who knows them—the Ace G-Man who, virtually single-handed, blasted the most vicious peacetime attack ever made upon this country!"

US Attorney Lamar Hardy took one look at the paper, rushed before a federal judge, and obtained a court order to prevent the *Post* from publishing, alongside the boxing coverage in the next afternoon's paper, sensitive material that might jeopardize his prosecution. The *Post*'s publisher, J. David Stern, a committed anti-Nazi liberal who also owned the *Philadelphia Record* and Camden, New Jersey, *Courier-Post,* blasted the "unprecedented attempt to erase the freedom of the press from the Constitution." On the hangover morning after the "Brown Bomber" knocked out Hitler's hero in 124 seconds, perhaps the most lopsided famous fight in boxing history, Lamar Hardy's assistant argued before a judge in the federal courthouse at 40 Centre Street that the *Post* should be enjoined from publishing confidential information that could taint the jury pool in obstruction of justice. Further, Agent Turrou had broken the law in providing the information to the *Post* in the first place, since his resignation from government service wouldn't become effective until September. "It is desirable for Turrou to make money," prosecutor John W. Burke told the court. "I would like to see him make money. It is desirable for the *Post* to extend its circulation. But not at the expense of the federal court."

Lawyers for the *Post* and Mr. Turrou countered that it was a central tenet of First Amendment law that the government was forbidden from exercising prior restraint of controversial speech. And anyway, Turrou's attorney charged, J. Edgar Hoover had achieved national fame by doing the same thing, publishing articles and books that used materials from the "secret files" of the FBI. "If it's all right for Mr. Hoover to get his name in the papers and his picture in the papers, then it is all right for humble Mr. Turrou to do the same," said lawyer Simon Rifkind. Understanding that he was being asked to render judgment on what could become a landmark press-freedom case, Judge Murray Hulbert threw up his hands and retreated to chambers, communicating the message that no decision would be forthcoming that day.

On the next morning, June 24, a reporter asked President Roosevelt during a press conference around his desk in the Oval Office, "Any comment you care to make on the New York spy inquiry—espionage?"

The president "sat silently considering the question, obviously aware of the significance that would be attached to his reply, and after a long pause he answered in the affirmative," wrote the *Times*.

"Yes, I think so," he said, according to the transcript. "I have been a good deal disturbed by that because it raises a fundamental double question in relation to the press. Perhaps I should not say 'the press' because there is only one syndicate involved in this particular thing. The issue is, frankly and squarely, an issue of patriotism and ethics combined. As I understand the facts, a government employee, in the pursuance of his regular duty, unearthed a great deal of information relating to foreign spies in this country. Well, that is a pretty serious thing. It was information which seemed to call for criminal action on the part of the government. The Department of Justice undertook that crim-

inal action. This government employee, having obtained all of the details on which the presentment to a grand jury would be based, and before the grand jury had taken any action and before the trial, resigned from the government services and within fifteen minutes signed a syndicate contract."

Press secretary Stephen Early interjected, "Not before the grand jury."

"Not before the grand jury," FDR corrected himself, "but before the trial—thereby in a very serious case relating to the national defense possibly jeopardizing the criminal prosecution by the government."

The president continued, "I am not talking about the law of this case, I am talking about the patriotism and the ethics; first, of a government employee doing that, and secondly, any newspaper undertaking to syndicate information of that kind. I think that is the proper way to present this particular problem that faces the government of the United States today. I think that is all the comment that could be made."

After dodging a question about whether the US ambassador in Berlin would make a formal protest over the spy issue, President Roosevelt was asked whether "the Army and Navy and their intelligence units should have more money and more men for counterespionage." The questioner was referring to the nearly moribund Military Intelligence Division and Office of Naval Intelligence.

"Yes, I think so, frankly. Both the Army and Navy intelligence have been held pretty low on funds."

"Do you mean by that answer, sir, to approve activities of counterespionage?"

"What do you mean?" FDR said. "Do you mean running down spies in this country? That is what I mean by counterespionage. I think we ought to have more money for that purpose."

With a presidential rebuke stinging in his ears, the *Post's* FDR-supporting publisher caved. A few hours later, that afternoon's edition carried a front-page notice announcing that the Turrou series had been postponed until after the trial. "The *Post* believes that nothing in this series of articles would have, in any way, interfered with the course of justice," the notice read. "But it desires to avoid setting a precedent which might handicap the government in guarding itself against other spy activities." The paper understandably focused the bulk of its coverage on the second part of the president's comments, when he seemed to propose a new counterintelligence policy for the United States, which, the paper noted, was the whole point of the prosecution to begin with. "Roosevelt Asks Spy Hunt Fund," read the banner across the top of the *Post*. But other papers also fronted with this angle. The *New York Times* began its page 1 article ("President Urges Fund to Fight Spies") with the news that the president "favors larger appropriations for the Army and Navy Intelligence Services for the expansion of counterespionage activities within the United States." The *Los Angeles Times* ("Counter Spy Fund Sought") said more generally that FDR "came out in favor of more cash to detect and apprehend spies."

Hoover, who refused to accept Turrou's resignation and instead fired him "with prejudice," now set about ensuring that the FBI would lead the counterespionage initiative that the president had publicly committed himself to launching. Like the rest of the nation, he was now certain that many more Nazi spies were yet to be uncovered.

CHAPTER FOUR

TRUE FAITH AND ALLEGIANCE

What is America but millionaires, beauty queens, stupid records, and Hollywood?

—Adolf Hitler in conversation
with his friend Ernst Hanfstaengl

Wilhelm Gottlieb Sebold wanted nothing to do with the Aryan cause. He was a not-atypical German immigrant living in Yorkville who had experienced the horrors of the trenches and emigrated during the volatility of the Weimar era. If his early history had been characterized by anything, it was by a desire to forget all about the troubles that disfigured the Old Country. He saw his adopted homeland as "a sanctuary for those whom the misrule of Europe may compel to seek happiness in other climes," as Thomas Jefferson wrote in 1817. "I came to America to forget all this," Sebold said in less exalted language when asked his ideological views. "Don't you talk to me about politics."

He was born in 1899, the eldest child of a beer-wagon operator who christened him in the name of the reigning monarch. Wilhelm quit school as a young teenager at about the time his father's death left his mother as the sole supporter of his two brothers and sister. He began apprenticing as a mechanical draftsman in the heavy-metal works that defined his home city of Mülheim on the Ruhr River in a smoke- and soot-filled region near the French border often compared with the Monongahela Valley surrounding Pittsburgh. Over four years of rigorous instruction, Sebold gained a thorough grounding in machine sciences that would carry him through the rest of his life. At age seventeen, he was drafted into the Imperial Army and, in early 1918, sent to the Western Front in the Somme District. Later asked about technology that was used during the war, he responded, "I don't know anything. We were only machine gunners." He spent eight months suffering along with hundreds of thousands of others from the malnutrition, infectious diseases, and mustard-gas poisoning that helped spell the doom of the German war effort, marking the beginning of physical maladies that would also remain constant until his dying days. "Every soldier was gassed, to a certain extent," he said.

But Sebold neither surrendered nor deserted as so many did during the miserable final onslaught. Afflicted with the influenza that was ravaging the ranks, he was transported to a military hospital at Göttingen "a couple of days or a week" before the end of the fighting on November 11, 1918, which means that, like his fellow soldier Adolf Hitler in Pasewalk Hospital, he was recuperating from injuries when he was informed of the outbreak of nationwide revolution, dissolution of the House of Hohenzollern, declaration of a republic, and signing of the armistice. Sebold supported the Kaiser's monarchy and was opposed to its usurpation. But his abiding purpose over the next three months at Göttingen was to recover his health with a steady regimen of medicine, nutrition, and sweat baths. "I was in the war, and a soldier is entitled to a rest," he said.

He returned to the Ruhr Valley, which, in keeping with its role as the nation's industrial heartland, was in the midst of the proletarian uprising. In Mülheim, the municipal government had been taken over by a workers' and soldiers' council (or soviet), which was serious enough about seizing the means of production that it arrested the elderly August Thyssen, the steel magnate in slouch hat known around town as King Thyssen and to American journalists as the Rockefeller of the Ruhr. Sebold began his journey from the military hospital in Göttingen in February or March 1919, which means that he would've arrived at about the time a battalion of the Freikorps, the right-wing militia of fearsome reputation that was helping put down the revolution on behalf of the Social Democratic government, marched into town and arrested the council without the bloodshed then occurring in neighboring cities. He stayed close to home for the next three tumultuous years, working in a machine shop and helping his mother maintain a business she was operating, a difficult proposition in a municipality that was prominent enough in the Communist movement to serve as the command headquarters for the second regional uprising in March–April 1920. A self-proclaimed Red Army of the Ruhr, composed of at least fifty thousand combatants, occupied the main cities of the region for less than two weeks before the army and its Freikorps allies ended the takeover in a five-day campaign of slaughter that left more than a thousand Communists dead, most of them shot after they had been taken prisoner. The Ruhr Valley of the immediate postwar period was a nightmare of wildcat strikes, fiery public meetings, running street battles, and worsening employment prospects. Asked about the political beliefs he held at the time, Sebold said, "I did not have any complaint about President Ebert's government, but in our industrial district we had a lot of Communists and there was a lot of shooting, and nobody knew what was what."

He sought escape to a more peaceful land. At age twenty-three, he signed on as a junior engineer on a Schindler Oil tanker that plied between Hamburg and Galveston, Texas, although he only stayed aboard long enough to reach American soil. "When I left Germany, I had in mind never to go back," he said. He jumped ship with five dollars in his pocket, using three or four of them to take the train from Galveston to Houston, where he sauntered over to the fire department. "I did not get a steady job, but I made a dollar or two a day cleaning engines and carrying the lunches for the firemen," he said. A German American member of the force, part of an ethnic community that had been represented in significant numbers in the state since the nineteenth century, suggested he travel to the Texas panhandle, where the member's father owned a ranch. Sebold was hired there as a mule tender, giving him an opportunity to become conversant in the English language, his own version of a work-study program.

After six months, he moved on to Brenham, a city in east-central Texas with a sizable German and Bohemian population, where he spent another half year or so toiling at a furniture store, a funeral home, and a cotton mill. Then a letter from Mülheim alerted him to trouble on the home front. In the midst of the hyperinflation crisis, French and Belgian troops had occupied the Ruhr in an attempt to pry delinquent reparation payments owed under the Treaty of Versailles out of German industry. So young Willy Sebold, who had pledged himself to a lifetime of exile, agreed to come home to help. "My people were losing their homes in the inflation in Germany," he said. "I went back to see what I could do to save them." With the $150 he'd earned in Texas, he stowed away on a thousand-ton tramp steamer, the *Hans,* hiding in the chain box until he was discovered three days out and forced to work his way to Hamburg. Upon his return to Mülheim, Sebold opened a bicycle shop that enabled him to pay off the mortgage on his mother's home. He remained for a year until the government introduced a new currency to stabilize the economy and foreign troops began their withdrawal from the Ruhr. A lesson had been learned: Sebold could be counted on when it mattered.

Around Christmas 1924, he secured work on the SS *Rhodopis*, bound for South America. He jumped ship in the Antofagasta region of Chile, enticed ashore by a German saloon owner from the Ruhr looking for someone to fill a bartender job. He spent five or six months slinging drinks for the workers in the mining camps, who were extracting profits from the region's nitrate deposits on behalf of European and American companies. "I did not like it," he said. "I wanted to go to work at my profession."

He saved up 150 pesos, enough to get him to the coastal town of Iquique, Chile, where he was hired by a German company as a specialist in the diesel engines that were bringing greater automation to the processing plants. "I worked in the saltpeter mines there," he said. He was soon lured away, given the title of diesel foreman with an American concern, the Anglo-Chilean Consolidated Nitrate Co., based in Tocopilla, Chile. He gained such a firm understanding of diesel technology that he took a short trip to Oakland, California, in 1927, in an unsuccessful attempt to interest the Atlas Imperial Manufacturing Company in an innovation he had devised. He returned to South America for another two years, following his boss from Anglo-Chilean to a new position with a company over the border at Callao, Peru, where he was paid $250 a month. But his health problems emerged again: he was struck by typhoid fever that probably was exacerbated by the internal injuries he'd suffered in the trenches of the Great War. Two months of hospitalization would be required before he was healthy enough to return to work.

In 1929, Sebold boarded the *Cuzco* for San Francisco. On February 13, 1929, just a few weeks shy of his thirtieth birthday and less than a year before the stock market crashed, he entered the United States as a legal immigrant. His route to New York was typically wayward. He was employed for several months at a gold-dredging company in Alaska and another several at various regional outposts of the Bucyrus-Erie Steam Shovel Company of Milwaukee, which laid him off in the early days of the Depression. Like any good German, he set out for Yorkville, where he struck up a friendship with a butcher, Victor Wien. Victor was married to a roundish fashion plate from northern Bavaria, Rosa "Rosie" Büchner, who was employed as one of a team of servants for a wealthy family on Park Avenue. Rosie had a demure younger sister, Lena (or Helen, in the Americanized form), also a maid on the Hilders family staff, responsible for tending to the particular needs of a daughter.

During a social evening sponsored by a German club, according to the story told in the family, "William" Sebold, captured in photographs during these days as tall and thin with jug ears and a vibrant grin, was introduced to Helen Büchner, who with her strong jawline and unfussed-over bob seemed the picture of Bavarian constancy. They were married with little fanfare on May 2, 1931, at the German Catholic church on East Eighty-Seventh Street, St. Joseph's, located just around the corner from the apartment on Eighty-Eighth near First Avenue that they might have been sharing before Monsignor Gallus Bruder formalized the union. Sebold was such an indifferent Catholic that he could remember neither the name of the church ("St. John's?" he ventured) nor the identity of its pastor when the subject came up a decade later. "And did you meet Father Bruder?" No, he said, although he insisted he attended the church "several times."

While his wife kept her position on Park Avenue, Sebold hopped from job to job in the midst of a woeful labor market, just another laborer in New York trying to survive a time of soup lines and homeless encampments. He worked as a maintenance man for an orphanage on the Upper West Side, a "great big real estate concern in New York," and the Hudson Terminal at 30 Church Street. He built a boathouse and installed steampipe for Mrs. Ida

Oschlag of Madison Avenue. He was a porter and relief elevator operator for the apartment building at 151 West Seventy-Fourth Street, "giving the best of satisfaction in his work and at all times doing his utmost in every detail entrusted to him," according to a recommendation written by his boss, A. S. Lupez. "I worked in building work, as a handyman, and superintending," Sebold said.

Of his political associations, this much is known: one of the two sworn witnesses on his petition for naturalization, which he submitted on July 15, 1935, was a relative of his wife's, Lorenz Büchner, who operated a *Bierstube* underneath the Second Avenue el that advertised itself in pro-Nazi publications as a cozy gathering place for *Gesinnungsgenossen* or like-minded political companions. Sebold, who lived a block and a half away from "Lorenz Büchner's," could not but have spent time around or near the rowdy ideologues who plotted their intrigues from just such drinking and dining establishments in the heart of German Yorkville. But we also know that he took seriously the pledge he made on February 10, 1936, when he raised his right hand before a deputy clerk in federal court in Manhattan and recited the following words: "I hereby declare, on oath, that I absolutely and entirely renounce and abjure all allegiance and fidelity to any foreign prince, potentate, state, or sovereignty, and particularly to the German Reich of which I have heretofore been a subject; that I will support and defend the Constitution and laws of the United States of America against all enemies, foreign and domestic; that I will bear true faith and allegiance to the same; and that I take this obligation freely without any mental reservation or purpose of evasion. So help me God."

He would later assert he meant every word he uttered: "I had nothing to do with Hitler anymore. I was an American citizen."

CHAPTER FIVE

WITH THE RESOURCES
WE HAVE ON HAND

The techniques of advanced scientific crime detection that had proved indispensable in conquering home-bred banditry were now set to work uncovering the enemy.

—J. Edgar Hoover

The summertime impasse over the Sudeten crisis ended when Adolf Hitler, still intending to launch his invasion of Czechoslovakia in the name of rescuing ethnic Germans by the first of October, delivered a violent speech on the final day of the Nazi Party meeting in Nuremberg on September 12, 1938. With an international audience hooked up to "the world-awaited talk on Germany's foreign policy to be delivered by Adolf Hitler," as the chirpy CBS radio announcer described it, the Führer ranted at length about the mostly imagined misery of his fellow members of the *Volksgemeinschaft* who were "being oppressed and humiliated in an unprecedented fashion." They "may not sing a song they like because the Czechs dislike it." They are "beaten until they bleed simply because they wear stockings which the Czechs care not to see." They are "terrorized and abused because they greet one another in a fashion the Czechs cannot bear even though they were merely greeting one another and no Czech."

He pledged that "if these tortured creatures can find neither justice nor help by themselves, then they will receive both from us. There must be an end to the injustice inflicted upon these people!" In the aftermath of the tirade, Konrad Henlein's storm troopers dutifully launched riots in the Sudeten regions, which were only quelled after the Czech government declared martial law on the following afternoon. Listening in from Rochester, Minnesota, where his son was being treated at the Mayo Clinic, President Roosevelt (who could understand German) turned to his aide Harry Hopkins and instructed him to go to the West Coast "to take a look at the aircraft industry with a view to its expansion." Hopkins felt that at that instant FDR knew "we were going to get into war and he believed that air power would win it." On the following evening in London, Prime Minister Neville Chamberlain sent his historic message to Hitler offering "to come over at once to see you with a view to trying to find a peaceful solution."

The story that follows is so deservedly ignominious that it is almost too painful to relate: On September 15, Chamberlain, who was sixty-nine years old, took the first airplane ride of his life, landing in Munich, traveling three hours by train to Berchtesgaden, and motoring up to Hitler's chalet, the Berghof. Escorted to Hitler's study on the first floor, Chamberlain listened as Hitler sputtered for a few hours about the plight of his *Volk* in a manner that somehow convinced Chamberlain that "here was a man who could be relied upon when he had given his word," as he actually wrote. After agreeing in principle that the Sudetenland should be handed over to German control, Chamberlain made the long slog home, convincing his cabinet and then the French that this gift would be, as Hitler had promised, his last territorial claim in Europe.

By September 21, the Czechs had been bullied into going

along. On the following day, Chamberlain flew in triumph to the Rhineland resort of Bad Godesberg and presented Hitler with his benefaction. "I'm sorry," Hitler responded after a brief pause, "but that won't do anymore." He wanted a speedier occupation of a larger area of western Czechoslovakia, a more forceful expulsion ("no foodstuffs, goods, cattle, raw materials, etc., are to be removed") of the non-Germans residing there, and land grabs for neighboring Poland and Hungary to further weaken the Czech state. Chamberlain harrumphed about being "both puzzled and disappointed." Flying back to London, he "saw spread out like a map beneath him the mile upon mile of flimsy houses which constituted the East End of London," shuddering "to think of their inmates lying a prey to bombardment from the air," wrote an aide.

By September 26, Chamberlain's cabinet, the French, and the Czechs had all rejected Hitler's Bad Godesberg ultimatum. For the next two days, the world braced for war. French troops manned the Maginot Line, built for just this purpose after World War I, and Chamberlain mobilized the British fleet. The Allied capitals anticipated an aerial attack the likes of which humankind had never seen. Charles Lindbergh, who had been given the privilege of touring Reich aviation facilities a year earlier with his friend Ernst Udet, was in London meeting with senior British officials and influential notables and communicated his expert opinion that "German air strength is greater than that of all other European countries combined" and "has the means of destroying London, Paris, and Prague," according to a memo he wrote at the request of that most fervent of appeasers, US ambassador Joseph P. Kennedy. Lindbergh said the Luftwaffe possessed eight to ten thousand aircraft with the capacity to produce five to eight hundred more a month, vast overestimates that would become conventional wisdom among military, political, and opinion leaders throughout the world. On the evening of the twenty-seventh, Chamberlain told his nation over the wireless, "How horrible, fantastic, incredible, it is that we should be digging trenches and trying on gas masks here because of a quarrel in a faraway country between people of whom we know nothing!"

In Berlin, Hermann Göring received a memorandum from the Luftwaffe general who had been asked to draw up a war plan for Great Britain. Citing a lack of sufficient airfields in northern Germany, bomber pilots without training over water, and a poor weather-reporting service, the general concluded, "A war of destruction against England with the resources we have on hand is ruled out." The Luftwaffe had about 2,900 planes, just 1,669 of which could've been mobilized during the crisis, with the ability to build less than 450 a month. Without at least the services of runways in the Low Countries or France, the Luftwaffe's medium bombers had no chance of mounting effective attacks against the British mainland. Several other German generals, fearful that Hitler was leading the nation to certain defeat, were apparently ready to launch a putsch, according to their postwar claims. But before the plan could be activated, Hitler (at the decisive urging of Benito Mussolini) agreed to a British plan to convene a four-power summit to try to avoid war. On the afternoon of September 28, Chamberlain was speaking in the House of Commons when Sir John Simon handed him a note. "I have something further to say to the House yet," he said after looking it over, one of the most dramatic moments in the body's history. "I have now been informed by Herr Hitler that he invites me to meet him in Munich tomorrow morning. . . . I am sure that the House will be ready to release me now to go and see what I can make of this last effort." The applause from the assembled MPs was thunderous. Talks between Hitler, Chamberlain, French premier Édouard Daladier, and Mussolini (an interested neutral who spoke the languages of the other three) began at noon on September 29 and ended at 3:00 a.m. on September 30 with the signing of the Munich Agreement, essentially Hitler's once-rejected counterproposal from Bad Godesberg. The Soviets hadn't been invited to participate. The Czechs were waiting in the next room to be informed of the fate of their sovereignty. Not content to let well enough alone, Chamberlain took the Führer aside later that morning and had him scrawl his name to a sheet of paper pledging that Germany and Great Britain would never go to war against each other. Returning to the acclamation of a grateful nation on October 1, Chamberlain waved the document on the tarmac at Heston and later from the windows of 10 Downing Street, where he told the crowd that he believed he had achieved "peace for our time." From the backbenches, Winston Churchill had to pause for the protests to die down after he told his colleagues, "We have sustained a total and unmitigated defeat."

On that same day, German troops crossed the border into the Sudetenland as joyous crowds flung flowers before their path and heiled praises to the great leader who had once again proved the master of his opponents. In swift order, the invaders took control of the mountain fortress line that represented Czechoslovakia's best protection against a land invasion, arrested the eight thousand ethnic German and two thousand Czech political opponents of Nazism who hadn't joined their comrades in flight, seized the Skoda Works munitions plant and other industrial structures, and installed Konrad "Little Hitler" Henlein as the first commissioner of the new Reich Region Sudetenland. Charles Lindbergh flew to Berlin, where an appreciative Hermann Göring presented him with the Service Cross of the German Eagle with Star, the highest decoration that the Nazi state could bestow on a foreigner, honoring him for delivering (willfully or not) misinformation that enhanced the Luftwaffe's sinister renown while giving it greater time to build up its strength.

On October 14, Hitler told Göring to "execute a gigantic production program, against which previous efforts would pale into insignificance" that would increase the size of the Luftwaffe by *five* times. With a war against long-range enemies now a distinct possibility, Nazi air planners ordered the mass production of two planes that were said to have the capacity to fly more than two thousand miles and finally provide Hitler with the ability to strike into the heart of the worldwide Jewish conspiracy. Yet Ernst Udet insisted that both planes function as dive-bombers, heedlessly brushing away concerns about the technical difficulty of manufacturing such machines and guaranteeing a significant delay in the creation of a mature air force to serve Hitler's most delusional ambitions of international conquest. Orders were issued to develop a dive-bombing sight rather than the kind of precision bombsight for level flight that Hermann Lang had stolen from America, which meant that the hard work of turning the Norden blueprints into an instrument that German industry could replicate in numbers was yet to begin. "It is comparatively easy to build two or three bombsights," Ted Barth, president of Norden Inc., later said. "To get sizable production takes a terrific effort." On October 21, Hitler told his military to begin preparations for a strike against the rest of the tottering Czech state in the belief that Chamberlain and Daladier weren't serious when they promised to guarantee the integrity of its newly drawn borders. "That fellow Chamberlain has spoiled my entry into Prague," Hitler was heard muttering on the way home from Munich.

With his clamorous HUAC hearings earning him a national reputation for smoking out un-American enemies, Congress-

man Martin Dies ("rhymes with 'spies,'" noted *Time* magazine) wanted a greater hand in suppressing the spy menace that
everyone seemed to agree was a growing threat to the country.
The president would have none of his meddling. When asked
by reporters about a meeting he had with US Attorney Lamar
Hardy to discuss the "spy situation," Roosevelt went out of his
way to note that the administration wasn't interested in suppressing "propaganda activity" of the sort the Dies Committee
had been investigating but only in "military and naval spy activity" that "goes by the generic term of 'foreign spies.'" He said
"very, very deep study" was being conducted to determine how
to "counteract the continuance of foreign government spying on
our national defenses." Congressman Dies responded the next
day by proposing a legislative angle to Roosevelt's effort, suggesting the creation of a central intelligence agency, a ban on foreign-
controlled groups, and a drastic tightening of immigration and
deportation laws. "The president has taken cognizance of this
grave situation in a splendid move," Dies said.

The newspapers didn't need to seek comment from FDR to
know he had no interest in cooperating with Dies. In a cabinet
meeting on Friday, October 14, 1938, Roosevelt asked Attorney
General Homer Cummings to chair a committee "to inquire into
the so-called espionage situation" and report back in a week with
recommendations for Roosevelt to implement. He asked that
the proposed system "be confined to the investigation of espionage on the part of foreigners" and arranged "so that the budget
could supply the funds without attracting too much attention,"
according to Cummings's notes.

But first Lamar Hardy had a spy trial to conduct. He caught
a break when young Guenther Rumrich pleaded guilty, agreeing to testify against his codefendants and leave unchallenged
any incriminating statements he had made to Special Agent

Leon Turrou. On the Monday following FDR's Friday cabinet meeting, Hardy delivered an epic opening statement before a courtroom full of reporters from throughout the world, a diplomatic assault against an ostensibly friendly nation that the press described as unprecedented. He charged that a conspiracy "conceived in and directed from Germany" had sought to steal "information respecting our national defense" for "the advantage of a foreign government, namely Germany." Hardy identified eighteen defendants—five regime officials in Germany, six transatlantic couriers, six spies, and a Scottish woman whose Dundee address served as a mail drop (and who was already serving time in a British jail)—but could only point jurors to the four unprepossessing individuals in custody, whom most observers dismissed as "small fries."

The first week of the trial was dominated by the unchallenged testimony of Rumrich, described by the *Times* as a "United States Army deserter and unsuccessful dishwasher," whose stories were so odd that it was "almost impossible to learn from his recital where fiction ended and fact began." Many column inches in the nation's newspapers were nonetheless expended on his revelations about a plot to entice an Army colonel to the McAlpin Hotel, where a courier dressed as a window washer was to subdue him with a fountain pen filled with gas, and an equally ludicrous daydream about obtaining the plans for the aircraft carriers *Yorktown* and *Enterprise* by falsifying President Roosevelt's signature on faked White House stationery. (*Daily News* front page: "Spies Plotted F.D.R. Forgery.") Rumrich testified about seeing a photograph of a courier posing with Hitler aide Fritz Wiedemann and Ambassador Hans Dieckhoff at the German embassy in Washington, which resulted in international headlines suggesting that figures of truly prominent stature were tied up with the plot.

The press coverage was still favorable when Attorney General Cummings delivered his promised espionage report to President Roosevelt on the trial's fourth day, October 20. The six-page memo was written not by Cummings, who would only serve for another few months and would quickly recede into history's shadows, but by J. Edgar Hoover. The director made the case that the Federal Bureau of Investigation was perfectly situated to transform itself into the nation's premier spy-chasing agency. He reminded the president that the FBI already had his authorization to conduct broad-picture surveillance of Fascist and Communist threats, which enabled agents "to collect through investigative activity and other contact and to correlate for ready reference information dealing with various forms of activities of either a subversive or a so-called intelligence type," Hoover wrote. He said there were "approximately 2500 names now in the index of the various types of individuals engaged in activities of Communism, Nazism, and various types of foreign espionage."

Since the FBI already had the legal authority to conduct occasional spy investigations at the instigation of the State Department and other agencies, he wrote, it didn't need any "special legislation which would draw attention to the fact that it was proposed to develop a special counterespionage drive of any great magnitude." Instead, the Bureau needed money. He asked for a vast increase in funding to hire and train new personnel that should be obtained "with the utmost degree of secrecy in order to avoid criticism or objections which might be raised to such an expansion by either ill-informed persons or individuals having some ulterior motive," a wily suggestion that would allow the FBI to accrue power before its intragovernmental rivals knew what was happening. And the director needed control: Yes, Hoover was willing to coordinate spy efforts with military and naval intelligence, whose leaders, he told the president, had already agreed to the arrangement. But he wanted to end the State Department's role in authorizing investigations, arguing "that the more circumscribed this program is, the more effective it will be and the less danger there is of its becoming a matter of general public knowledge." There was no need for "a larger departmental committee" because "other agencies of the government are less interested in matters of counterespionage and general intelligence." In his best bureaucratese, the nation's number one G-man was making the case that he, and he alone, should be its number one spymaster.

By the end of the trial's second week, with FDR continuing to mull Hoover's proposal, the government's case still appeared to be strong. On Thursday, October 27, the prosecution spent much of the day discussing how the spies had obtained plans for an experimental dive-bomber developed by Curtiss-Wright and a machine-gun sighting system for naval airplanes built by an unnamed contractor that enabled "a gunner to lead an enemy plane much as a duck hunter leads a bird," testified Lieutenant Commander Daniel V. Gallery of the Bureau of Ordnance. A gasp filled the courtroom when an assistant prosecutor reached under a pile of newspapers and pulled out a large weapon equipped with such a sight, a stunt that "unquestionably made a profound impression on the jury," wrote one reporter.

But the newspapers were more riveted upon Dr. Ignatz Griebl's mistress, Kate Moog, who took the stand at 3:55 p.m. after arriving at the courthouse resplendent in a sailor cap and black velvet suit with silver-fox scarves draped around her neck. She described traveling with Naz to Germany, where they met with Abwehr officers impressed with her boasted acquaintances with Rear Admiral William "Bull" Halsey, Secretary of the Navy Claude Swanson, and President Roosevelt, for whom she had once served as a nurse. Over tea at the roof garden of the Hotel

Eden, she had been asked if she would be interested in using her society connections to host a salon in Washington to instruct politicians, military men, reporters, and other DC players in the intimate glories of National Socialism, a barely disguised attempt to send her into the field as a new Mata Hari, the stage name of the Dutch exotic dancer and seductress executed by a French firing squad in 1917 for allegedly employing her sexual wiles on behalf of Imperial Germany. "He thought I could extend a gweat service to them if I could make social contacts for them," she told jurors, according to the *Daily News'* phonetically precise transcription. Although she testified that the proposal was an innocent ploy to improve relations between the two countries, the coverage in the next day's papers made her out to be a dumb broad who was clearly being recruited as a femme fatale. "In the carefully modulated tone of a debutante trying out for a society play, a comely nurse told a jury in federal court yesterday that two 'fine gentlemen' she met at lunch in Berlin a year and a half ago wanted to cast her in the role of an American Mata Hari," began the *Times'* story.

When she returned to the witness stand on the next morning, she was a different woman. "The baby talk of Kate Moog Busch gave way to the ferocity of a tigress," wrote the *Daily News*. In her rage, she claimed to have forgotten all about spy conversations she once said she'd heard in a Bremen nightclub. "There was a floor show!" she said. "I was going to dance, have a good time. I was going to be a lady, not listen to gentlemen's talk." She angrily denied the suggestion that she was having an affair with Dr. Griebl. "Didn't you ever have a friend? If you ever had a good friend, then you know what a good friend means." In a teary-eyed appeal to the judge, she wailed, "When I came home, everything was hotsy-totsy [thirties slang for "A-OK"]. There was nothing doing about the spy business. I didn't know anything about the spy business until this investigation began." As the courtroom roared with delight, Judge Knox banged his hand on the bench and shouted, "Stop that!" And she turned on Leon Turrou, who "acted like a mental case or something." Asked during cross-examination if Turrou had informed Dr. Griebl that a subpoena was about to be issued for him, she said he did. And didn't Dr. Griebl then leave the country? "Yes," she said.

At this inopportune moment the trial was recessed for the weekend, and the government was forced to endure two days of speculation about whether the FBI's lead investigator had assisted—"connived," in the words of the papers—in the flight of a key figure in the ring. On Monday morning, Moog was guided through a lawyerly seeming-disavowal before the prosecution turned to other witnesses: "He never, at any time, told Dr. Griebl or me that we could leave the country or go anywhere," she said of Turrou, which didn't contradict her earlier testimony. "He told us we must stay right here."

On Tuesday, J. Edgar Hoover was asked by the White House to board the president's train in a day's time to discuss a matter of importance during the trip from Washington to Hyde Park. FDR aide Stephen Early didn't specify the purpose of the meeting nor indicate whether it would last until the end of the line. According to a memo Hoover wrote several days later, Roosevelt wanted to talk spies. "He stated that he had approved the plan which I had prepared and which had been sent to him by the Attorney General," Hoover wrote. FDR told him that he had just ordered his budget director to quietly allocate an increase in funds "to handle counterespionage activities," as suggested by the memo, although Hoover was disappointed to learn that he wouldn't receive all the money he requested (at least yet). But that's about all Hoover revealed of a momentous encounter that allowed the FBI to vastly expand the scope of its investigative responsibilities. What we do know is that the president issued his fiat in an atmosphere of such secrecy that he hadn't squared the matter with other branches in the government, especially the State Department, which was bound to protest the loss of its ability to shape policy regarding foreign spies. The discussion of what was essentially a private deal appears to have lasted all the way to Penn Station. Hoover wrote that the "special train was held until the conference with the President was concluded and I left the train at New York."

At the same time, Agent Turrou was appearing for a second day on the witness stand downtown, facing a barrage of hostile questions from defense attorney George C. Dix, who had traveled to the Reich in September and obtained a seventeen-thousand-word deposition from a gleefully vindictive Dr. Griebl. Turrou was forced to deny that the entire investigation was concocted "to serve the American Public for breakfast a sensational 'spy case' with highly interesting Anecdotes," as Griebl wrote in a letter proclaiming his innocence. "What these G-men, including Mr. Turrou, assert sounds like an interesting spy romance, which exists only in his brain, but never occurred. These little fellows are making themselves ridiculous." Over the remaining three weeks of the trial, Turrou would angrily deny a series of "damnable lies" that accused him of coercing confessions and assisting escapes. The most bizarre moment in the character-assassination campaign came when an elderly Russian landlord testified that Turrou lived under the name Leon Petroff in his house on Douglass Street in Brooklyn more than twenty years earlier. "One day Petroff say, 'I kill myself,'" the man recalled in his accented English. "I say, 'Listen, you no kill yourself in my house.' So he started to drink something from a bottle so I run for police. Police go for doctors. Doctors put ice in mouth. So they took him to hospital." Was it Kings County Hospital?

George Dix wondered. "Yes," the Russian said, "that's the hospital for crazy people."

But at this point in world events, the spy trial had become of less pressing interest. The public was focusing its attention on a shocking act of Nazi criminality that caused even the most disinterested observer to concede that Hitler was truly a menace: the pogrom against the Jewish population of the newly expanded Reich that the *Times'* correspondent in Berlin, Otto D. Tolischus, described on page 1 as "a wave of destruction, looting, and incendiarism unparalleled in Germany since the Thirty Years' War" of 1618 to 1648. During the night of November 9 and into the morning of November 10, Nazi hordes set fire to more than a thousand synagogues and destroyed at least seventy-five hundred Jewish businesses, smashing their Belgian plate-glass windows with such fervor that the night would be forever known as *Kristallnacht*. Jewish homes and apartments were ransacked, and thirty thousand Jewish men, "especially rich ones," were incarcerated in concentration camps. Jews were cursed at, slapped, spat upon, beaten, murdered. The official death toll was ninety-one, but the actual number, which should include the hundreds who died in the camps before most inmates were released, was many times higher. The violence was followed by a spate of legal measures that all but ended the possibility of a Jewish existence in the Third Reich. German Jews were ordered to pay a billion-reichsmark fine and robbed of their businesses, land, stock, jewels, and artworks in a process known as Aryanization. They were banned from collecting welfare payments, holding driver's licenses, owning carrier pigeons, attending German schools, publishing Jewish newspapers, possessing precious metals or stones, and visiting most public places. During a conference of high-ranking officials that discussed the restrictions, Hermann Göring joked about confining animals that resembled Jews to certain sections of forests ("the elk has a crooked nose like theirs") and mused to no one in particular, "I would not like to be a Jew in Germany." Yet Hitler didn't go so far as to require Jews to wear special badges on their clothing or force them to live within exclusionary ghettos, probably in the belief that the German people were still unprepared for a radicalism that recalled not the great war of the seventeenth century but the dark era of the Middle Ages. Although it wasn't easy for Jews to navigate the labyrinthine bureaucracy or gain access to the necessary funds, the official policy of Nazi Germany was to induce them to emigrate, in the hopes, according to a Foreign Ministry circular, of increasing anti-Semitism in Western countries and thus producing sympathy for Germany's plight.

Few outside of the ideologically blinkered believed that the night of horrors was a spontaneous eruption of what Goebbels called the "healthy instinct" of the German people. "The foreign press is very bad," he confided to his diary. "Mainly the American." George Gallup found that 94 percent of Americans now disapproved of Nazi policy toward Jews, "a vote of condemnation so nearly unanimous as to constitute one of the most decisive expressions of opinion in any of the more than 800 surveys conducted by the organization in the last three years," he said. In New York, more than five thousand sign-carrying protesters (YOUR SILENCE EMBOLDENS HITLER, KEEP NAZI SPY SHIPS OUT OF NEW YORK HARBOR) jeered and hooted as the *Bremen* pushed off from Pier 86 with only 381 passengers on board. "The ship was kept brilliantly illuminated so that no attacker might approach unseen," wrote the *Herald Tribune*. A group of women in black veils conducted a silent vigil in front of the German consulate at 17 Battery Place. Such figures as the author of *The Maltese Fal-*

con (Dashiell Hammett), the Irish Republican Army veteran now leading the union representing subway workers (Mike Quill), the eminent German exile teaching at Union Theological Seminary (Paul Tillich), and the president of the Harlem Bar Association (Albert G. Gilbert) were on the rostrum during a packed-to-overflowing event at Madison Square Garden that called for a complete cessation of US trade with Germany.

The US government was not unresponsive to public opinion when it refused to alter existing policy to make it easier for the Reich's Jews to enter the United States. "That is not in contemplation," said FDR. "We have the quota system." The percentage of Americans opposed to relaxing immigration restrictions actually increased from 75 percent at the time of the *Anschluss* to 83 percent in the aftermath of *Kristallnacht*. Yet President Roosevelt *was* shaken by events in Germany. On November 14, he ordered the return of the US ambassador from Berlin, which, while short of a formal recall or a severing of diplomatic relations, was seen as a move of considerable significance. On the same day, he met with senior military and economic advisers and railed about the need to transform the low-output American aircraft industry into a juggernaut of mass production that could build an air fleet to frighten Adolf Hitler in just the way the Luftwaffe had worked on the Western democracies at Munich. "A new regiment of field artillery, or new barracks at an Army post in Wyoming, or new machine tools in an ordnance arsenal, he said sharply, would not scare Hitler one blankety-blank-blank bit!" recalled Army Air Corps general Henry "Hap" Arnold of the president's language. "What he wanted was airplanes! Airplanes were the implements that *would* have an influence on Hitler's activities!" Although Roosevelt's hopes of increasing the number of US planes from a mostly unimpressive fleet of eighteen hundred to a strike force of at least ten thousand would be scaled back and balanced with the needs of ground forces by the time he unveiled his new national defense program in January, FDR had laid the groundwork for the scaling up of an industry that would construct far more aircraft than any other world power after 1940. "A battle was won in the White House that day which took its place with—or at least led to—the victories in combat later, for time is a most important factor in building an air force," wrote General Arnold in his memoirs. On the next afternoon, November 15, Roosevelt took the unusual step of reading a prepared statement to the press about the anti-Jewish actions in Germany, which he pointedly noted was for direct quotation. The third of its four sentences would be the most widely reproduced: "I myself could scarcely believe that such things could occur in a twentieth-century civilization."

Two weeks later, a jury of ten men and two women found compelling reasons to deliver guilty verdicts again the spy defendants. On December 3, Judge Knox sentenced Gus Rumrich and his Air Corps friend to two years, providing leniency to Rumrich for his cooperation and to his pal for his near innocence. Even though Judge Knox didn't believe the *Europa* hairdresser/courier merited more than a deportation order, he gave her two years as a warning to any other employees of the German passenger liners who might wish to participate in "a system that cannot be tolerated." The technician from Seversky Aircraft, a man "inspired by a dream of *Deutschland über alles,*" was sentenced to a mere six years. In his closing oration, Judge Knox boasted that he was offering a lesson in the mercies of a just democracy to the emissaries of a cruel totalitarianism. On the same day in Berlin, the Reich issued a response of sorts. It executed two soldiers of the Wehrmacht, Bruno Trojaner and Berthold Koehne, dropping the blade of the guillotine upon them for "revealing military secrets to unnamed foreign powers," according to the Associated

Press. The AP dispatch noted that both men had deserted their units and fled abroad to serve a foreign espionage organization, although it didn't detail how they had been returned to the care of Germany. The formal charge against them was treason.

At the White House, President Roosevelt was full of praise for US Attorney Hardy's "perfectly amazing job in this spy trial in New York," but cautioned that "the root of this thing, the roots go down pretty deep." He explained to reporters that he didn't want Congress to allocate funds for a secret police that would monitor the American people but one that would allow "our own people to watch the secret police of certain other nations, which is a very excellent distinction to make." Questioned about the particulars of the new counterespionage plan that he said was already being put in place, FDR deemed the topic out of bounds: "That is one of the things I am not going to tell you, and I don't think it ought to be asked about because, very obviously, if you run stories of the exact workings of the intelligence system you are going to destroy ninety percent of the value of that system."

"You do not contemplate the establishment of a new agency?" a reporter asked anyway.

"No."

"Has a coordinator been named?"

"There you go," the president quipped as the Oval Office filled with laughter.

It wouldn't remain a secret for long that J. Edgar Hoover was the only man for the job.

CHAPTER SIX

TO LEAD
AN ORGANIZATION THERE

I began to look around for a man whom I could train as an agent with a secret transmitter.

—Nikolaus Ritter

On or about January 30, 1939, according to his FBI file, William G. Sebold applied for and was issued his American passport, the first, unwitting step in his bizarre journey to the heart of the Nazi espionage underworld in New York.

In the nearly three years since he had been solemnized as a US citizen, Sebold had led a curiously wayward existence. In the spring of 1936, he moved with his wife to Southern California, where he found his first job with a US military contractor, the Consolidated Aircraft Corporation of San Diego, which was known for its line of seaplanes, in particular the US Navy–commissioned PBY Catalina. He worked for the company on two separate occasions in the coming year, from May 27 to June 29, and August 3 to October 26, for a total of just less than four months. "My function was as a bumper," he said. "Shaping things out of metal, out of aluminum." According to his service record, his official job title was "hull assembler." Then his health beckoned: "Well, I took sick and had to lay off and go back again." Sebold had to "leave this climate due to poor health," his employer stated.

Returning to New York, the couple moved into another Yorkville apartment, this time at 214 East Eighty-Fourth Street, and Helen resumed her maid duties with the Park Avenue family. In hopes of improving his lungs, Sebold obtained a summer job through an employment agency working as an on-site electrician/ handyman for the Workmen's Circle Camp on Sylvan Lake near Pawling, New York, which was operated by a Jewish fraternal order as a Yiddish-language experiment in Socialist immersion. According to the camp's literature, children from the city were instructed in "Yiddish stories, names of Yiddish writers, incidents in the workers' movement, biographies of people who fought for the freedom of mankind, and Yiddish folk-songs." By his very willingness to accept a paycheck from the indoctrination mills of the Judeo-Bolshevik conspiracy, Sebold showed that he was telling the truth when he said he was uninterested in the doctrinal delusions of Nazi Germany.

But the upstate air didn't cure him. Sometime in the winter of 1937, he was home with his wife when his stomach pain became so severe that he rushed to Bellevue Hospital. "The doctor looked me over and laid me on the table and knocked a couple times on my stomach and said, 'You are okay,' and gave me some drops. And I said, 'I am not okay,' and used some insulting language to the doctor, and he said, 'Okay, now we have to keep you here and look you over,' and they took me into the psychiatric ward." Sebold was punished for displaying the flash of anger that was his characteristic response to being pushed too far. "I had a violent look on me," he said. "I was aroused to anger." After a stay of "twenty-one days, two weeks, I don't remember," in the psych ward, a senior doctor examined him, recognized the problem, and ordered that he undergo ulcer surgery without delay. He would later say that "half of his stomach" was removed. Upon his release in the early winter of 1938, Sebold set out alone for the warmer climes of Murrieta, California, where he spent a month chopping wood and selling the resulting stacks as firewood. After another six weeks working various odd jobs in Southern California, he returned home to New York.

It's unclear how he spent the remainder of 1938, a period during which the actions of Nazi Germany emerged as a central issue in American foreign policy. He may have been thinking about his employment prospects when he decided to return to Mülheim in early 1939. The press was forever writing about how Hitler's military and industrial mobilization campaign had brought full employment to Germany. He could've been worried about the possibility of a repressive campaign against German Americans, a concern prevalent enough to inspire Hermann Göring to issue orders following *Kristallnacht* giving "all possible preferential treatment such as free passage, tax exemption for one year, and so on" to those "agricultural workers, skilled artisans, engineers, and technicians" of German descent in America willing to work in the fatherland. Sebold read about the Munich Conference in the *Daily News* and the *Journal-American,* he said, but didn't see how it mattered to him. Perhaps he chose to go back to Germany because he was having troubles with his wife, from whom he had been separated for months at a time over the past two years. Maybe he was worried about the welfare of his family— just as he was when he went home and assisted during the French occupation of the Ruhr in the early 1920s. Or he could've been telling the whole truth when he claimed he just wanted to relax in the warm confines of his mother's house. "I was run-down and not fully recuperated from my operation," he said.

"Did you hesitate to return to the Hitler Germany?" he was later asked.

"No, I had nothing to do with Hitler," Sebold said.

"Weren't you aware of the nature of the regime?"

"But Hitler could not touch me. I was an American citizen. I had nothing to do with the government, with Germany. My hometown, my people lived there."

"You knew there were critical times abroad?"

"There always were in Europe, for hundreds of years."

"So that you went to Germany to take a rest, absolutely oblivious to conditions that existed there?"

"Yes, sir. Just a rest, a good long rest."

"Fully confident that you were protected and surrounded by the blanket of American citizenship?"

"Sure."

His passport in hand, he boarded the Hamburg America liner *Deutschland* on February 2, 1939, carrying a single suitcase and a package. He did not know he was walking into a trap.

Leon Turrou's long-delayed articles about the infamous German spy case were published in the *New York Post* in twenty installments from December 5, 1938, to January 4, 1939, concluding on the same day President Roosevelt began a public campaign to bolster national defense and revise neutrality legislation, a campaign aimed directly at containing Germany. "A war which threatened to envelop the world in flames has been averted," FDR said during his State of the Union that evening, "but it has become increasingly clear that world peace is not assured." Congress was receptive to his plans for a military buildup but unmoved by his comment that neutrality restrictions forbidding the sale of American armaments to combatant nations "may operate unevenly and unfairly—may actually give aid to an aggressor and deny it to the victim." On January 12, Roosevelt asked for $525 million to fund an "emergency program for the strengthening of the defense of the United States," with $300 million to be directed to the US Army Air Corps for the purchase of a minimum of three thousand new aircraft. "I suggest that $50 million of the $300 million for airplanes be made immediately available in order to correct the present lag in aircraft production due to idle plants," he said, which promised an increase in work for contractors involved in every aspect of a warplane's function. The isolationists were supportive just as long as FDR was prevented from finding a way to draw America into a European fight that would allow him to assume autocratic powers. He "cares no more for what may happen to us in a war than the man in the moon," said Senator Hiram Johnson of California. "He has developed a dictator complex." When a newly developed Douglas medium bomber crashed in California with a French military observer aboard, an obvious breach of neutrality, the outrage was so overwrought that the entire Senate Military Affairs Committee tramped over to the White House for a private conference with the president, who stated forthrightly that the future of our civilization depended on ensuring the military strength of the Allies. "It is not a question of secrecy," he told them. "We have just one secret, and that is the question of the bombsight, and that has not been disclosed to the French and won't." The thought would've never occurred to him that the Nazis already had it.

On January 27, Random House released Turrou's *Post* series in a swastika-bedecked hardcover under the title *Nazi Spies in America*. The public seemed receptive to the former G-man's self-glorifying account of how he "grilled" various evildoers until they "broke" under the pressure of his investigative brilliance, although the book revealed little more (and sometimes less) about the workings of the spy ring than had already been broadcast at trial. "There is evidence that for every spy we exposed, dozens more lurk hidden here," he and his uncredited coauthor (David Wittels) wrote in the concluding pages. The book quickly sold out its first printing. A British edition was released as *The Nazi Spy Conspiracy in America*. The *New York Times* raved that Turrou's "intensely interesting" tale served as a warning to the country that "the business of spying is not finished, by any means!" while the *Los Angeles Times* worried that "hysterical accusations" would only cause us "to grow blind to our immediate danger from foreign agents."

The hysterical accusations—Dr. Griebl's fraudulent assertion that the German espionage system had embedded agents in *every* armament factory and shipyard in the United States—inspired the title of the film that Warner Brothers was rushing into production, *Confessions of a Nazi Spy,* which the studio's bosses intended as a new kind of Hollywood movie. It would be a pseudodocumentary exposé that would serve the dual function of performing well at the box office while delivering a propagandistic broadside against an actually named menace. In the first American film to utter the words *Adolf Hitler,* the foe would be identified as Nazi (pronounced "nazzy") spies who spoke in cartoonish accents, traveled on German passenger liners, plotted in an unidentified German neighborhood in New York, listened to raving speeches at "Nazi Bund" rallies and summer-camp outings, stole secrets from US defense installations, and *didn't* obsess about the Jews, whose plight goes unmentioned in apparent deference to audience sensibilities. Edward G. Robinson, who had become famous playing Italian American mobster Caesar Enrico "Rico" Bandello in *Little Caesar* (1931) but was born Emanuel Goldenberg in Bucharest, begged one of the producers to cast him in the "international spy ring story you are going to do." Robinson said, "I want to do that for my people."

As filming began on a soundstage in California, Bundesführer Fritz Kuhn was in the midst of planning for the last great
act of public Nazism in the United States. He hoped a "Mass
Demonstration for True Americanism" in Madison Square Garden would inspire the anti-Semites of America to join a German-
led fight to end the Jewish defilement of the nation's ideals.
Denied the right to represent the whole of German America,
he offered himself as the leader of a multiethnic Fascist movement that pledged itself as loyal to one country and one country only. "The Bund is an Organization of American Citizens
unequivocally committed to the Defense of the Flag, Constitution, and Sovereignty of these United States," according to a
handbill promoting the event, "and therefore to the Defense of
the right and duty to proportionate representation in the conduct of the Nation of the more than 100,000,000 Aryan (WHITE
GENTILE) Americans, as being the ONLY means of preserving
the Independence and the Christian Culture and Civilization of
this our Country!" The message was directly aimed at the Nazis'
newest ally on the streets of New York, the followers of the
country's most prominent non-German supporter of Hitler's
racial policies, the noxious radio priest Father Charles Coughlin
(pronounced "cawg-lin" or "cog-lin"). The Christian Front was a
thuggish band of (mostly) Irish Americans from neighborhoods
in upper Manhattan, Brooklyn, and the Bronx, an anti-Semitic
hate group that shouted slurs at highly trafficked intersections,
picketed Jewish-owned businesses, aggressively hawked copies
of the priest's 250,000-circulation weekly newspaper, and looked
to start fights with anyone who dared challenge them.

On February 19, the rally's eve, a note was delivered to City
Hall warning that three time bombs would be detonated if
the Nazis were allowed to speak, which led to security sweeps
within and around the Garden, then situated at its third location

on Eighth Avenue between Forty-Ninth and Fiftieth Streets, just to the west of the bustle of upper Times Square. In the hours before the event, a NYPD deployment that would grow to 1,745 cops, said to be the largest in the city's history up to that point, began closing off streets immediately surrounding the arena. "So strict were the police that even persons living and working within the guarded area were banned unless they could convince the police of their identity," wrote one reporter. "This caused some grumbling among residents of the area. Many spurious press cards were torn to pieces by the police and their bearers escorted back to the police lines." With Mayor Fiorello La Guardia out of town, acting mayor Newbold Morris took to the radio airwaves at 6:00 p.m., urging the citizenry "to shun this assemblage as one would a pestilence." All told, about ten thousand protesters gathered for an evening of picketing and sloganeering that included several attempts to break through barricades manned by cops who were unafraid to use physical force.

Upon entering the hall, spectators were greeted by a thirty-by-fourteen-foot likeness of George Washington behind an elevated speaker's platform that was flanked on either side by star-spangled banners and swastika-adorned Bund flags with the letters *AV* (Amerikadeutscher Volksbund) on a red background. Large signs decorated the upper decks: WAKE UP AMERICA—SMASH JEWISH COMMUNISM; 1,000,000 BUND MEMBERS BY 1940; and STOP JEWISH DOMINATION OF CHRISTIAN AMERICANS. The evening began with a color guard parading down the aisles and up onto the stage accompanied by a fife-and-drum corps playing the "Badenweiler March," Hitler's traditional entrance theme. A young woman identified in the program as Marguerite Rittershaus sang the American national anthem. By the time the main part of the evening began, the Garden was filled to its capacity of nineteen thousand customers, who paid forty cents for the cheap seats and $1.10 for the ones closer to the spittle. The addition of three thousand "ushers" of the uniformed Ordnungsdienst (OD) pushed the attendance figure to twenty-two thousand, according to the *Times'* estimate. In the rhetorical manner of Adolf Hitler, the speeches grew progressively more extreme as the evening went on. Talk of "the moral erosion and subsequent disintegration of our national unity" soon turned into paranoia about "the oriental cunning of the Jew Karl Marx-Mordecai!" Boos were heard at the mention of "President Rosenfeld," "the international Rothschilds," and "the Jewish Federal Reserve System." Hitler, Mussolini, and Father Coughlin received loud cheers. When one Nazi spoke of the "Golden Rule to treat all human beings with a human face," journalist Dorothy Thompson burst out in loud and sustained laughter, which caused angry Bundists sitting near the press box to demand her removal. "I was immediately seized by two policemen, whose salaries as a New York taxpayer I help to meet, and I was also set upon by a husky uniformed storm trooper, whose movement is following the detailed instructions of a foreign power," she wrote. "I was roughly hustled to the door."

Dressed in his Bund uniform with Iron Cross prominently displayed on the lapel, Fritz Kuhn delivered a belligerent keynote in broken English. The speech included a long disquisition on the history of Jewish crimes against America, beginning with the perfidious wire-puller who, he said, was responsible for Benedict Arnold's treachery and ending with the perfidious wire-puller (financier Bernard Baruch) who was "set to drive the United States into a European war on any old pretext." Near the end of the address, a young man in civilian clothes leapt from his seat and made a mad dash for the platform. "Down with Hitler!" shouted Isadore "Izzy" Greenbaum, a twenty-six-year-old plumber's assistant from Williamsburg, Brooklyn. "Down with Nazism!" He came within a few feet of the Bundesführer before

OD men tackled him, delivering a beating convulsive enough to tear his clothes from his body and cause a microphone to fall from the lectern. After a handful of NYPD officers carried him from the premises ("I'm no Communist!" he yelled on the way out), Kuhn described the nine items of the new Bund charter (which pledged to remove Jewish influence from various quarters of American life) and exhorted white gentiles of good character, patriotic zeal, and Aryan stock to consider filling out the membership application on an inside page of the program. "Free!" he thundered. "America!" the crowd responded. The chant was repeated two more times in imitation of the "Sieg"-followed-by-"Heil" routine indigenous to the Reich.

It was quite a showing. "There can be no doubt that the German-American Bund has by this massed demonstration scored a considerable success as regards organization," wrote Hans Borchers, the Nazi consul general in New York, in his report to Berlin. "It has been to the advantage of the Bund that it has understood how to make good use of the general trends of thought of the American people, such as, for instance, Coughlinism, to further its aspirations, although, as a result of this, the former far more exclusively *volksdeutsch* character of its meetings has been not a little modified." So appalling was the Bund's triumph that the American public was nearly united in its condemnation. "There isn't any sense in having these bunds in the country," said Senator John Gurney, a Republican of South Dakota. "I don't think we ought to allow it." From the other side of the aisle, Senator John Bankhead, an Alabama Democrat, suggested establishing "concentration camps for those trying to spread un-American propaganda." Martin Dies announced that the next session of his committee would devote renewed attention to the Bund. Even Father Coughlin distanced himself, suggesting that any of his followers who attended probably went out of curiosity's sake. "The meeting was held," said Mayor La Guardia upon his return home. "That's that." The mayor neglected to mention that he had devised a plan to take down Fritz Kuhn. He instructed his Department of Investigation to determine whether the Bund had paid all applicable sales and business taxes. At the same time, Manhattan district attorney Thomas E. Dewey, the mustachioed thirty-seven-year-old who was such a preternaturally gifted scourge of racketeers that he was seen as a serious contender to challenge President Roosevelt in 1940, ordered his own investigation into the Bund's fiscal affairs.

Within three months, Dewey's office had charged the Bundesführer with six counts of first-degree grand larceny, four counts of second-degree grand larceny, and two counts of third-degree forgery. Kuhn was accused of embezzling $14,548.59 in Bund funds, including $8,907.35 raised by the Madison Square Garden rally.

For all its elements of farce, the Turrou investigation had succeeded in destroying the Nest Bremen part of Germany's spy operation in New York, forcing its most experienced couriers off the Atlantic route and causing the flight or imprisonment of valuable in-country figures. The German passenger liners were livid at the besmirching of their reputation in the eyes of paying customers, who were less willing than ever to be associated with the swastikas flying at the West Side piers. The Foreign Ministry was predictably incensed that the task of keeping Americans from taking sides against the Reich had been made even harder. Nest Bremen's spymaster was able to convince Admiral Canaris that he didn't deserve to be punished for the debacle, but his career directing operations against the United States was effectively over. "The Nest was reduced to making a fresh start with new couriers buying magazines and newspapers in New York," according to the British postwar report.

The Abwehr's principal operation in the city was in the hands of Nikolaus Ritter, who, as the head of Ast Hamburg's office responsible for procuring air force intelligence, boasted a small cadre of agents whose most important members were Hermann Lang at Norden; "Colonel" Fritz Duquesne, the South African–born fraudster and veteran spy who was posing as a "consulting aeronautical engineer" under the banner of a front business, the Air Terminals Co.; and a high-level engineer at the Sperry Gyroscope Co. of Brooklyn who had been supplying technical data to Nazi Germany for nearly three years.

Everett Minster Roeder, forty-four, grew up as the brainy delinquent of an old-line German American family from the Bronx, a gun enthusiast and poker player who horrified his relatives by driving his pollution-emitting motorcycle into the kitchen, according to family legend. His father was Carl Roeder, a celebrated piano instructor who kept a studio at Carnegie Hall, taught at the Juilliard School of Music, and could be found every Sunday behind the organ at the Alexander Avenue Baptist Church. Young Everett did not have the musical precocity of his sister Dorothy, who was hailed in the pages of *Musical America* ("Piano Teacher's Young Daughter Surprises Hearers by Exceptional Talent") when she was nine years old. Instead, his ability lay in the intricacies of a draftsman's blueprints.

"Ed" Roeder, as he was known, was just fifteen when he enrolled at Cornell University's prestigious engineering school and almost certainly became acquainted with fellow students Edward Sperry and Elmer Sperry Jr. The brothers were known talent-spotters for their father, Elmer Sperry, who had founded his company just a few years earlier, in 1910, on the strength of contracts from the US Navy. The elder Sperry was a pioneer in the development of instruments that harnessed the stabilizing properties of the gyroscope (the spinning wheel with a carnivalesque ability to maintain its position in space despite the forces attempting to displace it) to bring command, control, and thus lethality to the increasingly powerful ships traveling on the ocean and in the air. The gyrocompass utilized an electrically powered gyroscope aligned to the earth's rotational axis to track true north, a marked improvement over the magnetic north of traditional compasses and a godsend in the age of the iron-hulled ship. The marine gyrostabilizer employed mammoth gyro wheels wired to the stabilizing fins in a ship's hull to lessen the roll caused by the sea's turbulence. The company's airplane stabilizer, which sought to tame "that particular beast of burden which is obsessed with motions, side pressure, skidding, acceleration pressures, and strong centrifugal moments . . . all in endless variety and endless combination," as Sperry described it, was the first autopilot, an avionic advancement that is probably second only to the Wright brothers' original invention in its revolutionizing impact. Utilizing the technology of the airplane stabilizer, Sperry developed an aerial torpedo, or flying bomb, which, when it traveled a thousand yards without a human pilot in March 1918, became the first cruise missile in history, "an extremely significant engine of war" in Mr. Sperry's accurate estimation.

At eighteen, Roeder quit Cornell to marry his pregnant girlfriend without the blessing of the church, committing an early act of fraud by providing the marriage bureau with a fake age (twenty-one) and a fake name (Edward Morgan Randolph), which would cause his wife many headaches with the Social Security Administration in later years. After surviving Elmer Sperry's notoriously intensive interview process—only gifted engineers with a "mechanical touch" able to keep up with the torrent of his imagination were allowed in the door—Roeder joined Sperry Gyroscope around the time of his marriage in the first quarter of 1913, which means he was one of the first seventeen employees at a founding institution of the research and development branch of the military-industrial complex.

His arrival coincided with the armament boom that preceded and followed the outbreak of the Great War in Europe in August 1914, which led some of Sperry's most talented employees to start their own ventures in service to specialized military requirements. Hannibal Ford, Sperry's chief engineer, decamped to an industrial building in lower Manhattan and won the right to be the secret supplier of the US Navy's fire-control system for battleships, the central plotting machine that used the gyrocompass's reference line to guide a battery of long-range guns in the complex matter of tracking and hitting moving targets as far as ten miles away. Roeder, who had apparently shown promise during his two years at Sperry, was lured away to join him. There is no evidence that Ed Roeder committed espionage over the next four years of wartime employment with the Ford Instrument Co. He was merely a draftsman learning the skills that would make him as knowledgeable as anyone else in the country in the field of precision instruments for military application. His time was yet to come.

In the years after World War I, Roeder utilized his experience to become a kind of gyro-systems consultant, jumping from one start-up to another as a designer with a central role in developing the products each produced. But he always returned to Sperry. He rejoined the staff from 1922 to 1924, early 1928 to late 1928, 1930 to 1932, and returned again in 1933. Now employing a thousand workers in its imposing building at 40 Flatbush Avenue Extension within sight of the Manhattan and Brooklyn Bridges, Sperry Gyroscope had become the core business of a global enterprise officially known as Sperry Corporation (with executive offices at the new Rockefeller Center), but still referred to as "Sperry's" by the average New Yorker. In 1933, when Wiley Post made history by piloting the first solo flight around the world, he gave all credit to the Sperry A-2 autopilot, "my robot," which was "uncanny in the way it takes over the job of flying," an endorsement that Sperry's publicity department had no part in arranging. (On the other hand, Amelia Earhart's Lockheed Electra was equipped with a Sperry autopilot when it plunged into the Pacific in 1937, a fact unmentioned in company literature.) Aircraft manufacturers, merchant marines, and foreign militaries were permitted to purchase some of the company's gyrocompasses, direction-finding radios, blind-flying instruments, gyro horizons, anti-aircraft searchlights, rate-of-turn indicators, directional gyros, and ship stabilizers, but the most advanced versions of each product were always reserved for the Air Corps and the Navy, which, in addition, funded the development of weapons systems that were intended for no other contractor but the US military.

With his toothbrush mustache and silver-rimmed spectacles, Roeder was one of an elite staff of a few dozen engineers (including Elmer Sperry Jr.) charged with coming up with innovations at least five years ahead of the current design, a collection of deep thinkers who were allowed to remain absent from the shop for weeks at a time while they mulled their ideas. Roeder was probably involved in the effort to perfect an antiaircraft-gun-directing system, which used data transmitters, a stereoscopic range finder, and tracking telescopes to enable its multiple human operators to feed information (about ground speed, wind, ballistics, air-speed) into an analog computer that determined where to aim a fusillade of artillery shells to destroy an approaching warplane. He likely also had a hand in an equally confidential product that made some of the same time-space calculations, Sperry's S-1 bombsight, which the Air Corps had determined would be its second-string bomb-aimer behind the Norden.

In 1936, Roeder came to Germany's notice through the efforts of a friend of his on the West Side who had connections with the Abwehr. Impressed, Ast Hamburg provided $300 to pay for Roeder's passage to Germany, a major vote of confidence for a service that was eager to rely on the incidental support of Nazi devotees pledged to the greater glory of the Reich. Which appears *not* to have been Roeder's main motivation. On his way to Germany during the summer of 1936, he stopped off in England, where he granted exclusive rights for an invention of his that "used as an emitter the cathode structure of a Coolidge tube" to determine the hardness of materials to a company that was a subsidiary of Vickers Ltd., the conglomerate that would play a significant role in rearming the British Army for World War II. With this success in hand, he continued on to Hamburg and the warm embrace of three Abwehr officers. The men quizzed him on the latest advances in high-intensity searchlights and autopilot systems for aircraft, both areas in which Sperry Gyroscope was a world pioneer. During off hours, he was plied with so many drinks that he couldn't keep up and was even offered a woman, though he said he declined. Then he was taken to Berlin to meet with half a dozen technical experts, who provided him with a drafting board in his hotel room. Suitably awed by his handiwork, the Abwehr agreed to furnish him with a salary of $200 a month, not including bonuses for valuable deliveries, which made him Nazi Germany's highest-paid agent in the United States.

Once he returned to New York, Roeder moved with his family to suburban Merrick, Long Island, where he registered his phone under a friend's name and developed new acquaintances "so as not to arouse suspicion" and "to please the German authorities," he later confided. He disappeared into his basement laboratory to continue experimentation on his own inventions, including a "speech secrecy system" that he was developing with a friend of his, a lieutenant commander in the US Navy who would later direct naval radio operations in the Panama Canal Zone. Instead of returning immediately to his work at Sperry, Roeder took a job in September or October 1936 at the Airplane and Marine Division Finder Company of Lindenhurst, Long Island, which produced gyro-based guidance systems for air- and watercraft. He was chagrined when Abwehr couriers began showing up at his door to pick up his packages, disrupting the tranquillity of his sleepy block. He arranged for them to take the Long Island Rail Road out only as far as the Baldwin station, which was not the closest, or even second closest, stop to his home in Merrick. At the designated time, Roeder would be waiting in the parking lot in his Buick sedan. The Abwehr had a code name for him: Carr.

On May 10, 1937, Roeder was hired back at Sperry (for the fifth time in his career), quickly winning the promotions necessary to return to the top tier of the design department. He would later say that he rejoined Sperry at the express wishes of the "organization in Germany." He maintained his cover even as the company's staff came under scrutiny during the Turrou investigation. Gus Rumrich had told investigators of a drunken evening he spent in Yorkville with a courier—they started at the Café Hindenburg nightclub before stumbling across Eighty-Sixth Street to the famously rowdy *Brauhaus* Maxl's—who flashed an envelope containing two $1,000 bills meant for a prized agent that Rumrich thought worked for a *periscope* company in Brooklyn "or something like that." The comment led agents to apprehend four German Americans working in the assembly and inspection divisions at Sperry, including an old-timer who had been accused of spying for the Kaiser during World War I. All four were released without charge. At trial, Rumrich didn't clear things up when he said he believed the unnamed agent was being handsomely rewarded for delivering plans that "were for some sort of gyroscope made in a submarine factory in Brooklyn." Roeder was lucky he was never questioned.

But Nikolaus Ritter's ring was deemed insufficient to handle the more expansive responsibilities that would be required in the event of the outbreak of war. Efforts were redoubled to recruit new agents to be sent to the city. "While we were trying to figure out how we could step up our work over there, I was summoned to Berlin, and I was asked whether I was ready personally to return to the United States in order, in case of war, to lead an organization there," Ritter wrote. "I did not really like the idea. But when I talked about this with my wife and she offered to come with me, I decided to go along." He says the couple underwent training in the telegraphic language of Morse code, which would be an essential component of Ast Hamburg's communications operation once the Atlantic Ocean was transformed into a battle zone, constricting the effectiveness of the courier and mail-drop systems and requiring a speedier transfer of information. A wireless telegraphy (or W/T) station was established in a handful of rooms in a baronial estate in the Hamburg suburb of Wohldorf, which would soon include a few dozen radio sets and a busy staff of cryptologists.

Not long after his training commenced, Ritter began to have doubts about embarking on an assignment that would be more difficult than his previous one in 1937, when he was able to travel under his own name in the confident belief that the Americans weren't paying much attention to foreign spies. Although he doesn't say so in his memoir, he was in the midst of a court battle to win custody of his two American-born children from his ex-wife, Aurora Evans, the Alabama woman he had cast aside (in a strange country ruled by a foreigner-loathing dictator) in favor of his Abwehr secretary, the kind of subplot that isn't usually included in spy thrillers. In his book, Ritter says he declined the mission to America when he learned that it would require him to resign from the military. Still, the problem remained: Who could be sent in his place to serve as an "informant and contact man with our agents in the United States"? "As I gave up the idea of going to the United States myself I began to look around for a man whom I could train as an agent with a secret transmitter."

Nine days after the *Deutschland* left New York Harbor, on February 2, 1939, Bill Sebold landed in Germany, surely one of the few bearers of American citizenship seeking entry into a war-eager Third Reich. He described what happened next: "Well, when I arrived at Hamburg, there was a passport police, and I had to present my American passport, and as I showed my American passport there were two civilians, two men in civilian clothes, that took me in a nearby room and questioned me about my activities in the United States."

Sebold said he was specifically asked if he had ever worked at an airplane factory. He believed that his interrogators knew to ask this because he had been talking a little too freely with some Hitler Youth during the trip over. He told the men about his (brief) service at Consolidated Aircraft Corporation of San Diego, California. He was asked how long he intended to remain in Germany. He responded that he didn't know. Finally, he was asked for the address where he would be staying. Sebold provided them with his mother's, Duisburger Strasse 147, Mülheim-Ruhr.

"And then you were told they would get in touch with you sometime later in the event they needed you?" he was later asked.

"No."

Sebold said they told him, "You will hear from us."

CHAPTER SEVEN

IN THIS SOLEMN HOUR

The Führer had to come in order to hammer into all of us the fact that the German cannot choose and may not choose whether or not he will be German but that he was sent into this world by God as a German, that God thereby had laid upon him as a German duties of which he cannot divest himself without committing treason to providence.

—Gauleiter Ernst Bohle,
leader of the *Auslandsorganisation*
(Foreign Countries' Organization)
of the Nazi Party

In the four months after his arrival in Nazi Germany, Bill Sebold did little more than quietly pass the time in his mother's home on Duisburger Strasse. He was free to recuperate from his stomach surgery of the previous year and follow the propaganda campaign that was preparing the German people for the coming struggle.

In the second week of March, Nazi newspapers began "reporting" that evil Czechs were launching attacks against the small number of Germans living within the borders of what was now known as Czecho-Slovakia, the rump Czech state that included the regions of Bohemia, Moravia, Carpatho-Ukraine, and Slovakia. In a move of genuine tactical cunning, Hitler coerced the leaders of Slovakia into declaring independence on

March 14, which led Neville Chamberlain to announce in the Commons that Great Britain wouldn't honor its obligation to defend Czecho-Slovakia since the "frontiers we had proposed to guarantee" at Munich had been dissolved by Slovakia's action. In the early morning hours of March 15, Hitler met with Czech president Emil Hácha in the Reich Chancellery and told him that the German military was preparing to launch an invasion within hours. When Hácha hesitated to sign a surrender document that had been prepared for him, Hermann Göring added that "half of Prague would lie in ruins from bombing within two hours, and that this would only be the beginning," a threat of such horrendous imagining that the sixty-six-year-old president fainted. Revived by an injection from the needle of Hitler's personal physician, Hácha agreed to order his military and civilian leadership to stand down, giving the specter of the Luftwaffe a central role in another victory for Nazism. German troops confronted severe winter weather rather than armed resistance when they crossed the border at 6:00 a.m. There were no cheering crowds when Hitler swept into Prague in the early evening and assumed control of a nation populated mostly by non-Germans, his first truly foreign conquest. After a night's rest in the Hradschin Castle, he presided over the creation of the new Reich Protectorate of Bohemia and Moravia. Slovakia became a puppet republic, and Carpatho-Ukraine was given to the pro-Nazi rulers of Hungary.

Hitler decided to quickly seize two German-majority communities on the Baltic Sea that had been excluded from Germany by the Versailles Treaty. On March 20, Lithuania was informed that an aerial bombardment would be forthcoming unless the port of Memel was granted to the Reich, which was done without delay. In response to the annexation of the Memelland, the Polish government made the provocative decision to partially mobilize its army and concentrate troops around the other object of Hitler's desire, Danzig, the "free city" created by Versailles to provide Poland with access to a seaport, which was administered under the suzerainty of the League of Nations and separated from Germany by what was known as the Polish Corridor. The DNB News Agency duly reported that attacks against German women and children "are accumulating to a regrettable degree" in the Polish Corridor. Albert Forster, the ambitious former bank clerk who presided as gauleiter over the Nazi organization in Danzig, was granted personal access to the Führer to discuss the proper levels of "quasi-revolutionary" activity that should be fomented to facilitate German war aims.

Sixteen days after the disintegration of Czecho-Slovakia, Prime Minister Chamberlain stood before Parliament and delivered a speech that all but promised war if Hitler sought to overrun Danzig and the Polish Corridor: "In the event of any action which clearly threatened Polish independence and which the Polish government accordingly considered it vital to resist with their national forces, His Majesty's government would feel themselves bound at once to lend the Polish government all support in their power," he said. "They have given the Polish government an assurance to that effect. I may add that the French government have authorized me to make it plain that they stand in the same position in this matter."

Events were now moving rapidly and almost uniformly in Hitler's favor. In the final days of March, Franco's Fascists captured Madrid and declared victory in the Spanish Civil War. After gaining Hitler's permission, Mussolini sent his troops into Albania, conquering the nation within days and opening up an Axis path to southeastern Europe, causing France and Britain to issue security guarantees to Greece and Romania. On April 3, Hitler told his generals to draw up a plan for a surprise attack on Poland that "can be carried out at any time from September 1, 1939, onward." On April 28, Hitler announced the cancellation of his nonaggression pact with Poland and naval agreement with Great Britain. Even though Benito Mussolini believed his armed forces wouldn't be ready to fight a major conflict for another three years, he agreed to an upgraded military alliance, the Pact of Steel, that obligated Italy to side with Germany upon the outbreak of hostilities. On May 3, Stalin signaled his openness to an alliance with Nazi Germany by appointing Vyacheslav Molotov as his new foreign minister in place of Maxim Litvinov, the personification of the Popular Front policy of cooperating with anti-Fascists abroad, who was excoriated as "the Jew Finkelstein" in the Nazi press. On May 23, the Führer told his generals he was determined to make war on Poland "at the first suitable opportunity." Danzig would be the pretext for "expanding our living-space in the East and making food supplies secure." If the French and British decide to intervene, he vowed, the Reich would then conquer Holland and Belgium, from where attacks could easily be mounted against France and Britain.

In America, the isolationists retained their hold over American foreign policy by refusing FDR's request to repeal the arms-embargo portion of the neutrality laws, which would allow the United States to announce its intention to supply Britain and France in the event of war and thus perhaps deter Hitler from launching the attack on Poland in the first place. "No one can foretell what may happen," said Senator William Borah, the venerable Lion of Idaho, who was so uninterested in entangling alliances that he had never set foot out of the United States. "But my feeling and belief is that we are not going to have a war. Germany isn't ready for it." Congress did promptly pass its version of the president's national defense program, which now included $300 million for the US Army Air Corps to purchase not the three thousand planes FDR had originally requested in January but up to fifty-five hundred of them, with the isolationists ever watchful that the administration didn't fritter away national defense gains on the Western democracies that might soon be fighting for their lives. Which was bad news for the British military officials who witnessed a demonstration of the Norden bombsight at Fort Benning, Georgia. Three waves of B-17 heavy bombers and B-18 medium bombers, all equipped with the device, scored direct hits on the outline of a battleship on the ground. "The first B-17 was due to drop its bombs at 1:27 p.m.," wrote George Pirie, the British air attaché to Washington. "At about 1:26 p.m. everyone started to look and listen for it. Nothing was seen or heard. At 1:27 while everyone was still searching the sky six 300-pound bombs suddenly burst at split second intervals on the deck of the battleship, and it was at least thirty seconds later before someone spotted the B-17 at 12,000 feet." The British estimated that the Norden was three or four times superior to the RAF's sight. Ordered to do everything "humanly possible" to win one for the Crown, the officials were dismayed to learn that the Americans wouldn't let them anywhere near the marvel. Air Commodore Arthur Harris, later known as Bomber Harris for leading the RAF's onslaught against German cities in the closing stages of the war, wrote that he was "resolutely prevented from catching even a surreptitious glimpse of it."

J. Edgar Hoover responded to the German aggression overseas by sending an urgent letter (on the day after the Czech takeover) to the new attorney general, ex–Michigan governor Frank Murphy, telling him that the FBI's secretly granted authority "to ascertain the identity of persons engaged in espionage, counterespionage, and sabotage," given to Hoover by the president during their train ride from Washington to New York, was being infringed upon by "other governmental agencies, including the State Department, which are attempting to literally chisel into this type of work." Hoover asked Murphy, an ascetic liberal nicknamed Saint Francis, to persuade President Roosevelt to take appropriate action to end "continual bickering," which was not helpful "in view of the serious world conditions which are hourly growing more alarming."

At a press conference a few days later, Murphy strengthened Hoover's position against his bureaucratic enemies by going public with information about counterespionage policy that FDR had declared off-limits during his talk with reporters four months earlier. "In times like these, there should be central control and not a confused direction. It should be in the Department of Justice and under Mr. Hoover," Murphy said, with his use of the word *should* indicating that the matter hadn't fully been resolved within the government. "We should be able to keep abreast of the situation so that it cannot take hold. We are working toward this. It is a good thing for the country to know of the new awareness of the situation and the new preparedness."

It was a good thing because the release of *Confessions of a Nazi Spy*, which opened nationwide on April 28, 1939, was calculated to inflame filmgoers into believing that German agents were everywhere; this impressed the critics (who raved about the film's verisimilitude) more than it did the viewing public (still accustomed to going to movies to escape). The studio's promotional department provided theaters with flyers claiming Nazi reprisals would be meted out to anyone who went to the film and posters that encouraged Americans to question the motives of the man next door: "Where does he get his orders? To whom does he report? How many others like him are there in the United States . . . spying, stealing, taking photographs, betraying America?" Although *Confessions* was only a moderate box office success, it was a widely noted emblem of the culture; attacked as a Jewish conspiracy by Father Coughlin; protested by sometimes vandalizing Nazi sympathizers in Milwaukee and other cities; banned by any country that sought friendly relations with the Reich; and garlanded with honors, including best English-language picture from the National Board of Review of Motion Pictures, beating out *Wizard of Oz* and *Mr. Smith Goes to Washington*.

On June 5, Attorney General Murphy delivered an FBI-prepared memo to President Roosevelt, asking him to issue confidential instructions to his cabinet that would end State Department interference onto Hoover's turf and affirm that the FBI and its two subordinate partners, military and naval intelligence, were the *only* agencies of the government allowed to look "into cases involving actually or potentially espionage, counterespionage, or sabotage." Before the president could act, the US Senate Naval Committee issued a report alleging "widespread evidence of espionage not only in Hawaii, Puerto Rico, the Canal Zone and on the Pacific Coast, but also on the Atlantic Coast and in the Gulf States as well," a headline-producing revelation that required a response from the attorney general of the United States. Frank Murphy once again went public on behalf of the director, informing reporters on the day the report was released that J. Edgar had taken swift action to contain a situation that he admitted was worsening in light of "worldwide conditions." The headline over the *Herald Tribune* story was "Anti-Spy Work Centered Under J. Edgar Hoover." Ten days later, President Roosevelt issued a three-paragraph directive to his cabinet (but not the public), announcing his "desire" that "no investigations should be conducted by any investigative agency" but the FBI or its allies in military and naval intelligence. "The directors of these three agencies are to function as a committee to coordinate their activities," and they would meet each week at

Hoover's office in the Department of Justice building on Pennsylvania Avenue in Washington. On July 17, the FBI began its first in-service training session instructing selected special agents in such novel matters as "document identification, electrical equipment and sound recording; methods of concealing messages; secret codes and secret writings; detection of secret inks; photographic aspects of espionage work; technical equipment usages in espionage work . . ."

On June 1, 1939, Bill Sebold was well enough to join the German war economy by taking a position with the Siemens-Schuckertwerke (formerly Thyssen) steam-turbine machine plant, an indication that he had no immediate plans to return to his wife in New York.

After about a month and half on the job, he received a mysterious letter in the mail. "The contents of the letter were like this, written in German," remembered Sebold. "It said, 'My dear friend, I would like to see you . . . in the Hotel Duisburger Hof'" on the following Sunday. "He said he would like to go over old times with me in the United States. He learned my address through a friend of his." The letter was written by a "Dr. Gassner," who gave his return address as Kotterhamer Strasse 25, Solingen, a city thirty miles to the south of Mülheim. It was signed with a G written through the "Heil Hitler" valediction. "I showed the letter to some friends of mine and they looked the letter over and said, 'It is very phony. You had better see the Gestapo about that; there is something phony about this because you are a stranger; you come out of America, and you never know what they might cook up.' I went to the Gestapo with the letter and showed it to them, and they said, 'Okay, you go there; we will cover you. We will see who is approaching you.'"

Sebold bicycled to nearby Duisburg for the meeting, but

Dr. Gassner was not waiting at the hotel as arranged. Returning home, Sebold wrote a note expressing his displeasure at being stood up. "I said it was very mysterious, I would not deal with people who did not sign letters." Dr. Gassner responded by apologizing for his behavior and asking for notice of when and where they could try again. Sebold ignored him. Several days later, Gassner sent a letter that included a threat. "It said he is sick and tired of me, something like that, tired of being chased around by me, and he wanted to get results, and if I didn't meet him, he wanted to ask the assistance of the state, or something, to make me meet him."

Sufficiently moved, Sebold replied by inviting Dr. Gassner to his mother's place in Mülheim. "I said he could come to my home in case he wanted to deal with me."

On August 1 or thereabouts, Dr. Gassner showed up as scheduled and the two went to a nearby restaurant to talk. According to a later FBI report, he asked Sebold about "bombing plans, coast patrol boats, the equipment used, bombsights, bombing racks and similar matters, apparently being aware of the fact that Sebold had previously been employed in the aircraft industry in the United States." The suggestion is that the dockside officials who had quizzed Sebold upon his arrival at Hamburg had communicated his qualifications to Dr. Gassner, who, according to postwar testimony, was an Abwehr official working on behalf of the Luftwaffe. Sebold said he was asked if he'd ever laid eyes on an actual bombsight, which appeared to be a device of interest to Dr. Gassner. "I told him no, but I had seen a great big contraption, I says, like a stool, where the bombsight goes on—which is a lie," he said.

Apparently impressed with Sebold's boasts, Dr. Gassner suggested that he travel to the United States as an espionage agent of *"unsere Gesellschaft"*—our society. Sebold says he demurred. "If you want to find out, go there yourself, it is a wide-open country," he quoted himself as responding. Dr. Gassner then issued a verbal threat. "He referred to the funeral clothes they'd give me when I was stretched out there."

Although Sebold didn't mention it in his subsequent testimony, he may have been confronted with the accusation that he was a part-Jewish ex-con now living under an assumed Aryan identity, a story that would become conventional wisdom in Abwehr circles. "His real name was Debrovsky," wrote Nikolaus Ritter in his memoir. "He had a prior criminal record, he had changed his name, and his name now was William Seebold [*sic*]." Of his brush with the law, Sebold later told the FBI of an incident that occurred after he returned "from the strain and the confinement" of his World War I service. "He stated that he was singing on the streets when two policemen grabbed him by both arms and put screw chains on his wrists and began to tighten them," wrote the Bureau. "He claims to have swung at the two policemen, smashing their faces together. He was sent to prison for this act." It matters little to Sebold's predicament that the Debrovsky story was pure bunk. The birth certificate on record in the Mülheim archives shows that he was born to Adolf Sebold, a Protestant, and Maria Sebold, a Catholic. His marriage license in the New York City Clerk's office reveals that his mother's maiden name was Rohé. Whatever else was said in that restaurant in Mülheim, Sebold was now in fear for his life. "There was the *Fertigmachen,* 'make you ready,'" he said, referring to a term used by the Nazis (and apparently Gassner) to describe the terrorizing conducted prior to execution in concentration camps. "And anybody who knows Germany now knows what that means, and I know it, too." He asked for time to think the offer over. Dr. Gassner gave him the thirty-one days of August 1939.

■ ■ ■

The month began uneventfully. Neville Chamberlain was fishing for trout in Scotland, clad in waders and an anti-gnat helmet, while Hitler was ensconced in his Bavarian retreat, enjoying the mountain air and plotting to take Poland before the muddy conditions of the autumn slowed the progress of his ground forces. By the second week, the world's media were filled with reports about the instability in and around Danzig fomented by Nazi forces in service to the Little Hitler of the moment, Albert Forster. "In this solemn hour," Forster told a crowd of Danzig Nazis after flying back from an audience with Hitler at the Berghof, "we can do nothing better than pledge ourselves to hold together come what may, to beat off any attack on this wholly German soil with all the means at our disposal and to carry out every order of our Führer, Adolf Hitler."

German newspapers were competing with each other to tell more lurid tales about the savagery committed against ethnic Germans in a wide range of Polish territory. "German houses broken into with axes—Terrorized by Poles for weeks—Hundreds of refugees are arrested by Poles." On August 14, Victor Klemperer of Dresden wrote in his diary, "The same tension for weeks, always growing and always unchanged. Vox populi: He attacks in September, partitions Poland with Russia, England-France are impotent. Natscheff and some others: He does not dare attack, keeps the peace, and stays in power for years. Jewish opinion: bloody pogrom on the first day of the war. Whichever of these three things may happen: Our situation is desperate. We go on living, reading, working, but in an ever more depressed state." Then on August 23, the monumental news was announced that the Soviet Union had reached a nonaggression pact with Nazi Germany, joining together the two most savage political leaders of modern history in an alliance that prophesied imminent bloodletting. On August 25, Hitler ordered the war against Poland to begin on the following morning, but a postponement was issued when he learned in the early evening that Mussolini refused to commit his military in abrogation of the Pact of Steel (at least for now), and Great Britain proclaimed a formal treaty with Poland confirming its intention to fight upon outbreak.

On the same day, Hitler's naval high command assumed control of all German merchant ships, whose captains were instructed to return immediately to Germany or the nearest nonbelligerent port to avoid the possibility of being sunk by the British Navy following a war declaration. It marked the end of an era when the *Europa* turned around before docking at Southampton and steamed back to her berth in Bremerhaven, joining the other swastika-flagged passenger liners in the North Sea ports that were to be transformed into troop transports or auxiliary cruisers for military use. Farther along on the route across the Atlantic, the *Bremen* decided to continue to New York, where Captain Adolf Ahrens planned to quickly refuel and find safe passage back home. The ship was held at Pier 86 for two days under orders from President Roosevelt, who wanted a thorough search conducted to determine if armaments were hidden within the massive confines. A rumor was going around about a false bottom in the swimming pool. "I want to know whether *Bremen* is carrying guns or not," FDR said.

When clearance papers were finally issued, the ship was tugged out into the Hudson with none of the gaiety that once marked such occasions. At just after 6:00 p.m. on August 30, the great liner "slipped almost furtively down the river, with every light extinguished except the running lights required for navigation," wrote the *Times*. "But the band kept playing, loudly enough to be heard from the pier-end behind. It played first a march known to Germans as the *'Hohenfriedberge,'* and then *'Deutschland über Alles,'* a band piece known to every passenger who has walked a German deck. Then, as the American shore receded, strains of the Nazi *'Horst Wessel'* song came across the blue-gray water."

Back in London, Neville Chamberlain took time away from mobilizing the nation's defenses, and making final attempts to reach a settlement with Hitler, to send "an urgent personal request" to President Roosevelt "because Great Britain today faces the possibility of entering on a tremendous struggle, confronted as she is with a challenge to her fundamental values and ideals." Under the scrawled salutation "My Dear Mr. President," the typed letter of three short pages asked for the "new type of automatic air bombsight known as the Norden bombsight," which "I understand is the most efficient instrument of its kind in existence." Chamberlain said the gift would allow the Royal Air Force to avoid committing civilian casualties, pledging that his country would not resort to terror bombing of the sort made famous by the Luftwaffe bandits in Spain. "Air power is, of course, a relatively new weapon which is so far untried on a large scale; there is the danger of unrestricted air attack which we for our part would never initiate," he wrote with a certitude that history would mock. "I am however most anxious to do all in my power to lessen the practical difficulties which may arise in operations even against legitimate military targets, and I feel that in air bombardment accuracy and humanity really go together. For this reason again I am certain that you would render the greatest service if you could enable us to make use of the magnificent apparatus which your services have developed."

Roosevelt turned him down, citing neutrality legislation that wouldn't allow the transfer "unless the sight desired by the British government were made available to all other governments at the same time it was made available to Great Britain," he wrote. FDR was afraid that the Norden would be lost to the Germans as soon as the first RAF bomber equipped with it was shot down over German-controlled territory.

On the last day of the month, the SS orchestrated a series of fake raids against German outposts along the border in an attempt to convince the world that the actions of "Polish insurrectionists" necessitated a monumental act of German self-defense. Before dawn on the next morning, more than fifty divisions of upward of 1.5 million men crossed the frontier with instructions to show no mercy upon enemies they had been taught to regard as subhuman, launching a "lightning war" or "blitzkrieg" exemplified by fast-moving panzer columns and mechanized infantry units closely supported by a brutal air force of dive-bombers (equipped with high-pitched sirens called Trumpets of Jericho), machine-gun-strafing Messerschmitt fighters, and level-flying medium bombers that had little trouble in eliminating the threat from the Polish Air Force.

The invasion officially began when the old German battleship *Schleswig-Holstein*, moored in Danzig harbor, fired its guns upon the Westerplatte munitions depot, which gave Albert Forster the signal to declare the *Anschluss* of Danzig with the Reich and appoint himself administrator of the region, making him an important ally of the *Einsatzgruppen* death squads that followed the troops into the occupied lands to liquidate prominent anti-Nazi elements with an emphasis on Catholic clergy, intelligentsia, and the Jews. Forster pledged his assistance in the task of turning the parts of western Poland to be incorporated directly into the Reich into a "blossoming, pure German" zone without Poles and Jews, who were to be sent eastward into a slave colony known as the General Government, a "dumping ground" in Hitler's description. In a sign that the Luftwaffe was not yet

designed to fight a war against far-flung enemies with significant air defense systems, the precision bombardment responsibilities were handled by what would become the most famous German plane of the war, the single-engine Junkers Ju 87, which could dive within thirty feet of targets on the ground in the risky hope that it would be able to withstand close contact with the adversary. In the minutes before the *Schleswig-Holstein* opened up on Danzig, three Ju-87 Stukas scored direct hits on a blasting device that the Poles were planning to use to detonate the Dirschau Bridge and slow the Wehrmacht's advance across the Vistula, possibly the actual first shots of World War II. Yet the most lethal of the Luftwaffe's air weapons remained the still-imprecise medium bombers, which were instrumental payload carriers in dozens of Guernica-style slaughters in settlements large and small. Incendiaries were literally shoveled out the cargo doors of the creaky Junkers Ju 52 (known as Tante Ju or Aunt Ju) transport planes sent over Warsaw. From neutral Washington, President Roosevelt issued an "urgent appeal to every government which may be engaged in hostilities publicly to affirm its determination that its armed forces shall in no event, and under no circumstances, undertake the bombardment from the air of civilian populations or of unfortified cities." It was already too late.

His thirty-one days now up, William Sebold chose this moment to escape from a war that was no longer theoretical. Probably at about the time in the late morning when Hitler was telling the Reichstag that he would lead Germany to victory or sacrifice his life in the attempt, Sebold traveled from Mülheim to the American consulate in Cologne, where he showed Dr. Gassner's incriminating letters to a young clerk named Rosenberg, who was no more than nineteen or twenty years old. "He looked the

letters over and said, 'That is too bad; you had better run away on the next day to Ostend,'" the port in neutral Belgium where a ship might be found to America, Sebold recalled. "I was hurt a little, you know. I didn't demonstrate anything, but inside I was a little hurt." He described how he went out into the streets of the frantic city, flagged down two motorists with foreign license plates, and pleaded with them to sneak him over the border. Both refused. After spending the night in Cologne, he went the next morning to the train station but was certain the Gestapo was following him. "Well, they stood there and looked at me," he said, providing a glimpse into his nightmare. Although he possessed a valid American passport, Sebold was mindful that he hadn't received permission to leave his job at Siemens-Schuckertwerke. "I could not do it," he said of boarding a train for Belgium. "There is a lot of official red tape. I have to have a permit to be properly discharged by the proper authorities in Germany. In the town I worked there is a labor bureau. . . . I just looked over the chances to get away and I thought it over and said I had better turn back again." From Cologne, he took a streetcar to Düsseldorf, where he sent a cryptic cablegram to his wife, telling her not to worry about anything that might happen to him in the future. Then he returned to Mülheim and wrote a letter to Dr. Gassner. "I said I accepted his proposition one hundred percent."

On September 3, with London and Paris evacuated of children and hunkered down for air strikes that were not (yet) coming, Britain and France made the reluctant decision to declare war on Germany. Chamberlain had barely finished announcing the news when air raid sirens sounded for the first time in London. In the early evening in the North Atlantic waters a few hundred miles west of the Hebrides, a German U-boat sent a torpedo into an unarmed British passenger liner, the *Athenia*, killing 112 of its 1,418 passengers and crew, which was the wayward shot

that announced the beginning of the Kriegsmarine's hit-and-run campaign against the Royal Navy and the British merchant ships that delivered the food, fuel, and supplies, mostly from North America, that meant the survival of the island nation. Of the three hundred Americans aboard the *Athenia,* twenty-eight perished, a propaganda disaster for the Germans that led the Nazi press to accuse the British of sinking the ship in an attempt to pull America into the war.

In his fireside chat that evening, President Roosevelt pledged to keep America out in the face of such provocations but noted that even "a neutral cannot be asked to close his mind or his conscience." As required by the neutrality statutes, the British and French became subject to the arms embargo, which spurred FDR to call Congress into special session to once again consider revising a law that now actively conspired to keep Hitler's enemies weak. Incensed to learn that the NYPD was forming a special sabotage squad to investigate acts that might be committed by violent Nazi supporters in the city, J. Edgar Hoover (through the reliable vehicle of Attorney General Murphy) persuaded FDR to issue a statement informing "all local law enforcement officers to cooperate with the FBI in the drive against espionage, sabotage, subversive activities, and violation of the neutrality laws," the president's first public comment on the Bureau's expanded authority. He told the press he wanted "to protect this country against . . . some of the things that happened over here in 1914 and 1915 and 1916 and the beginning of 1917, before we got into the war." He was referring to the violent campaign directed by German diplomats and military officials to prevent American-made war materials from reaching the Allied nations of Britain, France, and Tsarist Russia. Nearly two hundred acts of sabotage were credited to German initiative, committed by a small army of militant German Americans, German sailors stranded in New York Harbor, and Irish and other anti-British agitators. The most infamous attack occurred on July 30, 1916, when a massive explosion rocked the principal depot for Europe-bound munitions on Black Tom Island on the New Jersey side of New York's harbor, a blast so ferocious that it blew shrapnel holes in the Statue of Liberty, shattered thousands of windows in lower Manhattan, and caused the Brooklyn Bridge to sway. Seven people were killed, hundreds injured.

In his own comment to the media, Murphy said the FBI was assuming counterespionage primacy in order to prevent the "inhuman and cruel things" that were committed against ethnic Germans *after* America entered World War I, making particular mention of the scourge of vigilantism. From April 1917 to November 1918, the Justice Department had encouraged average citizens to join amateur sleuthing societies, such as the 260,000-member American Protective League, which, according to a supporter, "apprehended plotters and prevented consummation of conspiracies beyond number," but actually did little more than commit grievous violations of civil liberties. In the popular imagination, fueled by a government-sponsored propaganda offensive urging antipathy toward the treacherous "Hun," the German immigrant was *assumed* to be a covert agent unless proved otherwise. Anyone suspected of being pro-German could be harassed (forced to sing "The Star-Spangled Banner" to prove their Americanism), horsewhipped (as six farmers in Texas were for refusing to contribute to the Red Cross), or tarred and feathered (such as the California brewery worker caught uttering sympathy for the Kaiser). In what was only the most severe instance of violence, a German-born drifter was lynched outside Collinsville, Illinois, on April 5, 1918, accused without evidence and despite his protestations of innocence, of planning to destroy a nearby mine. "All right, boys!" were reportedly his last words. "Go ahead and kill me, but wrap me in the flag when you bury me."

Upon learning the happy news that Sebold had agreed to join *unsere Gesellschaft,* Dr. Gassner asked to meet at the Metropole Hotel in Mülheim to discuss the arrangements. When Dr. Gassner arrived as scheduled, Sebold told him he wanted to go somewhere else. "I said, 'I don't like this hotel. It is too high-class. Let us go to the Handelshof,'" which was apparently a more downscale inn. Sitting at a table in the rear of the Handelshof's restaurant, Dr. Gassner informed Sebold that he would soon be introduced to the man from Hamburg who would supervise his training. Sebold responded by telling Dr. Gassner that he was leaving his mother's home to take up residence in the Handelshof, a generous attempt to shield his family from his new associations. Over the next two weeks, he heard nothing but the news that the Germans were overrunning Poland without the British and French making any move against the (poorly defended) Siegfried Line in western Germany. The RAF was more interested in protecting its naval interests when it dispatched twenty-nine medium bombers to attack warships docked in two Kriegsmarine bases on the North Sea coast. Seven of the planes were shot down by Germany's impressive antiaircraft guns, which may indicate just how valuable to the German war effort was Sperry Gyroscope's Ed Roeder, one of America's foremost experts in such fire-control systems.

On September 17, the Soviet Union accepted Hitler's invitation and invaded Poland, easily seizing the eastern half of the country (and beginning its own campaign to exterminate Polish national identity) in accord with the secret protocols of the

Hitler-Stalin Pact, which carved up Eastern Europe between the two tyrannies. As Sebold made his way to and from the job at the steam-turbine plant that he wasn't yet allowed to quit, he may have caught a glimpse of the leaflets that the RAF was dropping on the countryside in lieu of bombs because of Chamberlain's worries about retaliatory strikes against British cities. "Your rulers have condemned you to massacre, misery, and the privations of war," the flyers said. "They cannot hope to win."

The next phase of Sebold's ordeal began on the morning of September 22, when he awoke to discover that his US passport, which was in the breast pocket of his coat hanging on a chair, had been stolen while he slept. Sometime later in the day, Dr. Gassner arrived at the Handelshof and introduced Sebold to his Hamburg controller, "Dr. Renken," who was not identified to him as Nikolaus Ritter. In his postwar statements, Ritter revealed that he made no attempt to discern Sebold's feelings about serving the Reich, a failure of basic competence that he would come to rue.

"Since I had been assured that this man had been checked out, I did not do my own review," he wrote, adding with aristocratic scorn, "He did not particularly impress me. He looked quite ordinary, was of average intelligence, and obviously came from modest means." In his British interrogation, Ritter claimed that Sebold "showed no reluctance" to work for the Abwehr. During an interview with the German newsmagazine *Stern* in 1953, Ritter said that Sebold made a "nationalistic impression" and revealed "a pronounced willingness to work for Germany in the United States." Ritter described as "absolute invention" the suggestion that he threatened Sebold into cooperating. "The decisive point in this matter for me was the fact that he was born a German and that he fought as a German soldier during the first war," Ritter said in his memoir. "Since I had his personal data, I did not waste any time with any other questions but went straight to the point: 'We are afraid that the United States might enter the war against us,' I said. 'We need information from over there, and we can get that only from somebody who not only lives over there but who is also an American citizen.'"

According to Ritter's story, Sebold then requested permission to visit the US consulate in Cologne because he wanted to apply for a visa for his wife so she could come to Germany for his training, a convenient misremembering of the facts that attempts to obscure Ritter's blame for all that would follow. Sebold's version is confirmed by contemporaneous State Department documents: it was Gassner and Renken who requested that Sebold go to the consulate, where he was to apply for the replacement passport that would be required before he could begin his (legal) journey to New York. Whoever came up with the idea, Sebold was proving himself trustworthy enough to be allowed to walk into the enemy camp.

During that same meeting, Sebold remembered that he underwent a cursory physical examination. "I did not have to take off my clothes, but they looked me over and said, 'Well, this guy can't hurt a fly,'" which may have contributed to a belief that Sebold didn't have the inclination *or* the capability to turn against them. According to the FBI report, "This statement is probably well founded as by this time he was practically a physical wreck from worry about this matter." On the following day, he collapsed and was admitted to St. Marien Hospital for what he described in one statement as a "nervous breakdown" and in another as a "physical breakdown." Six days later, he had regained his strength enough to send an inquiry to Cologne about the procedure for obtaining a new passport and received a response that told him to arrive "in person to make affidavit explaining the circumstances of this case."

After thirteen days in the hospital, Sebold was discharged on October 5, the same day that Hitler was reviewing his triumphant troops in Warsaw and directing reporters' attention to the ruins that he promised to replicate in Paris and London. Sebold traveled to Cologne, where he filled out his passport application without mentioning his new life as a German spy. On the following day, as Hitler was offering a peace settlement to Britain and France that consolidated his gains and forswore any desire for further foreign conquest, Sebold returned to drop off the necessary photographs. Once he made it back to Mülheim, Sebold penned a note to Dr. Renken (at Rothenbaumchaussee 135, Hamburg), informing him that the consulate had assured him the passport would be forthcoming. Renken/Ritter responded in a letter the following day that asked Sebold to return to the consulate in two weeks to see if he could speed up the process. "The passport affair is indeed very regrettable, but it can't be helped and I can only hope that you will succeed in getting out before America declares war on Germany," the letter read. Renken reminded Sebold of the necessity of coming to Hamburg "so that I can show you around my plant and you can get to know the German methods of manufacture here." Nine days later, Sebold received another letter from Dr. Renken, this one instructing him to visit the consulate to obtain a bulletin on the repatriation of American citizens. On the next day, October 17, Sebold did as requested, arriving at a time when the hysteria of the war's early days had subsided. With Dr. Renken's "German methods of manufacture" note in hand, he asked for a meeting with the American consul general, Alfred W. Klieforth. It was granted.

Sebold later testified that Klieforth was less than welcoming to an American citizen who was desperate for the assistance of his government. "He said, 'Okay, let me see the letter,'" Sebold said. "I showed him that letter. And then he said, 'Well, we cannot help you. You are in a bad spot. You have to know yourself what you are going to do. We have nothing to do with this. But I have to take this letter and copy it and send it to the State Department.'"

"Is that all he said?" Sebold was asked.

"That is all he said."

Nine days later, on October 26, Klieforth offered his version in a dispatch to Washington. William Sebold "appeared at the consulate and related a story which may or may not be important," he wrote. "Mr. Sebold claims that through a strange set of circumstances he is now at the mercy of certain German secret organizations interested in the production of American military aeroplanes." Klieforth said Sebold was being forced to undergo training in Hamburg in preparation for service in the United States. "Mr. Sebold was interviewed by Vice Consul Parker and myself and impressed us with his integrity," Klieforth wrote. "I take it that he involved himself in the beginning believing that the affair was harmless but now that it has reached a serious stage, he is in fear of his own life." Klieforth passed along the news that Sebold "requests that he be met upon his arrival in New York by representatives of the State Department in order to convey his story to them by word of mouth." Klieforth concluded, "I will report Mr. Sebold's departure by telegraph to the Department."

The American public didn't want to fight in the new war, but a *Washington Post* poll showed that 62 percent supported President Roosevelt's proposed revision of the neutrality laws, which would repeal the arms embargo and allow Britain and France to obtain guns, ammunition, and planes from US private industry through a cash-and-carry arrangement that required payment up front and the use of non-American ships for the journey across the Atlantic. With his ear attuned to popular sentiment, FDR argued that cash-and-carry would *ensure* neutrality by giving the Allies the ability to purchase the tools necessary to defeat Germany on their own and also assist in the nation's economic recovery by putting more Americans to work in the war industry. He made the solemn pledge that he had no intention of sending our boys overseas. Believing that the legislation was the first step to war, a third of the country opposed it, an unlikely coalition of libertarians, literary intellectuals, religious pacifists, Midwestern business leaders, left-wing revolutionaries, Anglophobes, concerned mothers, college students, and Hitler-sympathetic bigots and anti-Semites. Charles Lindbergh was granted time on all three national networks to urge Americans to resist the propagandistic emotionalism that would draw us into a fight against our racial equals.

"These wars in Europe are not wars in which our civilization is defending itself against some Asiatic intruder," he said in his maiden speech as America's most prominent isolationist. "There is no Genghis Khan or Xerxes marching against our Western nations. This is not a question of banding together to defend our white race."

With the Hitler-Stalin Pact marking the end of the Popular Front against Fascism, American Communists and those still willing to be fellow travelers came out against aiding the capitalistic imperialists of Britain and France, maintaining that fighting Fascism on behalf of a glorious future in Spain was one thing, but doing so in service of "so-called" democracies was another. Reactionaries such as *Chicago Tribune* publisher Colonel Robert

McCormick (whose paper portrayed the president as a puppet of Moscow) joined hands with progressives such as Wisconsin senator Robert La Follette Jr. (who regarded the New Deal as too moderate), united in their common belief, as La Follette said on the Senate floor, that the president would "inevitably" establish a wartime dictatorship that "will not evaporate into thin air after the war is over."

In New York, the FBI was monitoring the most extremist manifestation of antiadministration sentiment, an Irish German gang of Coughlinites that had graduated from street-corner demonstrations and meeting-hall harangues to devising a plan to bomb Jewish-controlled institutions (the *Daily Worker* newspaper, the US Post Office, the Flatbush branch of the American League for Peace and Democracy, the Brooklyn Navy Yard, the New York Customs House, etc.), hoping to spark a violent reaction from the Jewish-controlled US government that would rouse the slumbering (anti-Semitic, they hoped) masses and create the chaos necessary for a Fascist counterrevolution, resulting in the seizure of the government and the slaughter of the Jews. The plotters (most of them Irish American members of the Christian Front with a few Germans connected to the Bundist movement) wanted to marry the tactics of the Irish Republican Army, which had been engaged in its "S-plan" bombing campaign against installations in English cities since January 1939, to a Nazi-like wave of street violence that would achieve the objective of "driving Judaism out of government."

Although Congress was deluged with a million pieces of protest mail, and antiwar rallies were held in towns and cities throughout the country, the new neutrality bill made it through both the House and Senate by early November. Passage was secured even though the press was full of stories about the sinking of Allied merchant and military ships, more than two hundred of which would go down by the end of 1939, seeming to prove cash-and-carry would bring the war at least as close as the New York piers. FDR was so fearful of arousing isolationist fury that he didn't follow the signing ceremony with a public call for a more rapid increase in the capacity of the armed forces. The US Army included 227,000 men, just 80,000 of whom (five divisions) were equipped for duty, vastly inferior to the Polish Army, which had been annihilated with relative ease. The US Navy was mostly based in the Pacific to protect against the threat from Japan, which, not yet joined in a military alliance with Germany, boasted a naval force at least equal to our own. Of the Air Corps' more than two thousand planes, only eight hundred could be deployed as first-line units. A bare fourteen of the B-17 Flying Fortresses intended to be America's nation-conquerors had yet come off the factory floor.

But the United States did have something to distinguish it from potential enemies, the Air Corps publicity staff was keen to inform selected correspondents. "The American bombsight is the envy of the entire world," wrote *Collier's* in its October 14, 1939, issue. "It is our most closely guarded military secret. It is used by our Air Corps, but really belongs to the Navy." The "precious" instrument is "made in a small factory in the East, run by two civilian engineers who developed it," an obvious reference to 80 Lafayette Street and Carl Norden and his partner, Ted Barth, who in fact left the technical matters to Mr. Norden. "Details of the shop's location and name are not bandied around; yet recently it received a letter from the Japanese asking for a quotation on the bombsights in lots of 500!" In its October 23 edition, *Time* said the "new" American bombsight "makes U.S. aviators boast they can drop a bomb in a barrel from 18,000 feet." The Navy's Admiral W. R. Furlong demanded an end to the publicity, which "only makes foreign agents try harder to steal the sight from our various stations."

The country could also boast the elimination of the gifted organizer with a demonstrated ability to mobilize thousands on behalf of Nazism. It can literally be said that Bundesführer Fritz Kuhn was brought down for the love of a woman. During a three-week trial in General Sessions Court in downtown Manhattan, Assistant District Attorney Herman J. McCarthy devoted the bulk of his case to proving that Kuhn stole from his membership by spending $717.02 in Bund funds to pay for the transportation of the furniture of a Mrs. Florence Camp of California, who was one of two Kuhn mistresses named during the proceedings. (The other, Virginia Cogswell, was a former beauty queen and minor celebrity known to the papers as the "Marrying Georgia Peach" for her seven—or was it nine?—ex-husbands.) The *Daily News* spoke for many in finding it "difficult to imagine a smitten damsel stroking his rocklike jaw and murmuring, 'Whose itsie bitsie Nazi is 'oo.'" The papers ran long excerpts from three love letters that the "flirtatious Fuehrer," "Teutonic two-timer," and "hotsy-totsy Nazi" wrote to Mrs. Camp, which obscured the news that the judge had now dismissed seven of twelve charges for lack of evidence, meaning that Kuhn was alleged to have stolen $1,217.02 rather than the original $14,548.59.

On November 29, a jury of twelve businessmen, all non-Jews, deliberated for about eight hours before finding Kuhn guilty of two counts of grand larceny in the matter of Mrs. Camp's furniture and three counts of larceny and forgery in the unexplained disappearance of $500 earmarked for a Bund lawyer, concluding that his dictatorial powers over the organization (attested to by a parade of Bundist witnesses) didn't permit him to spend its money however he wished. On December 4, Judge

James G. Wallace delivered a sentence of two and a half to five years, sending him away "as an ordinary small-time forger and thief and not because of any gospels of hate or anything of that sort." Two days later, Kuhn was hauled off to Sing Sing, where an AP photographer captured him crossing the threshold, his left wrist handcuffed to a burly deputy sheriff and his right to two fellow prisoners. It must've pained the avatar of racial purity that one of them was an African American. Back in town, Deputy Bundesführer G. Wilhelm Kunze was elevated to the top spot, pledging to continue cultivating the pro-Nazi sentiment that was still apparent in the German American community. When poet W. H. Auden went to view a German film in Yorkville at almost exactly the moment of Kuhn's incarceration, he was stunned by the vile shouts of moviegoers incited to bloodlust by a Reich-produced newsreel of the invasion. "Every time a Pole appeared on the screen," he told a friend, "the audience shouted, 'Kill him!'"

In the six weeks since he'd told the American government of his agreement to work for the German espionage service, William Sebold had heard nothing from Ast Hamburg. It was his own version of the lull that had settled over Europe, called variously the phony war, the *drôle de guerre,* the twilight war, the bore war, or the Sitzkrieg, as the Allies launched no attack against the German mainland and Hitler kept postponing his move against the West (even while the Battle of the Atlantic continued and the Soviet Union launched its brutal "winter war" against Finland).

In hopes perhaps that the Germans would never contact him again, Sebold tried to raise his own funds for a one-way ticket to New York. On November 6, Consul General Klieforth sent a telegram to the State Department in Washington, requesting that a message be delivered to Mrs. Sebold, who could be contacted at her employer's address, M. Hilders, 993 Park Avenue. On November 7, Helen Sebold received a note signed by none other than the secretary of state of the United States, Cordell Hull. "Telegram from American Consul Cologne transmits the following message for you QUOTE Telegraph $200 my account American Express Company Rotterdam, William Sebold. UNQUOTE," it read. The response eventually came back from Washington: "Wife unable assist Sebold. Government funds not available." With the consulate unwilling to issue a US passport until he had a ticket in hand, Sebold was left with no choice but to write a letter to Dr. Renken in mid-November, reminding him of his existence and asking for help in paying his travel costs. Dr. Renken didn't respond, probably because he was immersed in training spies to be placed in the British Isles and Western Europe, a more pressing priority.

Another three weeks passed. Then on the evening of December 6, Sebold was startled awake by someone standing in the darkness of his hotel room. He was not charmed to hear the man say, "I am your uncle Hugo," particularly since he had no such relative by that name. The man informed Sebold that it was now time to prepare for his departure for America. On the following morning, the two traveled to Siemens-Schuckertwerke, where Hugo flashed his credentials to the guard, who snapped to attention and identified him as *Hauptmann* (or Captain) Sandel. In the meeting that followed with the general manager of the factory and Sebold's immediate superior, Uncle Hugo/Captain Sandel demanded that Sebold be honorably discharged from his job and provided with a letter of recommendation, which was promptly done. The two Sebolds then returned to the Handelshof for celebratory drinks. Uncle Hugo spun yarns about his adventures as a young traveler in America ("all of which, he, William Sebold, now thinks are false," according to the FBI debriefing) and provided a clue about Sebold's coming assignment. "He talked about the radio business, did I know something about radio, if I would be able to set up a radio station in the United States," Sebold remembered. Yet after Uncle Hugo left early the next morning, Sebold heard nothing for the remaining three weeks of December, a period of increasingly frigid temperatures during which he tried to stay out of sight and became ever more anxious about his fate, an isolated figure toyed with by malign forces. "He also lost a great deal of weight and became very sick," according to the FBI. Finally, he wrote a letter to Dr. Renken, demanding to know why he had been stranded without guidance or source of income. "I said something, why have they forgot all about me, I did not hear anything from them," he said.

Dr. Renken speedily informed him that $200 was being deposited in an American Express account in Amsterdam, which enabled Sebold to make a reservation on a Holland America Line ship traveling from Amsterdam to New York. But the US consulate deemed it too dangerous for him to sail on a Dutch vessel that would be required to pass through the minefields of the English Channel. He was told his passport wouldn't be issued until he switched to the United States Lines, which had just announced that two passenger liners (SS *Manhattan* and her sister ship, SS *Washington*) would begin service between New York and still-neutral Italy in accord with the neutrality law's prohibition against American ships entering "war zones," which encompassed the Northern European ports. Sebold booked on the *Manhattan*, scheduled to depart from Genoa on January 15, but Dr. Renken protested that this wouldn't allow enough time to complete his training. Sebold then changed to the *Washington*, which would leave from the same Mediterranean port two weeks after the *Manhattan*. In Cologne, Sebold used the $200 wired to his account to purchase the ticket, which he took to the consulate in the hopes of finally receiving his passport. But he didn't get it until the next day, apparently because the consulate had lost his photographs and he had to arrange to have new ones taken. During this, his final visit with US diplomatic officials before leaving Germany, he stated explicitly that he wanted to be met in New York by the FBI. "I said, 'G-men,'" recalled Sebold, confirming that he had chosen sides.

He went to Hamburg, where he was registered at the Abwehr's guest residence near the Alster River, the Pension Klopstock at Klopstock Strasse 2, later describing a pension to American interrogators as "a better class of boardinghouse." At 10:00 or 10:30 a.m. on each of roughly seven days, Sebold was picked up by car and taken to a building on Glockengiesserwall next to the police presidium, as he remembered it. Under the supervision of Uncle Hugo, who kept an office on the fourth floor, Sebold was given lessons in the art of sending and receiving secret communications. He was offered a brief tutorial in using a radio key to tap out messages via Morse code, which he picked up so quickly that the old man who trained him said, "If you can do everything else that well, you are okay." He was taught a coding system based upon the letter arrangements of a particular page (which would change each day) in the British edition of Rachel Field's bestselling historical romance, *All This, and Heaven Too*. He was instructed in the operation of a Leica camera, which, when outfitted with a special lens and attached to a perpendicular rod as Hugo demonstrated, could reproduce a blueprint or document onto a postage-stamp-sized microphotograph readable only with a magnifying instrument. And he was shown how to operate a microscope to examine written letters for a speck known as a *Mikropunkt* (or microdot), about the size of a period, which could contain dispatches of about

fifty words, "the enemy's masterpiece of espionage," J. Edgar
Hoover would later exult. Uncle Hugo told him to watch out
for such pencil-point marks in any communications he received
from Germany.

Since Sebold was only occupied with his spy work for a total
of ten hours, he had time to hang around the pension, which
housed a roster of apprentice agents who mostly kept to themselves except for the occasional comment from one of them
about just returning from Holland or Czechoslovakia. Sebold
struck up a friendship with proprietor Georg Gut, who scrubbed
the pots and pans while his wife answered the phone calls from
Ast Hamburg. Gut informed Sebold that he "was disgusted with
the whole matter" and admitted he wanted to sell the business
and move to America, which revealed that Sebold may have had
a natural ability to draw out seditious confessions whether he
was trying to or not.

Final discussions were conducted in Uncle Hugo's office
on January 26, 1940. Sebold was handed two leather money
pouches—one contained $500 in $5 bills to be used for the purchase of a Leica camera and "a radio transmitting outfit"; the
other had $500 in $10 bills to be delivered to Everett Roeder of
210 Smith Street, Merrick, Long Island. Sebold was given five
microphotographs of instructions, which were hidden within
the innards of his watch, two for his own elucidation and one
each for Roeder, Colonel Duquesne, and a woman, Lilly Stein,
whose address was given as 127 East Fifty-Fourth Street, just to
the east of Park Avenue. He was ordered to seek out an amateur
broadcaster who could help him with radio transmittal work, to
join the National Guard to learn about firearms developments,
to find a job at an aircraft factory, and to refrain from any unnec-
essary contacts with Germans, with a particular admonition "to
stay out of Yorkville." Provided with three mail-drop addresses

(in Shanghai, São Paolo, and Coimbra, Portugal), he was to establish himself under the undemonstrative all-American name Harry Sawyer, presumably a relation of Mark Twain's Tom. Although he wasn't aware of it yet, he had been bestowed with the code name Tramp, an obvious acknowledgment of his foot-loose life up until then that carried with it a hint of disdain.

During the meeting, Dr. Renken entered the room and revealed why Hermann Lang was not receiving a microphoto-graph like the others: his work was done. Renken / Ritter told Sebold to visit Lang at his Queens home, utter the words "Greet-ings from Rantzau, Berlin-Hamburg," and ask him to prepare for an all-expenses-paid trip that would return him to the Reich by way of the Far East. In his memoir, Ritter said that Lang was being called home because of worries that his theft of the Nor-den bombsight would become known to the American author-ities once a Luftwaffe bomber equipped with a Norden-like instrument was recovered by the Allies. Yet nothing of this was said to Sebold, who, quite by coincidence, took it upon himself to bring up the great secret that he had first learned about from Dr. Gassner.

"Up to that point the bombsight had never been mentioned definitcly?" attorney George Herz later asked Sebold.

"Never; never anything, micros, nothing—only radio."

"Exactly what was said to you? What did they say about the bombsight? Tell me as best you can recollect everything they said."

"I said, 'I might bring back the famous American bombsight and give it to you as a present.'"

"I want you to tell everything they said," said Herz.

"That was all that was said about it," responded Sebold. "He said, 'Don't bother about it. We already have it in our possession.'"

On the next morning, Sebold went by himself to the

Hamburg-Altona railway station, wearing an old sheepskin-lined coat and tattered blue suit that made him look like the tramp that Ast Hamburg said he was. He arrived in Munich in the evening and changed for the sleeper that took him through the Alps via the Brenner Pass. He reached Milan at noon on January 28, switched trains again, and made it to Genoa in the late afternoon of the same day. He spent the night at the Hotel Britannia. On the following morning, he was one of 427 passengers who boarded the *Washington,* including Irish novelist Liam O'Flaherty, Chicago construction engineer Hugh Rodman (who was returning after fourteen months of work in the Soviet Union), and three hundred Jewish refugees from Nazi Germany. Although Sebold thought of giving his spy materials to another traveler (and apparently did so briefly), absconding with the money and starting a new life, and even committing suicide, he decided to carry through with the plan in deference to the promise he'd made to the American consulate in Cologne. After all, he figured he probably wouldn't be subject to any more than a few days of unpleasantness in New York.

CHAPTER EIGHT

"YOU ARE HARRY SAWYER"

Keep still your former face, and mix again
With these lost spirits; run all their mazes with them;
For such are treasons: find their windings out,
And subtle turnings; watch their snaky ways,
Through brakes and hedges, into woods of darkness
Where they are fain to creep upon their breasts
In paths ne'er trod by men, but wolves and panthers.
—from *Catiline His Conspiracy* (1611)
by Ben Jonson

On February 8, 1940, the *Washington* made its first stop in American waters at the quarantine station at the entrance of Upper New York Bay, which enabled US officials to board and conduct required inspections before landfall. Arriving by Coast Guard cutter were State Department officer Hall Kinsey and FBI special agent Albert Franz, who sought out Sebold, heard a portion of his story, and asked if he would be willing to come to Foley Square for further discussions. He agreed. When the *Washington* docked at Pier 59 at the foot of West Eighteenth Street, reporters gathered around O'Flaherty, most famous as the author of *The Informer*, the tale of an Irish revolutionist who accepts twenty pounds to betray a comrade and suffers such torment for his violation of societal norms that death becomes his only redemption, which was made into a critically acclaimed film by John Ford in 1935. The papers that day carried prominent stories about the arraignment in the Brooklyn federal court of seventeen Coughlinites on charges of conspiring to steal munitions from National Guard armories and carry out a plot to overthrow the government, the result of a five-month investigation that represented the FBI's first major sedition case since receiving expanded powers. J. Edgar Hoover had come to town to announce the arrests three weeks earlier, charging that a faction of the Christian Front wanted "to spread a reign of terrorism so that the authorities would become thoroughly demoralized" and "a dictatorship could be set up here, similar to the Hitler dictatorship in Germany," a notion so ludicrous that it contributed to a growing sense among some that the FBI was using its new authority to transform into a state secret police. Hoover told the press that Bureau agents had employed the novel investigative tool of a motion-picture camera to record members of the group as they fired weapons at an upstate rifle range, which suggested a significant level of intimacy with the plot's workings. "Is it possible that in this country there exists a movement of any appreciable size to reproduce a Hitlerian dictatorship by way of IRA methods?" wondered the *Herald Tribune*, which noted the Celtic and Germanic surnames among the defendants. "We shall have to wait on developments for the answer."

Sebold was escorted unnoticed past reporters and driven downtown as two cars of FBI men trailed close behind. He spent the next two days explaining all that had befallen him in Germany, which was passed on to Hoover, who shared it directly with President Roosevelt. "The story, to say the least, seemed preposterous," wrote an agent assigned to the case, Raymond Newkirk, in his unpublished memoirs. "To send a head spy to the U.S. who did not want to be a spy in the first place and give him information as to the other spies in the U.S. did not show good sense." On February 10, Sebold was "asked whether or not he would be willing to follow the instructions given him in Germany and assist the Federal Bureau of Investigation in making an investigation concerning this matter," the offer to become the first counterspy in FBI history. (The phrase *double agent* was not yet in common currency.) All we know is that he agreed. "Was there an arrangement made whereby you were to cooperate with the FBI? Just say yes or no," he was asked in court. "Yes," he said without elaboration. He was offered a salary of $50 a week plus reimbursement for expenses. He would later receive a raise to $60 a week.

On the next day, he followed his Hamburg orders and sent a Western Union telegram to Mr. Hugo Sebold c/o Pension Klopstock, delivering the requested message that indicated he didn't believe he was being followed. "Arrived safe. Had pleasant trip. Bill." (If he feared trouble, he was to say, "Am in doctor's care.") On February 12, he went to Abe Cohen's Exchange at 142 Fulton Street ("The House of Photographic Values") and placed a $20 down payment on a Leica camera. "Easy terms arranged," promised the store's newspaper ad.

At 11:30 a.m. on the following morning, a Trans World Airways red-eye from the West Coast arrived at the newly opened La Guardia Airport, carrying James Claridge Ellsworth, a thirty-one-year-old special agent from the Los Angeles office who was recovering from a bout of airsickness suffered over Pittsburgh. A devoted family man with two young children and a profound commitment to his Mormon faith, he had gained fluency in German during his thirty-four months of missionary service in the late Weimar Republic from 1927 to 1929. He was so faithful to his religion's strictures that he dutifully sought repentance after once drinking from a barrel of iced tea to fend off dehydration during shooting practice at Quantico, violating a Mormon commandment against the consumption of coffee and tea. "He never wanted to be out of favor with God or with God's Church," according to one of his sons. "He never wanted to be disloyal to his employer, nor disappoint. In every case he would do everything he could to do what was 'right.' And if he made a mistake, he'd do everything he could to make it right." Lacking a bachelor's or graduate degree or seemingly any applicable work experience (as the manager of a beauty-products company), he was hired by the FBI at the urging of a fellow Mormon and close friend, the legendary G-man Reed Vetterli, whose name is etched in Bureau lore as one of three survivors of the Kansas City Massacre, the bullet-ridden attempt by Pretty Boy Floyd and his criminal associates (or so it was initially claimed) to free bank robber Frank Nash from federal custody outside Union Station, resulting in the death of Nash and four law enforcement officers, including one FBI agent. Ellsworth and Vetterli's friendship was such that Ellsworth and his wife, Nell, were dinner guests of the Vetterlis on the evening of the shoot-out. "I know this applicant to be a morally clean individual and think he can be relied upon to be a conscientious, ambitious worker and will be amenable to discipline and the division will never have any trouble with him," wrote Vetterli, who, in his capacity as special agent in charge (SAC) of the Indianapolis office, interviewed Ellsworth and recommended his appointment. In his five years with the Bureau, Ellsworth had risen to assistant SAC in Los Angeles. He was described in his most recent evaluation as "alert, intelligent, well-acquainted with the Bureau's work, and well-qualified to handle general assignments," but lacking "a sufficiently pleasing personality to be a good salesman," which wasn't regarded as a hindrance to administrative advancement. When he touched down in New York, Ellsworth had completed all of five days of espionage training at the Washington headquarters.

"I took a taxi to the city, took the subway (8th Avenue) to Chambers Street, and carried my suitcases over to Foley Square and the U.S. Courthouse," he wrote in his diary of the case, which he composed a year and a half later. During a meeting with the SAC of the New York office on the sixth floor, Ellsworth was informed that he was being assigned as the double agent's handler or body man, a heady role for his first spy case. "My job was to live with Sebold, check his story, see that he carried out German instructions, learn the code, and develop the case," he wrote. "I am on an important matter that may keep me here weeks," he told Nell in a letter that day. "I hope not. But if I make it, I'll really be in big. Please telephone to heaven often for my success. I need it."

Sebold was allowed to spend that evening with his wife, Helen, but was instructed to tell her nothing of his service with the FBI. "He at this time feels very badly about having to lie to his wife and tell her that he is employed as an electrical appliance salesman at $50 a week," according to the FBI. "Undoubtedly some day he will let some information slip and she will become aware of his activities. Such an occurrence, of course, will have to be taken care of at the proper time." Whatever the previous status of the relationship, it appears that Mrs. Sebold welcomed her husband home with love and support.

"Another agent and I were assigned to follow him the first night he went out," wrote Agent Newkirk. "There were two entrances to the apartment he visited and the agent with me watched one door to the building and I watched the front door. The only place I could find partly out of the snow and cold was in the entrance of a church across the street. There was hardly anyone on the streets. After a while a priest entered the church and said hello as he went by. He came back out in a little while and asked me if there was anything he could do for me—did I want a cup of coffee, a sandwich, or anything?—and I told him no I was just waiting for a friend. In about an hour the priest came out again. He explained that he was a priest and if I were in trouble he would not inform the law and would help me in any way he could. I told him I was still waiting for my friend and was perfectly all right. He went back to his church, I'm sure, puzzled and hurt. Sebold came out later and went back to his room and I ended up in bed for a week with a mild case of pneumonia."

Sebold returned to the Hotel Imperial at Broadway and Thirty-Second where the Bureau had reserved two adjoining rooms, one for him, the other for agents. On the following morning, Ellsworth met him for the first time. "As I was getting out of the shower in the hotel room, Sebold came in," he wrote. "Franz introduced me to him. I found Sebold to be a tall (6'3"), thin (157 pounds) German. He was big-boned, brown-eyed, and had brown hair. He spoke English brokenly but as time went on he spoke English very well. He was very nervous and irritable and I saw at once that he did not get along with Franz."

During their first day together, Sebold and Ellsworth took out a PO box in the Church Street Annex under the name Harry Sawyer (the first in a series of PO addresses Sebold would use) and paid the additional money ($108.30) owed on the Leica camera, soon returning to purchase the accessories necessary to create microphotographs. On February 15, they rented a typewriter from the American Typewriter and Adding Machine Company and reserved an apartment in Yorkville under the name of Harry Büchner, his wife's maiden name, which was soon replaced by another Germantown residence taken out under his real name. But Sebold and Ellsworth didn't live at either location, instead moving into separate rooms on the second floor of a German-run boardinghouse on the West Side. "Franz and I had previously looked the place over," Ellsworth wrote. "Bill and I were the only tenants as the place had been remodeled and opened for business. I was hard put to meet Bill there casually so I walked over to his door and knocked just as the landlord came down the stairs—I walked in. The landlord said someone was in there and went to stop me but I saw Bill there and said my name was End-icott and I wanted to get acquainted. The landlord said okay and walked on. I had taken the room as J.C. Endicott. Bill had used the name assigned to him in Germany—Harry Sawyer." But the FBI man couldn't stand the dump. He complained in a letter to his parents about being attacked by bedbugs ("who left red lumps over one arm and all over my neck"), forced to bathe in rusty water ("you can't see the bottom of the tub when the tub is full of fresh water"), tormented by the radiator ("the heat is on full force all the time so I suffocate with the windows closed, and the wind blows the room away when the windows are open"), and cramped by the too-short bed. "Last night I stacked the three couch pillows at the head end and put the bed pillow on them and thus made the thing long enough," he wrote. After a week or two of slum living, they moved to the twentieth floor of the Man-hattan Towers at Seventy-Sixth and Broadway, where Ellsworth lived as J. C. Elliott and Sebold as William Sutheor, an uncle's last name. "We had to keep initials straight due to laundry and cleaning marks." Ellsworth was pleased that the hotel was built over a Gothic-style church, which took up the first three floors of the building and hosted services by the Manhattan Ward of his Church of Jesus Christ of Latter-day Saints. "The Mormons love it so I had an easy time getting to Sunday School and evening ser-vices," he told his diary. "Some Sunday afternoons I also attended St. Bartholomew's Church [on Park Avenue] at 4 p.m. as they had a swell choral group and organ music for an hour."

■ ■ ■

But Bill Sebold was not happy. Soon after his arrival from Germany, he informed Ellsworth that "he would not go through with this case; that he was not being treated right; that he was being kept under suspicion by the Bureau and that he did not have the full confidence of the agents," wrote Percy "Sam" Foxworth, the SAC of the New York office, in a "personal and strictly confidential" message to the director. "He claimed to be unable to sleep or eat and said the nervous tension was becoming too great for him. He expressed a desire to talk over this situation with me and I had a long conversation with him."

The lengthy talk convinced Foxworth that Sebold might not have the coolly duplicitous nature required to operate effectively as an undercover.

"Sebold has an honesty complex," he wrote. "In fact, he is so honest that I am afraid some day he will give himself away because of his inability to act his part. He has a mania for doing just what he feels is right; for example, he says that if the German government really knew him they would never have entrusted him with the assignment which they gave to him, and that he took this assignment knowing that he would never go through with it, but knowing that he had to do something in order to get out of Germany alive."

Further, Sebold's feelings for America were unequivocal. "He states that an oath to him is a sacred thing and that when he swore to be loyal to the United States and a loyal United States citizen at the time he was naturalized, he considered that a sacred oath and he considers he renewed that oath at the time he was given a passport. He is of the opinion that if a man breaks faith with him in any respect whatever that man is not deserving of any further consideration with him. It is, therefore, apparent that if Sebold ever feels that the Bureau does not trust him or would fail to carry out any part of what he thinks is its contract with him, he would blow up and probably ruin the case."

And he was just the type to blow up. "He admits that he has a violent temper which he claims to have inherited from his Swedish father," Foxworth wrote. "It is sometimes difficult for him to control this temper and it is possible that in a moment of stress and anger he may say or do something in the presence of the subjects of this case which would give away his operations in connection with the Bureau." Sebold beat up "a prankster in Mülheim during the past year in the office where he worked when the latter hit him on the head with a tomato."

Foxworth said Sebold "cooled down considerably" when he assured him that "the Bureau knows his whole background and is now able to trust him and is confident that he is telling the truth. I told him we would see that he had proper medical care. This appeared to satisfy him and appropriate arrangements were made."

Sebold was instructed to make an appointment with an expert in nervous disorders, Dr. Phillip Goodhardt, who was to be told nothing of his work with the FBI. According to Sebold's account, the doctor "immediately diagnosed his case as being one of considerable nervous strain and told him he was in a very rundown condition; that his mind was overactive and that he had apparently recently been under severe nervous shock and strain." Sebold said he told the doctor "that he had a terrible experience in Germany and had nearly lost his life there; that he had, however, succeeded in getting away to America and that he is now working with the Federal Bureau of Investigation." The doctor feared he was a few days away from a nervous breakdown. His recommendation was "a lot of rest and mental ease," said Sebold.

According to Dr. Goodhardt's account, which was provided to a Bureau agent, Sebold told him "he had lost 40 pounds in the past two years; that when he lies down his head twists so that it causes him considerable inconvenience; that he is quite worried and two years ago was operated upon for stomach ulcers at the Bellevue Hospital, New York City." The doctor said he wasn't sure "whether Sebold is a 'paranoiac' which is a person troubled with a chronic form of insanity with delusions. However, the fact that he states he is not being followed at the present time would seem to indicate that this is not the case." Dr. Goodhardt told the agent that he thought "Sebold was a German spy; that he appeared indiscreet to him in mentioning any connection at all with the federal government and, frankly, he had been turning over in his mind considerably the possibility that Sebold might be a 'paranoiac' as previously mentioned."

In his own conclusion, Foxworth described Sebold as a "definitely eccentric" individual whose "usefulness to the Bureau is very definitely limited." He wanted Hoover to be aware of Sebold's "personal make-up as there is no way of telling what he might do to this case when he is outside the care of an agent and handling his contacts by himself."

Of this episode, Jim Ellsworth makes only a brief mention in his diary. "We sent him to a nerve specialist who attested that he was on the verge of a nervous breakdown, prescribed rest, and plenty of good food," he wrote in a line that suggests he didn't believe Sebold's state of mind would jeopardize the investigation. Now convinced of Sebold's "honesty and desire to cooperate," Ellsworth wrote, the Bureau allowed him to spend every evening and all day on Sundays with his wife. The case was going forward.

On February 16, with the assistance of Ellsworth and another agent, Sebold typed out the letters that Hamburg wanted him to send to Everett Roeder ("I should be very much obliged to

you if you would let me know by return mail when and where
a meeting between us can take place"), to Colonel Duquesne ("I
have had the pleasure of meeting your old friends Nicholas and
Joy and they have asked me to get in contact with you"), and, in
German, to Lilly Stein ("My dear Miss, I met your friend Heinrich and I have regards from Bachenkel and Grinzig to extend
to you"). The first to respond was Ms. Stein, who sent a note
seeking a meeting to "talk with you about our mutual acquaintances." On February 19, Sebold called her from a phone booth
in a drugstore on the corner of West Eighty-Sixth and Columbus and took a cab with Ellsworth to the vicinity of Stein's building in the East Fifties. At 7:20 p.m., he rang her bell and was
buzzed into the building. Answering the door of the ground-
floor apartment was a twenty-four-year-old woman with hazel
eyes and bushy brown hair, a seductive native of Vienna who was
five foot four, of medium build, with "better than average looks"
and a "Jewish appearance," according to her FBI description.
Sebold was so startled by her youth and beauty that he asked
at least twice if she was indeed Ms. Stein. When he muttered
his Hamburg-dictated introduction about "your friend Heinrich" and "regards from Bachenkel and Grinzig," she responded,
"I know. I know." With little concern about Sebold's identity,
she blithely spoke of two of her contacts, one of whom she
described as a well-known American diplomat. She also mentioned that she had received a payment of $200 without a prob-
lem but hadn't heard a response to several letters she'd sent to
Germany. When Sebold handed her the microphotograph that
he had hidden in his hat, she extracted a powerful lens from her
purse, placed it in a socket, and glanced at the message, which
she could make out fine. Once the bothersome matter of spy
business was concluded, she asked him to sit down, have a drink,
get comfortable. Sebold declined, saying he didn't want to get

caught in her apartment, which he later described as "very luxuriously furnished." As he was leaving, she pouted, "Now you are going and leave me all alone." Waiting outside in the rain and sleet was Ellsworth, who, despite a red face, runny nose, and cracked lips, was thrilled at how well the case was going. "Everything is working out just lovely," he told his wife in a letter the next day. "It reads like a novel and I am the ace in the hole so am enjoying it immensely."

A few days later, Lilly mailed a request for another meeting. This time, the two met at the corner of Lexington and Fifty-Seventh Street, where Bureau agents captured the scene on film, and then proceeded to Child's Restaurant at Fifth and Fifty-Ninth, the cafeteria-style chain known for its impeccably clean interiors, strong coffee, and flapjack-tossing cook viewable to pedestrians through the front window. Here she revealed more of her story: She said she was a "prostitute" in the midst of an ongoing relationship with Ogden Hammond Jr., a twenty-seven-year-old son of the American aristocracy whom she had met a year earlier when he was vice consul at the US consulate in Vienna and she was a pretty girl of Jewish lineage who would do just about anything to obtain a precious visa to the United States. Without "Oggie" Hammond's help, she would admit, "I might be still now in Vienna." She told Sebold that her principal contact at Ast Hamburg was "Heinrich Sorau," apparently the subordinate of Nikolaus Ritter's known to Sebold as Uncle Hugo, who told her in a letter she had received since the first meeting, "By now you have probably met Harry Sawyer, who is a funny looking animal but very reliable." The story, as she would later reveal, was that she met Sorau through her connections to European high society, which she was able to cultivate because of her family's considerable wealth in the cold-storage business. In early 1939, he had provided her with a German passport that identified her as

THE DIRECTOR—In 1938, in response to public fears about Nazi spies active in the United States, J. Edgar Hoover was granted the authority by President Franklin Roosevelt to protect "the internal security of the United States against foreign enemies," as Hoover put it. "The techniques of advanced scientific crime detection that had proved indispensable in conquering home-bred banditry were now set to work uncovering the enemy."

THE IDEOLOGUE—Hermann Lang, *pictured at far left*, entering Brooklyn federal court on July 1, 1941, was a Bavarian-born resident of Queens who provided the Nazi regime with the plans for the most precious instrument created for the American military before World War II, the Norden bombsight, which enabled planes to drop bombs with unprecedented accuracy. "We have just one secret," President Roosevelt said during a private meeting with congressional leaders in 1939, "and that is the question of the bombsight."

HITLER'S SPYMASTER—The United States had no counterespionage system in place when Nikolaus Ritter, an English-fluent Luftwaffe officer assigned to the Abwehr, the German military's espionage service, visited the United States in late 1937 and recruited the founding members of his ring, Hermann Lang and Fritz Duquesne. In early 1940, he sent William G. Sebold to New York as an "informant and contact man," unaware that Sebold had already communicated with a newly empowered FBI.

THE GRIFTER—Guenther "Gus" Rumrich, who volunteered to become a Nazi spy because he found life as a dishwasher "quite a strain," was arrested on a Manhattan street corner in early 1938, which led to blanket coverage in the press about the failure of the United States to protect itself from foreign intrigue.

THE PIONEER—Everett M. Roeder, *second from right,* was a high-level engineer at the Sperry Gyroscope Co., where he first began developing precision weapons systems in 1913. When Sebold first met him in a train station parking lot on Long Island in 1940, he'd been passing information to the Nazi regime for four years. Roeder was blind in his right eye, "which gives it a peculiar stare," wrote the Bureau.

THE GLORY HOUND—FBI special agent Leon G. Turrou, *right,* botched the investigation that followed Gus Rumrich's arrest, which didn't prevent him from writing a bestselling book about the expansiveness of Nazi operations in the United States that served as the source material for Warner Bros.' *Confessions of a Nazi Spy,* starring Edward G. Robinson, *left.* The 1939 film was calculated to inflame the public into believing that German agents were everywhere.

THE CAPITAL OF GERMAN AMERICA—East Eighty-Sixth Street between Second and Third Avenues was the heart of the Manhattan neighborhood of Yorkville, a favorite rendezvous point for German spies and tourists in search of rowdy beer gardens.

THE BUNDESFÜHRER—Fritz Kuhn, *second from left,* was the leader of the pro-Nazi German American Bund, the proud face of National Socialism in the United States. The Bund and its affiliates had enough public support to fill Madison Square Garden in February 1939. Within a year, Kuhn was convicted of embezzling from his own membership and sent to Sing Sing.

THE DOUBLE AGENT—Wilhelm "William" Gottlieb Sebold, a native of Mülheim in the Ruhr Valley, was a peripatetic soul who became a US citizen in 1936. During a visit to his mother in Germany in 1939, he was coerced into the Abwehr but never carried out a single act on its behalf because he regarded his oath of allegiance to America as "a sacred thing." He is pictured with his wife, Helen, also an American of German birth.

The photo attached to Sebold's "Declaration of Intention" to become a US citizen.

THE HANDLER—Special Agent Jim Ellsworth, pictured with his wife, Nell, was assigned to be Sebold's handler or body man, responsible for shadowing his every move during the sixteen-month investigation. "It reads like a novel and I am the ace in the hole so am enjoying it immensely," Ellsworth wrote in a letter to Nell.

A RADIO STATION—The two-room cottage in Centerport on the north shore of Long Island housed the short-wave transmitter set up by the FBI to establish a communications link with Hamburg. A total of 468 messages—301 from Centerport to Hamburg; 167 from Hamburg to Centerport—were exchanged via a cipher system based on the letter arrangements in a bestselling novel, *All This, and Heaven Too* by Rachel Field.

Special Agent Richard Millen, *right,* was brought in from Washington to help launch the station.

THE FEMME FATALE—A Jewish native of Vienna with connections among European high society, Lilly Stein was assigned by the Abwehr to hit Manhattan nightclubs in search of men who could whisper in her ear "about all sorts of war developments and deals in industry and finance," as she later admitted. When Sebold spurned her amorous advances, she said, "Why is it you American men are always afraid of women?" At *left*, an FBI surveillance photo captures Stein walking near her midtown apartment with Sebold, whose face was obscured by the Bureau.

THE MAN WHO "KILLED" KITCHENER—"Colonel" Fritz Duquesne was a South African–born adventurer who dined out for years on tales of his spy exploits during the Boer War and World War I. His claim that he was responsible for the death of Lord Horatio Herbert Kitchener during the Great War was unsupported by evidence, but the British government believed he had a hand in the explosion on the SS *Tennyson* that killed three British seamen on February 21, 1916. He told Sebold that he could pick out FBI men by the way they walked, "sort of pigeon-toed and with a peculiar halting step."

THE COUP DE GRÂCE—In the final phase of the Sebold investigation, the FBI rented three rooms in the Newsweek building at the corner of Broadway and Forty-Second Street in Times Square, transforming Room 627 into the office of WILLIAM G. SEBOLD DIESEL ENG. The double agent met with a procession of spies who were unaware that they were being filmed behind a two-way mirror by a Bureau agent. When the films were shown in court, the American experience with hidden motion-picture footage was born.

Fritz Duquesne made a single visit to the office on June 25, 1941, just days before the arrests. At one point, he raised the leg of his trousers and pulled an envelope from his sock, a cloak-and-dagger detail that would be much remembered in later years by the agents who worked the case. During the trial, this son of the nineteenth century claimed it was all an optical illusion. "The taking of anything out of my stocking never happened," he said.

Paul Fehse, *left,* and his sidekick Leo Waalen wandered the Manhattan and Brooklyn docks picking up information about British merchant ships that were being loaded with goods in preparation for running the U-boat gauntlet. They submitted such detailed reports that Sebold admonished them to provide only the most essential information for transmittal to Germany.

Erwin W. Siegler, the chief butcher of the SS *Manhattan,* later transferred to the SS *America,* was one of several German-born spies working on the kitchen staffs of American-flagged liners, who were hired because they produced the European dishes that sophisticated travelers expected during their transatlantic passage. Siegler bragged that he was "the biggest whoremaster in Hamburg."

PAUL BANTE   MAX BLANK   ALFRED E. BROKHOFF   HEINRICH CLAUSING   CONRADINE DOLD   FREDERICK DUQUESNE

RUDOLPH EBELING   RICHARD EICHENLAUB   HEINRICH CARL EILERS   PAUL FEHSE   EDMUND CARL HEINE   FELIX JAHNKE

GUSTAVE KAERCHER   JOSEF KLEIN   HARTWIG KLEISS   HERMAN LANG   EVELYN CLAYTON LEWIS   RENE EMANUEL MEZENEN

CARL REUPER   EVERETT ROEDER   PAUL SCHOLZ   GEORGE GOTTLOB SCHUH   ERWIN WILHELM SIEGLER   OSCAR STABLER

HEINRICH STADE   LILLY STEIN   FRANZ JOSEPH STIGLER   ERICK STRUNK   LEO WAALEN   ADOLF WALISCHEWSKI

ELSE WEUSTENFELD   AXEL WHEELER-HILL   BERTRAM W. ZENZINGER

THE 33 CONVICTED MEMBERS OF THE DUQUESNE SPY RING

The "Duquesne" Spy "Ring," shown here in FBI mugshots, was in fact made up of four separate rings with a smattering of lone wolves, a diverse collection of Hitler supporters that included a convicted counterfeiter from Dusseldorf and a former auto executive with Ford and Chrysler, an employee of a boat basin in the Bronx and a secretary for the law firm representing the German Consulate in downtown Manhattan. J. Edgar Hoover described the investigation as "the greatest of its kind in the nation's history."

Bill and Helen Sebold were relocated after the case to a small home outside San Francisco in an early version of the witness protection program. As the years passed, Sebold grew fearful of Nazi reprisals, which may have contributed to an increasing mental instability. But he never disavowed his service to the United States. He told an FBI agent in 1954 that he "did not take advantage of making money from his story or from radio or movie because he felt he had done what he did for the good of the country."

"Jewish first degree mixture," a *Mischling* or half Jew, sparing her from the worse of anti-Semitic excesses in post-*Anschluss* Austria even though both of her late parents (Hugo Stein and Ida Lowey Halpern) were Jews who had been married in a synagogue. The passport allowed her to spend much of 1939 traveling between Vienna, Brussels, London, Budapest, San Remo, and Venice, cavorting with a sporty circle of the beau monde that included her close friend Friederike "Fritzi" Burger, the figure-skating champion who was known for always coming in second to Sonja Henie. The understanding was that "I would be willing to help him maybe later on in some business deals," she said.

Since arriving in New York in October 1939, entering the country by way of a visa obtained through the personal intervention of an overly friendly Oggie Hammond and a passport furnished by Nazi spymasters eager to try another Mata Hari operation, she set up a beach-hat and beach-accessories business and hit the nightclubs in search of men who could whisper in her ear "about all sorts of war developments and deals in industry and finance," as Sorau instructed her. "She was to my way of thinking a well-built, good-looking nymphomaniac with a good sense of humor," said Agent Newkirk, who was part of a team that tapped her phone line and placed a recording device in her fireplace. During this, his second experience as an actor, Sebold told her to look upon him as a father figure rather than one of her boyfriends, someone she could, on a strictly platonic basis, share her concerns with about the confidential business of espionage. Which didn't prevent her from seeking closer intimacy during a later get-together: She "then tried to make some subtle advances toward him," according to the chaste language of the FBI report, "and among other things said, 'Why is it you American men are always afraid of women?'"

At their following meeting, Stein revealed that Oggie Ham-

mond was "a very patriotic American" with such a hatred of the Nazis that he would have her shot if he knew she was a spy. He was also a member of what one left-wing magazine called "official Washington's first fascist family," which included his father, a former US ambassador to Spain and outspoken supporter of Franco, and his brother-in-law, an Italian count who had served as an attaché in Mussolini's embassy in Washington. Young Hammond was once overheard musing that he would've liked to fight on the Fascist side in the Spanish Civil War, according to one of his pampered peers, Cornelius Vanderbilt Jr. Yet his feelings about German militarism couldn't have been unconflicted: both parents were aboard the British liner *Lusitania* when a U-boat struck on May 7, 1915, sinking the ship and killing 1,198 people, including his mother, Mary Picton Stevens Hammond. Stein told Sebold that Oggie had just returned from Europe and was planning to visit her in a few days, but she was more preoccupied with a subject that would come to dominate her talks with Sebold: her perpetual need for funds. She said she'd received no response from letters and telegrams she sent to Hamburg seeking more "Mary," her code word for money, which she said she needed so she could socialize with gentlemen of a sufficiently elevated stature. Two days later, agents were listening in when Hammond arrived to ease her financial woes, handing over a $100 check and a gold watch. "The visit was seemingly social in nature and the conversation failed to indicate that he had any knowledge of her activities and interests," according to the FBI. During Sebold's next stop at the apartment, she struggled to rouse herself from bed, later admitting that she was recovering from an abortion that cost $100, but was well enough to pass along a tip from Hammond. He had told her there is "no chance of America getting into the war."

■　■　■

Next to make contact with Sebold was Colonel Duquesne, whom Hoover called "a particularly interesting element" of the case in a memo he sent to President Roosevelt four days after Sebold landed in the country. The Bureau provided a summary of Duquesne's "colorful career and adventures," describing him as an "excellent talker," who, because of a partially paralyzed right leg, always carried a cane. (Actually, the paralysis was one of his old hustles: he could walk just fine.) The president may have been piqued by the revelation that "Duquesne has, on occasion, boasted of friendship with former President Theodore Roosevelt." One of the episodes detailed in the short biography told of how Duquesne had briefly resided in the home of an H. A. Spanuth, president of the Commonwealth Film Company. He "was asked to leave, according to information subsequently furnished by Spanuth, when the latter's wife informed Spanuth that she had fallen in love with Duquesne. Spanuth thereafter left New York and proceeded to Chicago, obtaining a divorce from his wife during 1918." Duquesne was said to have an "intense hatred for England and apparently expressed strong sympathy for Germany and her Allies during the World War period," the president was told. "No information, whatsoever, concerning the whereabouts and activities of Duquesne since June 6, 1932, is possessed by the Federal Bureau of Investigation."

Sebold's microfilm information enabled Bureau agents to begin surveillance of Duquesne's front business, Air Terminals Co., which had moved from an East Forty-Second Street location to a thirty-four-story art deco skyscraper at 120 Wall Street on the East River waterfront. From his rented desk, Duquesne employed his greatest gift in service of the Reich, his brazen willingness to pretend he was someone he wasn't. On a typical day in the office, he wrote a letter to the president of Grumman Aircraft Engineering Co. in Bethpage, New York, requesting photographs of the G-21 twin-engine seaplane for lectures he said he was delivering "on the art of docking planes at sea," which were sent to him with warm regards. On another occasion, he mailed a note to the Mine Safety Appliance Company of Pittsburgh, Pennsylvania, asking for a component of its "M.S.A. All-Service Gas Mask, BURRELL type," because "my own was destroyed by coming in contact with a live wire which fused the component parts," part of his efforts to procure the latest protective gear for chemical warfare. "He was a go-getter with iron nerves, and he got what he wanted," claimed Nikolaus Ritter. "When, for example, he read an item in the newspaper about a new military product, he did not hesitate to drop in at the office of the general manager of the company and boldly assert that he needed details for a lecture about future American weapons. He was rarely turned down, and his information promptly was passed on to Germany. Sometimes he also, without advance notice, dropped in at a factory and quite calmly demanded to see a certain product. Here again, he was mostly successful."

While agents were able to monitor his activities during working hours, they failed in their initial attempts to follow the elusive fantasist to his residence. "The Duke had been a spy all of his life and automatically used all the tricks in the book to avoid anyone following him," wrote Agent Newkirk. "He would take a local train, change to an express, change back to a local, go through a revolving door and keep going on right around, take an elevator up a floor, get off, walk back to the ground, and take off in a different entrance of the building." He was eventually discovered to be living in a studio apartment on the second-floor front of 24 West Seventy-Sixth Street. Now one of the most exclusive properties in the city, it was then merely a Renaissance Revival boardinghouse a half a block from Central Park operated by a Polish woman who hated the Nazis and was more than happy to permit the FBI to occupy a room above Duquesne's apartment and put a microphone in his door buzzer. (He didn't have a phone.) Agents learned that the apartment was rented by his girlfriend, Evelyn Clayton Lewis, an artsy Southerner more than twenty years his junior, a playwright, sculptress, and toy designer who knew full well what he was up to with the Germans. "I love you," the FBI microphone overheard her telling him one day. "But I realize that you have things to do, that's your job. You have to do it and that's all there is to it." The Bureau described both as "sexual perverts," although the nature of their perversion is unexplained in the files.

When Sebold reached the Air Terminals desk in Room 17–18 on the thirty-first floor of 120 Wall Street, Duquesne handed him a pink slip of paper. "We will go out," it said. "Cannot talk here." They exited the building and walked crosstown for several blocks to the Automat at Broadway and John Street, where each purchased a coffee by dropping a nickel into the slot and watching as a spout filled the cup to the rim, participating in one of the early rituals of American fast food. Sebold sought to play upon Duquesne's vanity, describing himself as a "greenhorn" who was eager for the old master's tutelage. Duquesne obliged at great length, telling Sebold to always send the third carbon copy of any message he typed; to wear gloves when handling documents; to avoid all Germans, whom Duquesne regarded as "squealers"; to burn everything; to become a loud opponent of the Nazis so as to avoid suspicion; to never speak to the authorities "even though he is placed against the wall and shot down"; etc. Duquesne delved into his feelings about the Jewish people, noting "that this war is no war with England but a war of the Jews against Germany, and the English are fighting the Jews' fight," and that Bundesführer Fritz Kuhn was framed "by the Jews" and imprisoned "for nothing." In a later session, Duquesne would repeat a favorite canard of the anti-Semitic right, describing President Roosevelt as "a darned Jew." In the midst of the long talk, Sebold gave Duquesne an English-language translation of the instructions contained within Duquesne's microphotograph and asked him to mail word when he wanted to schedule another session. "Intimate contact to be avoided for the time" was one of his orders, apparently a reference to sabotage, which was forbidden for now in accord with Hitler's policy of encouraging US isolationism. "Remain exclusively in an auxiliary position."

After the two parted, Duquesne sent a telegram informing Sebold that he believed they had been under surveillance, which they were—by six agents: INVESTMENT DANGEROUS. FOLLOWED AFTER MEETING. STOCK BAD POSITION. HOLD OFF. S. FRANK. Sebold responded with a telegram to Air Terminals: I AM HOLDING STOCK. HARRY. At their next appointment, which was mostly conducted at a downtown Automat (this one at Chambers and West Broadway) and on the corner of Fulton and Broadway (where they remained for "perhaps an hour," said the FBI), Duquesne spent much time obsessing in a low voice about the "Pinkerton detectives and FBI agents" he was certain were watching him. He spoke of how he could pick out G-men by the way they walked, "sort of pigeon-toed and with a peculiar halting step," which he figured was a method taught to them at the academy so they could be identifiable to each other. He told Sebold he went up to one of his pigeon-toed antagonists and demanded that he stop tracking him, a story confirmed by Agent Newkirk, who wrote of how an "inexperienced but quick-witted" agent responded to the provocation by grabbing Duquesne by the lapels and telling him "that he had heard about queers approaching people on the street but never had the experience of being approached before and he had a good mind to knock the Duke's block off," which brought forth a stream of obsequious beg-your-pardons from the chastened spy.

■ ■ ■

Then came word from Ed Roeder, who was among the most esteemed members of a Sperry Corporation workforce that had doubled in size over the last two years, from 1,594 in 1938 to the current 3,345, and was in the midst of a hiring spree that would increase that number to 5,582 by January 1, 1941, which was just the beginning. "Operations in Sperry Gyro's 11-story Brooklyn plant are romantically secret," wrote *Time* magazine in an article upon the outbreak of the European war that noted the company was already enjoying record profits. "Sperry employees (all US citizens) wear colored badges (a different color for each division), come and go under the vigilant eyes of watchmen. Except for a few top officials, no Sperry employee knows much about what is going on outside his own division. In a spy-fearing industry, most of them would rather have it that way." Now forty-five, Roeder had a role in one of the US military's most important projects, the attempt to perfect an autopilot system that could be connected to a plane's bombsight, which in effect turned the *entire aircraft* into a bombing platform during the sighting run and further removed the unstable human element from the munitions-delivery process. "In 1939–1940, the writer, while employed by the Sperry Gyroscope Company, designed an electro-hydraulic servo unit for use with the U.S. Army Air Corps Type A-5 Gyro Pilot," he later wrote from prison, referring to the advanced mechanism that the Air Corps considered linking not merely to the Sperry bombsight but also to the Norden bombsight. Roeder's life revolved around marksmanship. He was an avid weapons collector and gun-club member who in his spare time developed an electrical timer unit for skeet shooting that he sold to the Remington Arms Company, which was earning him royalties. "Roeder maintains a shop in the basement of his residence, filled with tools, guns, et cetera, and his activities have been viewed with suspicion by his landlord for some time," according to the FBI memo written to President Roosevelt. He cultivated his love of aiming and firing despite (or perhaps because of) an inability to see out of his right eye, "which gives it a peculiar stare," the Bureau wrote of a malady that may have been caused by injury.

As he apparently did with previous messengers from Germany, Roeder asked Sebold to take the 7:17 p.m. Long Island Rail Road commuter train from Penn Station to the Baldwin stop on the Babylon Line, where Roeder would be waiting in the parking lot in his dark green 1939 Buick sedan, license number 5R 1698. "I drove out in a Bureau car with another agent, Birch O'Neal," wrote Ellsworth in his diary. "Franz drove another car and an agent followed Bill on the train. I parked at the Baldwin station and at about 7:50 p.m. saw a Buick sedan drive up with license 5R 1698. The train came in at 7:59 p.m. and Bill got off, walked up the platform, saw the car, entered it, and immediately they drove off eastward on Sunrise Highway to Merrick, where they parked for an hour."

The first words out of Roeder's mouth were "You are Harry Sawyer." Getting the hang of things, Sebold asked to see Roeder's identification before the discussion could proceed and later assured him he was an expert at "ditching" people he thought were following him. He performed his appointed tasks, handing over the microphotograph and $500 in $10 bills, which Roeder didn't regard as an impressive amount. He said he hadn't been paid in months and was owed no less than $2,000. Yet he wasn't dissuaded from conferring his own gift, a black briefcase with a nickel lock and nickel metal corners containing a handful of documents that he thought would be "of interest to the other side." Sebold said he would make micros of the items and mail them off to Hamburg, neglecting to mention that a committee in Washington would first conduct a review to determine whether national security would be compromised by the release. After a visit of about an hour and fifteen minutes, Roeder let Sebold off in front of a bar in Merrick, giving him the opportunity for a fortifying drink before catching the LIRR back into the city.

During follow-up meetings conducted over the next few weeks, Sebold recorded how Roeder brandished his German Walther automatic pistol and boasted of his "several very fine guns," gave a tour of the Suffolk Republican Club (where he was a member in good standing), asked numerous questions about the unsettling ordeal of Guenther Rumrich and Dr. Griebl, expressed concern about the possibility of arrest, made several informed suggestions regarding the establishment of radio contact with Germany, pledged to smuggle something "big" out of the Sperry building, and, finally, became so angry over Germany's failure to pay him his just wages that he decided to retire. "Roeder says that you owe him $1,500; that he was promised $200 a month," Sebold wrote in a coded letter to Uncle Hugo. "Yesterday he said, 'They will send me money within a month or I will quit this business.' He has promised me some important drawings within two weeks. He is experimenting with a bombing device." In truth, Sebold would've been content to allow Roeder to take that nonmunitions job in Pennsylvania that he kept saying would pay him better than Sperry. "Roeder had Bill very nervous because he always carried guns with him and often took Bill for long rides out on the Island where, if he had been suspicious, he could have killed Bill and dumped his body," wrote Ellsworth.

Finally, Sebold approached Hermann Lang, the Abwehr's man at Norden.

Sebold mailed to the address that had been provided to him by Hamburg, 59-36 Seventieth Avenue, Woodridge, New York. Since there was no such municipality in New York State, the US Post Office sent the letter to Woodridge, New Jersey, which bounced it back to Sebold's PO box as undeliverable. A little detective work determined that *Woodridge* obviously meant "Ridgewood," the German neighborhood of the outer boroughs, which led Sebold to travel out to the Seventieth Avenue apartment building that Lang hadn't lived in since returning from his triumphant visit to Hamburg and Berlin during the bombsight summer of 1938. A janitor sent him upstairs to talk to a friend of Lang's, a Mrs. Foster, who was hesitant at first but agreed to provide the forwarding information when Sebold said in German that he knew Hermann. On a cold Saturday three days later, Sebold returned to the neighborhood on the elevated subway train, walked over to 74-36 Sixty-Fourth Place on the other side of Myrtle Avenue in Glendale, and rang the buzzer at a few minutes after noon. Agent Ellsworth was watching from a safe distance. Lang descended the stairway and opened the door. Sebold asked if he was Mr. Lang. He said he was and invited Sebold upstairs.

"Well, he walked around me, didn't say anything, just stared at me all the time," said Sebold.

Sebold was invited to sit down in the living room.

"I said, 'I have been in Germany, I met some friends of yours, I give you greetings from Rantzau, Berlin, Hamburg, and you should return by way of Japan and Russia to Germany.' And his expense would be repaid, and he would get a pretty good job over there."

Lang responded that he was now a naturalized American citizen and had no desire to return to Germany.

When Sebold suggested that Lang had previously "sent over"

plans from Carl Norden Inc. (where he admitted he worked), Lang denied that he had any hand in such dealings.

Professing to be confused by the whole situation, Sebold said he would contact Hamburg once the radio was in working order and return when he had clarified Lang's position with the organization.

"He said, 'I don't want anything to do with you,'" Sebold recalled.

He left before he could be kicked out.

"Today I talked to your client and gave him the greetings Rantzau, Berlin, Hamburg," Sebold wrote to Ast Hamburg in a coded letter sent through China. "He said he doesn't know anything about your business and does not want to travel. I will not deal any more with him until further advice." He concluded the message with the words "Otherwise business okay," which was another way of saying that the deception operation was off to an impressive start.

CHAPTER NINE

A VILE RACE OF QUISLINGS

Knox brought up the question of the bombsight and the president indicated that his information indicated that the Germans already had it.

—Secretary of War Henry Stimson,
writing in his diary, July 16, 1940

By the middle of March 1940, with the ongoing "phony war" encouraging a belief among many that maybe a great European conflagration wasn't in the offing, J. Edgar Hoover was coming under such sustained attack from those who felt he was accruing too much power in the face of a perhaps-overblown threat that he feared for the future of his directorship. "No one outside the FBI and the Department of Justice knew how close they came to wrecking us," he later said. During testimony before Congress, he had revealed the existence of a General Intelligence unit, which "has now compiled extensive indices of individuals, groups, and organizations engaged in subversive activities, in espionage activities, or any activities that are possibly detrimental to the internal security of the United States." If "we enter into the conflict abroad we would be able to go into any of these communities and identify individuals or groups who might be a source of grave danger to the security of this country."

The announcement was bound to stir up memories of the

period immediately after World War I when America's anti-enemy anxiety shifted from ethnic Germans to radical leftists, many of them foreign-born and living in the big cities, who were instrumental in a wave of strikes, riots, and terrorist bombings seen as a prelude to a Bolshevik revolution. Attorney General A. Mitchell Palmer appointed Hoover, then twenty-four, to lead the first iteration of the office, the General Intelligence Division (or GID), which was responsible for the infamous raids of November 1919 to January 1920. The Bureau's agents arrested from five thousand to ten thousand alleged subversives in cities and towns across the country, ransacking their homes and meeting places without proper search warrants and holding them in pitiful conditions without access to legal counsel until they could be shipped "back where they came from." Initially lauded as a necessary curtailment of civil freedoms at a time of national crisis, public opinion quickly turned against the anti-Red drive. The Labor Department released the majority of the arrestees, arguing that there was little evidence they were intending to stage an uprising, and consented to the deportation of some 350 of them. An influential report issued by twelve prominent lawyers (including the dean of the Harvard Law School and a future Supreme Court justice) decried the "present assault" by the Bureau "upon the most sacred principles of our Constitutional liberty." Upon being named director in 1924, Hoover agreed to shutter the office under the orders of then Attorney General Harlan Fiske Stone, who determined that the Bureau shouldn't be involved in monitoring "political or other opinions of individuals."

In the aftermath of Hoover's statements to Congress, the *New Republic* wondered if he was the best person to lead the FBI "in view of his background and experience during its blackest period." The magazine recalled how he had once overseen "wholesale raids on thousands of defenseless and innocent citizens and aliens, the breaking up of strikes, and the violation of the most sacred civil rights." The *Philadelphia Inquirer* worried that "what we are heading into is the wanton rule of a bludgeoning spy system, arrogant and menacing, such as has been developed by the totalitarian governments of Europe." Hoover's greatest antagonist was Senator George Norris, a seventy-nine-year-old liberal Republican from Nebraska, who openly mocked the director as "the greatest hound for publicity on the North American continent" and "one of the greatest men who ever lived and who now held the future life of our country in the palm of his mighty hand."

Nothing seemed to exemplify Hoover's overreach like the FBI's practice of wiretapping suspects' telephone lines in violation of a congressional ban that had twice (in 1937 and 1939) been upheld by the US Supreme Court. Adding to Hoover's woes was a new attorney general who appeared inclined to be a greater friend of civil liberties than the pliant Frank Murphy, now an associate justice of the Supreme Court. Asked at a press conference whether "he found anything in Mr. Hoover's record that might justify his dismissal," the new man, Robert Jackson, later a Supreme Court justice himself and the chief US prosecutor at the Nuremberg Trials, gave the chilling reply that he had "not studied his record." For a brief moment, it appeared Hoover was on his way out. "The case of J. Edgar Hoover suggests that our No. 1 G-man may become the first American political casualty of World War No. 2," wrote one Washington correspondent in a story headlined "FBI's Difficulties Traced to Spy Scare."

But President Roosevelt wasn't interested in losing such a gifted and loyal snooper, especially with an impending reelection campaign inspiring him to think anew about his political opponents. Instead, the hounds were fed with Attorney General Jackson's announcement that the FBI "shall conform to the decisions of the Supreme Court in recent cases, which have held interception and divulgence of any wire communication to be forbidden by the terms of the Communications Act of 1934," which Jackson delivered on March 17. The director was shrewd enough to ensure that all the stories said the new rule was *his* idea, as the front-pager in the *Times* credulously proclaimed, "Justice Department Bans Wire Tapping; Jackson Acts on Hoover Recommendation."

The public's generosity toward enemies in its midst began to recede following Germany's invasions of Denmark and Norway on April 9, surprise acts of aggression that overwhelmed both neutral countries so quickly that it was universally believed that something more than the arriving military forces were at work. The world was introduced to the loathsome figure of Vidkun Quisling, the leader of Norway's tiny Fascist party, who took advantage of the flight of the country's leadership to the mountains to commandeer the radio airwaves, announce (with Hitler's approval) that he was assuming power, and insist that all resistance to the invaders cease. It didn't much matter that Hitler only allowed him to rule for six days (at least initially), and Norway, aided by Anglo-French land and sea counterattacks that at least succeeded in inflicting real damage on the Kriegsmarine destroyer and cruiser force, wouldn't officially capitulate until June 10. "Major Quisling," wrote the *Times* of London, "has added a new word to the English language." Peace-loving nations were now menaced by what Winston Churchill called a "vile race of Quislings," who are "hired to fawn upon the conqueror, to 'collaborate' in his designs, and to enforce his rule upon their fellow countrymen while groveling low themselves." A famous report by Leland Stowe of the *Chicago Daily News*, which was noteworthy for its breathlessness, wide distribution, and inaccuracy, alleged that Norway was felled "by means of a gigantic conspiracy which must undoubtedly rank among the most audacious, most perfectly oiled political plots of the last century." Through "bribery and extraordinary infiltration on the part of Nazi agents and by treason on the part of a few highly placed Norwegian civilian and defense officials," the German state "built a Trojan Horse inside of Norway. Then, when the hour struck, the German plotters spiked the guns of the Norwegian navy and reduced its formidable fortresses to impotence." Stowe was seeking to explain "How a Few Thousand Nazis Seized Norway," according to the headline over the eleven-page package devoted to his story in *Life* magazine.

The countries believed next on Hitler's list began targeting Germans and Austrians within their borders. Belgium placed several thousand in detention camps, and Holland declared a state of emergency that empowered police to deal "sternly" with supporters of Anton Mussert's Dutch Nazi party. The French had already instituted mass internment of enemy aliens, and the British were considering a policy of similar stringency, which would be adopted within weeks as the home isles became more directly threatened. "The French feel that many innocent refugees undoubtedly are suffering internment unnecessarily," wrote a European correspondent, but "the task of dividing the sheep from the goats is such a big job" that extraordinary precautions were required. The US branch of the Quisling movement was represented by the Christian Front cabal, which, as revealed by the ongoing trial in Brooklyn, had been betrayed by a disaffected plotter who allowed the FBI to place recording devices in the attic of his home, catching a junior führer advocating sabotage because it's just as well that they be "killed here as in a foreign war instigated by international Jewish bankers." J. Edgar took advantage of the changing mood to write to Attorney General Jackson, informing him that the Bureau's surveillance of "what appears definitely to be the real center of organized German espionage in the United States" had been "materially retarded" by the wiretapping ban, which must count as an exaggeration since Bill Sebold was in such a good position to know the mind of the (actual) Hitler operatives in New York. Robert Jackson was unmoved.

Then came Germany's historic onslaught against Holland, Luxembourg, Belgium, and France, which was launched on May 10, the same day Churchill replaced Neville Chamberlain as British prime minister and emerged as the principal representative of anti-Nazi resistance with "nothing to offer but blood, toil, tears, and sweat." Besieged by airborne troops that had been dropped behind the front by parachute or landed via transport plane, Holland held out until several dozen Heinkel He 111 medium bombers destroyed the center of Rotterdam on May 14, a deliberate act of terror that nonetheless killed far fewer civilians (814, according to the Dutch government figure offered at Nuremberg) than the initially reported 100,000. Just as responsible for the swift defeat, or so went the prevalent thinking, were the ethnic Germans and Nazi sympathizers among the population who had waited for the decisive moment to become active. These apparitions disguised themselves as farmers, train conductors, policemen, mail carriers, priests, and even nuns, handed out poison-spiked chocolates, cigarettes, and drinking water, used light signals to direct German bombers to their targets, scrawled messages on public walls about Dutch troop movements, and spread false rumors about such things as defective air-raid sirens.

The *New York Times* reported that refugees, "from Queen Wilhelmina down, have told amazing stories of the manner in which thousands of apparently innocent Germans turned out to be advance agents of the Nazi regime." On the same day as the Rotterdam bombing, the fate of European democracy was all but sealed when the panzer forces that had navigated through the supposedly impenetrable forests of the Ardennes north of the Maginot Line smashed through a French Army force that had been tormented by Stuka dive-bombers and began the rapid dash to the Channel that would trap a sizable Anglo-French force (including the whole of the British Expeditionary Force) in a pocket at the northern French port of Dunkirk. In statistically the worst moment of Royal Air Force history, seventy-one RAF light bombers were sent in to swoop low and destroy the pontoon bridges over the Meuse River that were facilitating the advance. At least forty of them were shot down by antiaircraft fire and Messerschmitt fighters, a national disgrace that caused the air marshal commanding the British air fleet in France to break down in tears when he heard the news.

On May 16, with the Allied armies in disarray and French diplomats burning documents in the gardens of the Quai d'Orsay, President Roosevelt spoke before a joint session of Congress, requesting a massive increase in rearmament spending (eventually pushing defense appropriations to $2.2 billion for the year) to fund the creation of a "two-ocean" Navy and a US aerial fleet of fifty thousand planes, pointedly asking legislators "not to take any action which would in any way hamper or delay the delivery of American-made planes to foreign nations." In surveying the "brutal force of modern offensive war" that was currently on display, he made a point of highlighting "the use of the 'fifth column' by which persons supposed to be peaceful visitors were actually a part of an enemy unit of occupation."

Four days later, Treasury Secretary Henry Morgenthau learned from Hoover that the FBI was still unable "to listen in on spies by tapping the wires" and so brought his concerns to the president, who on the following day ordered Attorney General Jackson to ignore the Supreme Court and "authorize the necessary investigative agencies that they are at liberty to secure information by listening devices . . . of persons suspected of subversive activities against the government of the United States, including suspected spies." The FBI would rely on this authority to conduct wiretaps for the next quarter century. During a fireside chat on May 26, FDR pledged the government's vigilance in combating the foe that everyone believed was hiding in the shadows. "The Trojan horse," he said over the crackling connection. "The fifth column that betrays a nation unprepared for treachery. Spies, saboteurs, and traitors are the actors in this new strategy. With all of these we must and will deal vigorously."

The country was gripped with panic. "Now, just a minute," began a column by Westbrook Pegler. "Wait a minute!" Rural Pennsylvanians were plotting how to defend against parachute troops, National Guardsmen in western New York started patrols along the Canadian border, Mayor Frank Hague of Jersey City announced that he would "exterminate all un-American plots and plotters," and Washington politicians secured easy passage of the Alien Registration Act of 1940 (or Smith Act), which set severe penalties for advocating the overthrow of the government and required data on all 3.6 million noncitizens thought to be living in the country, 1.1 million of them estimated to reside in New York City. One of the fifteen questions on the registration form, to be filled out at the nearest post office and forwarded along with fingerprint samples to the FBI, asked whether the foreign national had been "affiliated with or active in" any organization "devoted in whole or in part to influencing or furthering the political activities, public relations or public policy of a foreign government."

The next big German American Bund meeting was advertised as an "Anti-Fifth Column Rally," which brought a few hundred members to a meeting hall in Astoria, Queens, where they heard President Roosevelt denounced as the chief traitor who was seeking to betray America by involving it in a war on behalf of global monetarists. The new Bundesführer, Wilhelm Kunze, urged his fellow Germans "to have more guts and be proud of the blood in their veins and speak up for their rights as American citizens because we are only interested in the welfare of this nation," according to an NYPD detective conducting surveillance. Kunze spoke "about himself as a boy being beaten up in public school during the last war because his name was Wilhelm." The police report said that an unnamed Bundist attacked a photographer for the liberal daily *PM*, punching him in the ribs and breaking his camera.

In the meantime, Belgium's King Leopold III agreed to Hitler's demand for an unconditional surrender, and the Luftwaffe was accorded the honor of finishing off the Allied forces that were evacuating from Dunkirk in an improvised flotilla of eight hundred vessels ranging from Royal Navy destroyers to civilian fishing boats. By the time the port fell on June 4, the British Admiralty's Operation Dynamo had succeeded in rescuing 338,226 British and French soldiers, a justly celebrated "miracle" that was facilitated by the ability of the RAF's single-engine fighters to prevent German fighters and bombers from achieving control of the airspace during the few days when the cloud cover lifted, an embarrassing (first) defeat for the Luftwaffe that was a hopeful intimation of things to come.

"All of our types—the Hurricane, the Spitfire, and the new Defiant—and all our pilots have been vindicated as superior to what they have at present to face," Churchill said that day in his "We Shall Fight on the Beaches" speech in the Commons. "When we consider how much greater would be our advantage in defending the air above this island against an overseas attack, I must say that I find in these facts a sure basis upon which practical and reassuring thoughts may rest."

On the following morning, the German armies began the

campaign to capture the rest of France, sending the blitzkrieg against an ineffectual French army and a decimated Armée de l'Air. On June 10, Mussolini saw his chance and announced from the balcony of the Palazzo Venezia that Italy was joining the war against the "plutocratic and reactionary democracies of the West." ("The hand that held the dagger," President Roosevelt told the graduating class at the University of Virginia that afternoon, "has struck it into the back of its neighbor.") On the next day, Paris was declared an open city to forestall a repeat of Guernica, Warsaw, and Rotterdam. On June 14, the City of Light fell to German troops, who hoisted the swastika from the Eiffel Tower and the Arc de Triomphe. On June 22, French general Charles Huntziger signed the armistice on behalf of the new collaborationist regime of Marshal Philippe Pétain in the old railway dining car where the French High Command accepted Imperial Germany's surrender twenty-two years earlier. The battlefield losses of World War I had been avenged. Hitler was at the height of his powers, with a claim to being the greatest German of them all. It was "so unbelievable as to be almost surely unreal, and if not unreal then quite immeasurably catastrophic," wrote the British foreign secretary, Lord Halifax.

On July 4, the war seemed to come to New York City when an actual ticking time bomb was found in an upstairs ventilation room at the British Pavilion at the World's Fair in Queens. The buff-colored canvas bag was taken from the crowded building by the NYPD and carried to an isolated spot on the edge of the grounds behind the Polish Pavilion. An hour and a half later, it exploded, killing two Bomb Squad detectives and gravely wounding two other detectives. A livid Commissioner Lewis Valentine sought no assistance from the FBI in mobilizing the entire police force to round up every known Nazi, Fascist, Coughlinite, Christian Fronter, and Irish Republican in town. Investigators eventually focused on a Bundist employed by Sperry Gyroscope who resided in a furnished room on the West Side stocked with tear-gas pistols and cartridges and "littered with Nazi pamphlets, a swastika flag, and anti-Jewish banners and posters," reported the *Times*. But charges were never filed in the bombing. Colonel Duquesne, who boasted to Sebold that he had been questioned for two days, was probably the only one in the city who thought the perpetrator was a Frenchman angered over Britain's recent forcible seizure of the French fleet to keep it out of German hands. The FBI heard Duquesne telling two visitors to his apartment that he was regarded as the leader of the fifth column. He joked that he was "only a three and one-quarter column."

American popular opinion was broadly sympathetic to the Allied cause but resolutely opposed (86 percent) to declaring war on Germany and Italy with many believing "that the money we have spent on our military and naval forces during the last few years has gone down the rathole," as FDR colloquially put it. Even his own (isolationist) secretary of war opposed Roosevelt's decision to flout the neutrality laws by ordering the military to declare six hundred freight-car loads of guns and ammunition as "surplus," which enabled the munitions to be sold to U.S. Steel, which resold them five minutes later to the Allied purchasing commission hoping to rearm a British nation that had left everything behind on the beaches of Dunkirk.

In such a moment as this, the Sebold investigation represented America's only significant battle with Nazi Germany. And the good guys were winning. On May 15, a letter with several enclosures was discovered in Sebold's PO box at the Church Street Annex. It was not mailed by any of the four spies working directly with him but by the chief butcher of the SS *Manhattan*, the United States Lines ship that had arrived two days earlier from Genoa with 811 passengers, including 350 refugees from Central Europe. "Dear Harry," the butcher wrote in German, "I would like to speak to you."

On the following day at the entrance of Pier 59, Sebold met Erwin Siegler, a thirty-year-old American citizen of German birth in a snap-brim hat with a "swaggering, rolling walk" and "large, bulging chest," wrote the FBI. He would later explain that the scar on his cheek was the result of a violent encounter with a beer glass. He was "a brute in strength," wrote Ellsworth in his diary. Over drinks at a waterfront bar and grill, Siegler revealed that he was a novice courier assigned to procure secrets for the Kriegsmarine, part of the efforts of Referat I-M of Ast Hamburg, which signified that Sebold had stumbled upon *another* ring operating out of New York. The butcher said he was delivering the materials to Sebold (of Referat I-L) on behalf of "a man named Gerhoff" based in the Hotel Britannia in Genoa and was working with a fellow spy on the *Manhattan*'s kitchen staff who had access to large sums of money.

Fully cognizant of the next logical move of a skilled double agent, Sebold requested to see Siegler's friend, which led to a meeting on the following day in Columbus Circle at the southwest corner of Central Park, a favorite location of the soapboxers of the Fascist right, a brown version of Union Square. There Sebold met with Franz Stigler, the *Manhattan*'s chief baker and confectioner, its head *Zuckerbäcker*, who was a naturalized German American with a "heavy build" known by the code name of Aufzug. As agents in a Bureau truck filmed the proceedings from a distance, Sebold explained that he needed money to pay a disgruntled agent, not mentioning that he was referring to Ed Roeder. The pastry man handed over $240 in reserve notes and silver certificates, agreeing with Sebold that it was important to "try to get the material for Germany." Sebold asked the *Manhattan* duo to contact him when they returned from their next trip to Italy, providing the address of his summer residence, a rented room in Mrs. Allen's house at 144 Washington Street in Hempstead, the Nassau County village that kept him in proximity to Ellsworth (who received Bureau permission to bring his wife and two children out from California), the most valuable producer (Roeder), his dummy job (as a ladies'-stocking salesman for Real Silk Hosiery Mills of Jamaica), and the location selected for the radio outpost that Hamburg had assigned him to establish.

One of the letters in the butcher's envelope to Sebold outlined the technical specifications necessary to make Morse code contact with Ast Hamburg's Wohldorf station. Using the funds given to Sebold in Germany, Bureau agents obtained two receivers (a Hallicrafters Sky Champion and a Hammarlund Super-Pro), a refrigerator-size hundred-watt Hallicrafters HT-9 transmitter (later used to power a more powerful five-hundred-watt transmitter), and various antennas, cables, supports, and feed lines, which (after failed tests in the static-heavy New York office) were installed in a rented two-room cottage in a hilly area among the trees near Centerport on Long Island Sound. "As the last solder connection was made and the blowtorch silenced it was noted that the time was a few seconds before 7 p.m., the next regular calling time of the German control station according to information given to Sebold," wrote Richard L. Millen, a special agent flown up from Washington to help set up the system, of the evening of May 20. "The receivers were tuned to the designated frequency and the HT-9 warmed up. Very shortly, Morse code dots and dashes were heard. At first, they were copied as 'RAORAORAO' in that they were too closely spaced and run together. Realizing this fact, the engineers soon separated the dots and dashes into the desired call of 'AOR AOR AOR.' When the control station stopped sending, the Bureau's undercover station began sending a series of dots and dashes in accordance with Sawyer's instructions. The transmitter was stopped after five minutes and the receivers turned on. The German control returned briskly with congratulations and instructions for the next contact. A working link had been established. Groundwork had been laid for the case to evolve."

Given the task of delivering and receiving the Morse code signals was a special agent from the Milwaukee office with a ham license, Maurice Price, who worked with Sebold to learn his particular manner of tapping the telegraph key, which can be as recognizable to a skilled cryptologist as a written signature. The messages themselves were encoded and decoded by Ellsworth and Sebold based on the system that had been taught to the double agent by Uncle Hugo in Germany. "That code is a complicated thing," the federal prosecutor who tried the case later told jurors. "It takes you a good while to study it out."

Each message was assigned a page of Rachel Field's *All This, and Heaven Too,* which was determined by adding the date (10 for the tenth day of the month, 12 for December, for example) to an agreed-upon third number (20). Turning to page 42, Ellsworth and Sebold would look to the upper left-hand corner of text, along the left margin, and copy down the letters that began the first twenty lines of text. "That will be a mere jumble of letters, you see," the prosecutor said. "Because it won't form any sentence—*A, X, L, R,* and so forth." The letters would be written horizontally across a sheet of paper. Below each of the letters, they would jot a number corresponding to the letter's position in the alphabet. The first A among the twenty letters would be assigned the number 1. The second A would get a 2. If there were only two As, then the first B would be assigned the number 3. If there was only one B, then the first C would get the number 4.

Below the horizontal list of numbers, Ellsworth and Sebold would draw a rectangular grid of squares, twenty across and five down, with each vertical column corresponding to one of the twenty numbers determined from the twenty letters from page 42 of *All This, and Heaven Too.* They would write the message they wished to code into this twenty-by-five grid, one letter per box, working left to right horizontally. The resulting grid of letters would then be given to Price—not as horizontal rows, but as vertical columns, taken out of order and starting with the column marked 1, and continuing then with the column marked 2, then the column marked 3, and so on.

Ellsworth said of the procedure, "If the message was to be sent, I used the date of the sending of the message or the day we expected to send the message as the basis for preparing the code, and then prepared the square system, as explained by Mr. Sebold, and entered the message to be sent into that system of squares, and from that extracted a series of code groups of letters which I handed to Mr. Price for transmission."

To decode Ast Hamburg's messages, Ellsworth and Sebold would again turn to that day's specified page of *All This, and Heaven Too,* draw a twenty-by-five rectangular grid of empty squares, and run the process in reverse. "Agent Price would hand us a series of code groups, letters arranged under a code system at that time existing, on the date of the receipt of that message," Ellsworth said. "I would prepare a graph or chart using the system explained to me by Mr. Sebold. That series of code groups of letters which Mr. Price handed to us, I would then arrange into that system, and from that system extract the code message, and set it out either in German or in English, in whichever it was received. If it was received in the German language, I would work with Sebold on the translation of the German into English."

In the first message tapped to Hamburg, "H.S." told Station AOR that he had received $240 from the *Manhattan*. "Meet Roeder Monday. Shall I give him this money since he will not work longer without money." The response came three days later, a veritable instant in the transatlantic spy business: "The money is for Roeder." After Roeder received the cash during a ride-around in which he showed off a .357 Magnum and said he would "do a real job" if he ever decided to kill somebody, Roeder promised Sebold he would keep the secrets coming, soon producing a stream of intelligence that included the blueprints for the Lockheed Hudson, a light bomber and coastal reconnaissance aircraft that was being manufactured for the Royal Air Force.

When the *Manhattan* arrived back in New York from Genoa on June 10, the same day Mussolini's balcony declaration ended the neutral ship's journeys to the now-combatant port, it was overloaded with 1,907 passengers, nearly twice the capacity, "a confused and clamorous throng of many languages and diverse views," wrote the *Herald Tribune*. "There were men and women who had lived for years on the Riviera, at Cannes, or Monte Carlo, Americans to whom America may seem strange. There were businessmen abandoning commercial claims they had staked out in Europe. There were needy refugees, the women shawled and blank-eyed, some of them Jews from Germany or the lands overwhelmed by Germany. There were nuns and priests and actors. There were refugees from Denmark and from Norway who had traversed the length of Europe to find a port from which an American vessel sailed. There were dogs and cats and canary birds." And there were pro-Nazi travelers "who grinned and slapped each other on the back when the radio brought word of new German triumphs," including the chief butcher and head pastry chef on a kitchen staff full of the naturalized Germans who were favored by the dowdy American liners because they added the European dash that sophisticated travelers expected in their ocean passage.

Over the next three weeks, as the *Manhattan* prepared to sail to its new destination of Lisbon in pro-Fascist but still neutral Portugal, Sebold met with the butcher (sharing a boozy evening at the Lorelei and Café Hindenburg on Eighty-Sixth Street in Yorkville, which was de rigueur for Nazi spies), the baker, and, during an introductory session partly conducted on the grass opposite the Tavern on the Green in Central Park, a thirty-year-old former fish cook on the *Manhattan*, Paul Fehse, who was serving as the chief of the "marine division." Now living over the river in New Jersey with a fellow conspirator, Fehse (code name Fink) had graduated from a four-week training course at Ast Hamburg and returned to the United States via Genoa at about the time of Sebold's arrival, which means their instruction periods at least partially overlapped. He showed himself every bit the would-be spymaster when he asked to visit the Long Island radio station, a request that Sebold deflected by saying he was working with a native-born American of venerable background who refused to allow anyone on the property "for fear of involving him in trouble and ruining the reputation of his family." Sebold further asserted his supremacy when he informed the three that arrangements had already been made for the butcher and the baker to rendezvous with an Ast Hamburg contact at the Hotel Duas Nações on Rua Vitória in Lisbon, which would've been impossible to set up in the era before the radio. After uttering the phrase "Sesam greets Franz," they were to hand over Sebold's latest collection of micros containing reports from Roeder, Lilly Stein (now serving as a mail drop for a Nazi agent in Detroit code-named Heinrich), and Colonel Duquesne, who, operating out of a new office at 70 Pine Street in the Wall Street area, liked to confer with Sebold as they rode back and forth on the ferry between lower Manhattan and Jersey City. One day the old saboteur gazed upon the Hudson River docks and expressed his fond wish to blow them all up.

With the aid of the radio, Sebold and his FBI associates were able to gain solid proof that the Germans *had* stolen what everyone knew as "the secret bombsight," the miraculous invention that was entering the nation's folklore (although not yet publicly associated with the name Norden) at the same time that rumors about its theft were becoming widespread among the Washington–New York elite. In the brief period between the Nazi invasion of Denmark and Norway and the start of the operation against France and the Low Countries, Universal Pictures released *Enemy Agent,* which portrayed initially inept G-men getting their act together to prevent Euro-accented spies from making off with the "Wallis bombsight," which was "so accurate that a plane can drop a bomb into a pickle barrel from five miles up," says one character.

Just before the Nazis' offensive on the west, President Roosevelt asked a wealthy distant relation, Vincent Astor, to look into cocktail-party chatter that the Germans had gotten hold of the Norden, and Astor responded a few days later by ridiculing "the same old song and dance which has cropped up repeatedly in the past," a figment of the imagination of "the sort that [pseudonymous gossip columnist] Cholly Knickerbocker calls Café Society." On May 24, as the Germans were completing the encirclement of Dunkirk, the *Toronto Globe and Mail* urged the United States to release the sight to the Allies. "The immediate physical advantage to be gained from its possession would be numerous, but the moral effect on the German people, who through their spies have repeatedly tried to steal this bombsight, would be of equal if not greater value," the paper wrote in a front-page editorial. On the day before the evacuation ended, June 3, President Roosevelt dashed off a note to a supporter who made the same argument, telling her that the problem was "the article mentioned might fall into the hands of the enemy and help them more than our friends."

On June 15, with the European continent all but mastered by Hitler, Senator Styles Bridges of New Hampshire called for an investigation after a thinly sourced radio report claimed a captured German plane in France was discovered to possess a bombsight that was suspiciously similar to America's own. And on June 19, Sebold made his third visit to Hermann Lang's Queens apartment, where he handed over the *second* message sent by Germany to establish the legitimacy of his mission—"Further References for Lang are Beier, Eberhardt, and Aplohn Pop Sohn," the last phrase referring to his Norden coworker Fritz "Pop" Sohn, who had introduced Lang into the spy business.

"I said I couldn't make it out," testified Sebold, "and I said, 'Tell me the meaning of it, this something like Aplakson.' He said it was right, there was a fellow by the name of Sohn who worked with him in the Norden bomb plant and returned to Germany about a year ago."

It was enough to convince Lang to engage in a conversation that took for granted he had committed the larceny but didn't touch upon his method. Asked if his knowledge of the Norden was currently helpful to the Reich, Lang said it wasn't because the bombsight had been in German hands for two years, which meant 1938, the year he made the visit with his wife to Germany.

"I said, 'Don't you feel very important to have done such a thing for Germany?'" Sebold said. " 'How much did you get for it? How much did they pay you for it?'"

Lang said he worked for no payment except "a promise to be taken care of."

"Then I said, 'Aren't you afraid of being cheated out of this promise by Germany?'"

Lang said he wasn't because of his personal relationship with Hitler from the early days of the movement in Bavaria.

"You didn't think Lang was kidding, did you?" Sebold was later asked in reference to the Hitler comment.

"No. He is not a kidder."

Conceding that it would be difficult to leave his job on the sixteenth floor in the midst of such heightened watchfulness, Lang nonetheless asked Sebold to send a radio message asking for the best advice in escaping the country. "Lang feels secure," he wanted the statement to read.

On June 20, Hoover broke the news to the White House. "Without making any specific admission, Lang did indicate that two years ago he prepared a complete model of the United States secret bombsight or secured all of the details with regard to this bombsight (the informant is not entirely clear as to just what Lang indicated in this regard), and sent the data to Germany," the memo read. On the following day, isolationist Senator Gerald Nye took to the floor of the Senate and made headlines by repeating an unfounded rumor that Secretary of War Harry Woodring, who had just resigned at FDR's request because of his continued opposition to providing military aid to Great Britain, was let go specifically because he refused to give up "national defense secret number one—that all-valuable bombsight that every member of this Senate has been assured for months is being guarded with the utmost secrecy." The Senate majority leader, Alben Barkley, was required to step forward and say he spoke to Air Corps chief Hap Arnold, who told him "at no time or under any conditions has any consideration ever been given to revelation of any secret bombsight."

But President Roosevelt was looking for creative ways to

respond to Churchill's pleas for help in preventing what many regarded as a distinct possibility, the fall of Britain. On July 1, FDR mentioned nothing of the Lang revelation when he told the British ambassador, Lord Lothian, that he would provide the Norden to the RAF if it could be proved that the Germans were using a bombsight that "was more or less equivalent in efficiency." In fact, the British *didn't* have such proof: the recent examination of a Heinkel He 111 shot down on the Yorkshire coast revealed that it was equipped with a Lotfe 7B bombsight, which "is not adapted for high altitude precision bombing of ground targets and certainly not of moving ships," according to the RAF report. The truth was, the Luftwaffe's mismanaged Technical Office, long in possession of Hermann Lang's plans for the Norden, was still in the midst of developing a gyro-stabilized bombsight for installation in its medium bombers.

On July 16, with the Luftwaffe conducting the raids against coastal installations and shipping lanes that represented the opening phase of the Battle of Britain, President Roosevelt informed the newest cabinet members—Secretary of the Navy Frank Knox and Secretary of War Henry Stimson, both Republicans and interventionists—that the gossips were correct. "Knox brought up the question of the bombsight and the president indicated that his information indicated that the Germans already had it," wrote Stimson in his diary. "He said that of course if that was true, we certainly ought to give it to the British at once. He mentioned a number of striking facts which indicated carelessness on our part in the preservation of that bombsight from the work of the Fifth Column agents," confirmation of FDR's familiarity with the discoveries of Bill Sebold. But the president couldn't overcome a jittery military leadership that had just convinced him to shelve his idea of giving the Brits twelve (out of the Air Corps' current fifty-two) B-17 Flying Fortresses as an unconscionable breach of national security. Besides, the revelation that he had handed away *our most valuable secret* would be certain to hurt his now-active campaign against the tousled-haired utilities executive unexpectedly nominated by the Republicans, Wendell Willkie, who, like FDR, was an interventionist wary of doing or saying anything that might upset the isolationists now coalescing around a newly formed organization, the America First Committee. It is a measure of British desperation that Churchill approved a plan (which he initially regretted) to send a technical mission to the United States to reveal the UK's greatest innovations without an explicit promise that the bombsight the RAF had long sought would be made available in return. The delegation soon arrived with a large black metal deed box containing Britain's own holiest of holies, the resonant cavity magnetron tube, which was better than the Sperry Gyroscope–developed klystron tube at increasing the range of microwave radar and would prove an essential component of the Allied victory in World War II. The Norden had not yet been tested in combat and was already worth all the money spent in its development.

CHAPTER TEN

AND YOU BE CAREFUL

I noticed the beautiful dog that was following you on 42nd Street yesterday. I was very interested in it and a friend of mine wondered if you had it for sale or kept it for a companion. If you do neither, he will not be offended.

—Fritz Duquesne in a letter to Sebold,
August 9, 1940

J. Edgar Hoover couldn't have been more pleased with the progress of his premier case. In a memo to the White House, he crowed that the Bureau "has undercover agents actually participating in a German espionage group in such a manner as to enable the Director of the Federal Bureau of Investigation to know the entire activities of this ring," the only specific investigation mentioned in the nine-page letter. ". . . Special Agents of the Federal Bureau of Investigation as members of this German espionage group actually maintain and operate a short-wave radio station which is in daily contact with Germany, and through this station pass the messages of a number of German agents. All messages, of course, are surreptitiously submitted to the State, War, and Navy Departments prior to the time they are transmitted to Germany and, of course, information and instructions received from Germany are transmitted to interested agencies." During a gathering of 175 law enforcement officials, Hoover boasted of the depth of the Bureau's infiltration of secret networks of spies and saboteurs, explaining that the news media would be informed (and "honor and glory to all" duly accorded) when the evidence was ready for presentation in court. "The enemy does not know our actions," he said, "and cannot anticipate a time when he might plan his devious task with a minimum chance of detection."

Determined to prevent a repeat of the Turrou embarrassment, Hoover assigned one of his best men, Earl J. Connelly, who had led the celebrated raid on kidnapper Kate "Ma" Barker's Florida hideout in 1935, to relocate to the city and assume control from the New York office, probably at about the time he was promoted to assistant director in June. "They brought Froelich in from Pittsburgh to start a filing and index system on it," Ellsworth wrote. "Maxwell Chayfitz read and coordinated reports." A small team of stenographers and clerks was assembled. German-fluent agents such as Joseph Fellner, an Austrian-born graduate of the University of Wisconsin Law School, and William Gustav Friedemann, an Oklahoman with an LLB from George Washington University, arrived to work as interpreters. New men were assigned to follow the growing list of suspects, which was done clumsily in the case of Paul "Fink" Fehse, who noticed suspicious figures following him on the subway and parked out front of his house, prompting him to lie low for a while. Agents took jobs at Sperry Gyroscope and Norden Inc., went undercover on the SS *Manhattan*, initiated a twenty-four-hour watch on Hermann Lang's home to guard against his flight, and relaxed in the nicest of bars while Lilly Stein was charmed by her latest suitors. And just as E. J. Connelly began holding weekly conferences to discuss how to cope with unfamiliar challenges—"What do you fellows suggest?" Friedemann remembered the senior men asking. "What should we do here?"—a providential lesson came from Brooklyn in the form of the collapse of the Christian Front prosecution. Despite the Bureau's (grainy) motion pictures, (scratchy) sound recordings, and (untrustworthy) cooperating conspirator, the jury returned exactly zero convictions for the simple reason that the Coughlinite defendants hadn't done much in furtherance of their violent plan to turn America into a concentration camp. "An ill-timed arrest invariably will do more harm than good," Hoover now believed, according to a newspaper op-ed he wrote headlined, "Is There a Spy Menace?" ("The answer is emphatically, Yes!") "The real test of successful counterespionage, and that is our task, is locating the spy, ascertaining his contacts and methods of communication—and then closing off his sources of information."

After the *Manhattan* returned from Lisbon in late July— "Passengers Assert Many of Stewards are Pro-Hitler and Ship's Paper is 'Defeatist'" was the subheadline on the *Times*' story— Sebold met with the butcher, who gave him a gray paper package containing $1,350 to pay the salaries of the active I-L spies and $1,500 to purchase a bombsight other than the Norden, which further confirmed that the Germans had no need for the dream weapon the whole country was talking about. The butcher told Sebold that the *Manhattan* was ending its Lisbon run (because it was deemed too dangerous to have such a large passenger ship skirting the war zone in the manner of the *Lusitania*), and he and Stigler were taking senior kitchen jobs on the new SS *America*, which would be plying between New York and four ports in the Caribbean, a less propitious journey for Nazi espionage efforts. No worries about maintaining a courier connection to Europe, though. During a subsequent evening on the town, which ended with the butcher and the baker escorting a couple of young ladies to an Eighth Avenue flophouse, Sebold learned about a new man who was willing to make his first trip for the Abwehr, a waiter on the SS *Exochorda,* one of the four small ships of the American Export Lines still on the Lisbon passage, each with a capacity for just 130 passengers.

A naturalized German American of small stature and thinning blond hair who (like Ed Roeder) was blind in the right eye, Erich Strunck was something of a legend among the marine spies for maintaining his loyalty to Hitler even though he underwent three months of rough interrogation in a Hamburg jail, where he was serving time for a currency scam that defrauded refugees attempting to get their money out of the Reich. He was "a very tough fellow who refused to talk," said the butcher, who was incarcerated alongside him. When ringleader Fehse later asked Sebold if he was impressed with the waiter's "gallant" willingness to serve his native land even in the face of such *Fertigmachen* abuse, Sebold responded, "No, I think he is dumb to take such treatment."

After gathering up new materials and informing Ed Roeder of Germany's desire for the Sperry bombsight, Sebold met Strunck in Columbus Circle and handed him a brown manila envelope for delivery via the *Exochorda.* It was all going a little too well for Duquesne, who appears to have alerted Ast Hamburg to his belief that Sebold was an amateur who had been made by the authorities. "Friend reports you are under surveillance," according to a radio communication received from Germany. "Caution. You must stay off the air for two weeks." In response, Agent Price sent out a message insisting that "Dunn," one of Duquesne's code names, was actually the careless one, undeserving of his reputation as a master spy. "He might have seen me with Bill," wrote Ellsworth in his diary, citing the "beautiful dog" letter that Duquesne mailed to Sebold. "Lately it had appeared Duke was getting jealous because Bill was now in direct contact with Germany, handling all the spies, sending over all the materials etc. So he probably was trying to cut Bill out of the picture and place himself in control of the spy ring." The crisis passed when Hamburg responded, "Don't let Dunn make you nervous too, and you be careful."

On August 12, Ast Hamburg radioed its desire "to receive from you and friends regular accurate details" about aircraft deliveries from North America to England, which was now coming under more sustained attack as the Luftwaffe began its all-out effort to destroy the capacity of the RAF and establish the blanket of air superiority necessary for a cross-Channel landing. The invasion of Great Britain was code-named Operation Sea Lion and planned for the middle of September. Yet it was soon apparent that the Hurricanes and Spitfires, aided by radar installations lining the coast, cryptologists at Bletchley Park who had cracked the Germans' Enigma code, and binocular-wielding civilian spotters of the Royal Observer Corps, were more than a match for a German air force operating at the limits of its speed and range, haunted now by the failure to develop a four-engine heavy bomber with the capacity to readily traverse British airspace. "I never really thought there would be a war with Britain," complained the Technical Office's Ernst Udet, whose beloved Ju 87 dive-bombers, the scourge of the Continent, were shot down in such numbers that they were pulled from the battle within a week.

With the prospect of an easy invasion looking less likely by the day, President Roosevelt made two politically risky decisions that brought the United States closer to open hostility with the Axis powers, which, following the signing of the Tripartite Pact, now included Imperial Japan. Bypassing Congress, he used his executive authority to give Great Britain fifty World War I–era destroyers that had been certified by Navy admiral Harold R. Stark (at

FDR's demand) to be militarily insignificant, exchanging them for leases on several British military installations from Newfoundland to British Guiana, which was hailed by the public as a shrewd deal that gave America the means to repel an invasion from Europe. And FDR threw his full support behind the Selective Training and Service Act, the first peacetime draft in the nation's history, which earned the pivotal support of Willkie and made it through Congress in the face of hyperbolical warnings from the likes of Senator Burton K. Wheeler of Montana, who said the bill would "slit the throat of the last democracy still living."

By early September, with Hitler having second thoughts about Operation Sea Lion, the Luftwaffe was ordered to pivot away from eliminating the RAF as a prelude to invasion and begin pounding in and around cities in the hope that a collapse of British morale would force a capitulation. The months-long bombardment campaign that would come to be known as the Blitz began on the afternoon of September 7, when three hundred bombers accompanied by six hundred fighters spent hours dropping incendiaries upon the densely populated dock areas of London's East End, killing several hundred civilians at a minimum. Yet the daylight raids were too costly for the Luftwaffe, which lost 298 aircraft during the first week, forcing Göring to switch to nighttime sorties, less susceptible to fighter interception and perhaps more conducive to inducing panic in the British people. "The decisive thing is the ceaseless continuation of air attacks," Hitler said. In his cigarette-enriched basso profundo, CBS's Edward R. Murrow assured the American people that the plan wasn't working. "Today I saw shop windows in Oxford Street covered with plywood," he said in one of his "This Is London" broadcasts, which sometimes featured the sound of air-raid sirens and antiaircraft bursts in the background. "In front of one there was a redheaded girl in a blue smock, painting a sign on the board covering the place where the window used to be. The sign read OPEN AS USUAL."

On September 3, Lilly Stein informed Sebold that British factories were producing a thousand airplanes a month, a piece of intelligence that she could've obtained from a prominent English cricketer and military officer she was consorting with, Captain Hubert Martineau. She was not far off. The actual number was 1,601 for August and 1,341 for September, which, one of the major reasons for the RAF's resilience, exceeded the output of a German aircraft industry that was a victim of the Technical Office's misguided schemes, impossible demands, and increasingly unstable director. (Udet was now drinking heavily and taking Pervitin methamphetamine tablets.) Alas, Stein's information was never communicated to the Luftwaffe, then in the midst of fatally underestimating the ability of British plants to keep up with the rates of attrition. Probably sick of her constant demands for money in the face of her inability to come up with anything significant from diplomat Ogden Hammond Jr., Ast Hamburg ordered Sebold to stop seeing her. "Lilly should be careful and report in writing" were the instructions. "You personally will please sever connections as instructed." Also: "As reasons say that you don't work for us anymore." On September 11, Sebold let Stein talk awhile about an English gentleman she'd met at the Hotel Pierre before passing along a note that included a new contact address in Cologne, where Hermann Sandel (aka Heinrich Sorau and Uncle Hugo) had been transferred.

"What? Have you dropped me?" she said.

"No, they have dropped me," Sebold responded.

A few weeks after Sebold's final visit with Stein, Assistant Secretary of State Adolf Berle summoned Oggie Hammond to his office and told him that he knew all about the relationship. (Hammond had also mimicked the president "in a reprehensible manner" in front of eyewitnesses during a summertime party in Newport, another tidbit passed along by J. Edgar.) "This is nasty business," Berle said, according to Hammond. "We might as well get it over quickly. You had better resign." Incensed, Hammond refused. He assembled the lawyers and swore under oath that "at no time did I live with . . . or have intimate relations" with Lilly Stein. He was just returning the gold watch! The $100 was a repayment for a loan! With Berle unwilling to budge, Hammond took the unusual step of suing the State Department, which resulted in newspaper stories about the high-society scion's allegedly disloyal dealings with a "female agent of a foreign power," prompting Sebold to send a radio message notifying Ast Hamburg that one of its spies had been partially exposed.

Yet even without Sebold's cooperation, Stein continued to seek material on behalf of the Reich, often discussing her work with Else Weustenfeld, a secretary for the law firm representing the German consulate who had been brought into the spy business by her boyfriend, Hans Ritter, the affable younger brother of Nikolaus Ritter. The newspapers would later describe her as the "Blond Spy Mistress of Nazi Chief's Brother." In one of a handful of German-language conversations between Stein and Weustenfeld recorded by the microphones of the FBI, Weustenfeld complained of the way Sebold spoke to Stein "about her immoral conduct." Weustenfeld said she knew Lilly was "not clean, but that Harry had no reason for making such a great point" of it. Indeed, the FBI seemed to be mostly occupied with cataloging her love life. When she attended a prizefight at the Bronx Coliseum featuring Romuald Wernikowski, a heavyweight from Vienna who went by the ring name Rex Romus, G-men noted that Stein was "accosted" by Rudolph C. "Rudy" Schifter, another European with connections within elite athletic circles. A short time later, Romus (who knocked out his opponent in the first round) was recorded as a visitor to Stein's new apartment on East Seventy-Ninth Street in Yorkville. Another guest, Georg von Birgelen, a Zurich-born skating champion known for his daredevil jumps over card tables and the like, was described by the Bureau as Stein's Swiss boyfriend in an apparent attempt to distinguish him from the multinational pack. Still another companion, Hans Ruesch, a prominent driver on the European racing circuit who was beginning to make a name for himself as a writer, was thought by the New York office to have mailed letters on her behalf in Europe.

"Oh, I just look for them and they fall in love with me," she said.

During a discussion between Weustenfeld and Stein on October 18, the FBI learned that Stein thought of Sebold as a "swine" who had absconded with her money. "I always told you that you could not have any faith in that man," said Weustenfeld, who never met Sebold. In another conversation twelve days later, Weustenfeld broke the news that she'd heard a rumor about Sebold making "false statements over there." Stein responded by expressing further doubts about him, saying she was "certain" that "Harry had embezzled some money." She recalled that he had made "very unusual remarks concerning political affairs," an attempt at "shaking her," she believed. And now that she thought about it, he refused to look her square in the eye "as though he had a clear conscience." She "should have known that he was a dangerous man."

"So he made false reports—how could he do that?" Stein added.

"He's an American—it's no wonder," responded Weustenfeld.

Stein then brought up the possibility that Sebold was working for the British or the Americans.

Weustenfeld dismissed the suggestion. She didn't think Bill Sebold had "enough courage to do that."

■ ■ ■

Following his summertime interlude in Hempstead, Sebold was again based in the city, allowed by the FBI to live with Helen in an apartment on the top floor of 226 East Eighty-Fifth Street, in the heartland of German New York. In the midst of an investigation that was growing ever more hectic, he was able to cope with his anxieties in close communion with his wife, who was by now aware of his secret life in the spy underground. By the evidence of Dr. Goodhardt's statement that Sebold was susceptible to "considerable nervous strain," he was in need of occasional fortification. While the FBI files and Ellsworth's writings mention nothing about the nature of their relationship, the couple's relatives say they enjoyed a quiet bond. "They seemed to understand each other," a niece said. To their neighbors, the Sebolds couldn't have seemed more ordinary. Helen continued her work as a domestic with the rich Park Avenue family, a few blocks' walk to the west. And Bill, well, they weren't sure what he did, but he seemed nice enough.

With help from the marine spies, who appeared to have no suspicion of him, Sebold recruited two additional couriers following his break with Stein. The first was the chief steward on one of the other American Export Lines ships on the Lisbon run, the SS *Excambion*. A haughty ladies' man with relatives high up in the Nazi Party, he refused to meet Sebold in Columbus Circle or Central Park, forcing him to come to the steward's room at the Hotel Governor Clinton. The second was a Paris-born flight attendant for the wealthy and well connected on the only transatlantic airline service offered between Europe and New York, the Pan Am Clipper, the whale-shaped seaplane that took twenty-four hours to hop from Lisbon to the Azores, from the Azores to Bermuda, and from Bermuda to the Marine Air Terminal at La Guardia, where newsmen were waiting to see who was worth quoting.

At the suggestion of the butcher and the baker, who sought him out whenever they returned from their Caribbean cruises, Sebold began holding conferences at a Viennese restaurant on Second Avenue in Yorkville, Zum Schwarzen Adler, which they all agreed was much better than standing in the cold in Columbus Circle. The talks often "concerned inconsequential matters, such as women and the rewards that they were to get in Germany when the war is over," the FBI noted. Later at trial, the waiter (Erich Strunck) recalled an evening there when the butcher boasted of a new girl he had met in Havana. "She was a Hungarian fan dancer in the Eden Cabaret next door to Sloppy Joe's," Strunck testified. "So I told him that I had met a Spanish singer and dancer in the Arcadia Cabaret in Lisbon. And then he said, 'I think I know her, too.' Harry Sebold laughed—'You fellows are certainly having a good time.'" The butcher liked to brag that he was "the biggest whoremaster in Hamburg."

After weeks of trying, Sebold reestablished regular contact with the still-wary Paul Fehse, whose method was to wander the docks picking up information about British merchant ships that were being loaded with goods in preparation for running the U-boat gauntlet, submitting such detailed reports that Sebold admonished him to provide only the most essential information for transmittal to Germany. During a ride around the East Side in Fink's brown Ford coupe, Sebold was comfortable enough to laugh off Fehse's worries about being beheaded if he sought to return to Germany through Russian territory: "He told Fehse that would be all right; that the Germans would erect a monument and put his head on it in stone," according to the FBI report. Later in the conversation, Fehse spoke of his concern that he would be put into an American concentration camp if war broke out. Sebold scoffed, "About all you'll have to do is play football for three years."

"Yes, this is a pretty good country after all," Fehse conceded.

Sebold failed to glean much additional information from Hermann Lang, who remained hesitant about leaving the country even after Ast Hamburg agreed to his request to deposit $3,000 in a German bank for him. Sebold continued to indulge the spy theatrics of Colonel Duquesne, who wanted to send his reports via invisible writing and/or wax-paper impressions. After Sebold told him that Ast Hamburg was opposed to the latter—"Dunn should not use the wax system," according to the radio message—Duquesne wondered if "perhaps the British had gotten wise to it." And Sebold resumed taking the 7:17 from Penn Station out to Baldwin to see Ed Roeder, who was supplying a steady diet of air-gadgetry plans, production reports, informed rumors, and even service-issued incendiary bullets, earning such trust from Ast Hamburg that Roeder was asked to confer with a Japanese agent at the Nippon Club on West Ninety-Third Street, the first evidence that the Tripartite Pact was being observed in New York. Roeder did as he was told, meeting with "an elderly Japanese wearing glasses" who quizzed him about oil burners for fifteen minutes. Later, Roeder and Sebold were put in contact with a more senior Japanese operative during an evening that included a traditional Japanese meal in a brownstone on East Nineteenth Street. The man would be identified by the FBI as Takeo Ezima, a lieutenant commander in the Imperial Japanese Navy with connections to the Japanese consulate, another boon for the case.

By the middle of October, Roeder had again become angry over Sebold's inability to keep him supplied with sufficient funds. On October 11, Roeder waved two bills, complaining that he owed $200 to a Merrick bank and $320 for his newly overhauled furnace. On October 14, he said, "I have a sneaking idea that the material I am giving you is not getting into the right hands."

Sebold was forced to ask Hamburg for permission to dip into the $1,500 brought over by the butcher for the Sperry bombsight, which FDR had decided to give to the Brits in lieu of the Norden (soon resulting in articles that informed the country of the names of its two bombsights), and which Roeder refused to steal even for $50,000. He told Sebold that if he took the bombsight handbook a "big commotion" would be aroused and "he would have to leave the United States and could never return."

In response, Hamburg floated an idea that revealed how much the spymasters had come to trust Sebold. "If opportunity presents itself we have in mind to establish a large deposit with a New Yorker bank," according to the forty-eighth message received in Centerport. "We request recommendations as to how payments can be made unsuspiciously." For the next five days, the Bureau debated how to take full advantage of the matchless opportunity to control the flow (and thus the dispersal) of spy money into the United States, which would give Sebold an easy excuse to widen his circle of contacts. "We argued this one a great deal in the office," Ellsworth wrote in his diary. On the eve of Election Day, Centerport sent out its reply. "Since I have good connections in Diesel Lines, I recommend opening a small research office," the communication read. "Licensed business name and suitable space present no difficulties. As research offices continually need money, you can send me a large amount." On the following day, November 5, President Roosevelt was reelected to an unprecedented third term. And on November 7, the FBI received its fifty-second message from Germany:

"We are in agreement. Open office immediately. Advise when and where you want the remittance sent and the highest amount possible for you to handle without suspicion."

The FBI had never before contemplated such elaborate trickery. Thus began what Hoover called "the flytrap method."

CHAPTER ELEVEN

ROOM 627

Let us no longer blind ourselves to the undeniable fact that the evil forces which have crushed and undermined and corrupted so many others are already within our gates. Your government knows much about them and every day is ferreting them out.

—President Roosevelt, fireside chat,
December 29, 1940

The FBI chose the gaudy heart of America: the beaux arts building with French Renaissance ornamentation and copper mansard roof at the southeast corner of Broadway and Forty-Second Street in Times Square. Formerly the Knickerbocker Hotel, it was now an office building known for its most prominent tenant, *Newsweek* magazine, whose staffers would remain ignorant of the huge story that was taking place on the sixth floor. Dealing directly with the building's owner, who offered to replace the manager if he wasn't cooperative enough, the Bureau rented Room 627 and two adjacent offices, 628 and 629. In the days after the deal was reached in late November, agents created a stage set with the largest space occupied by the office of WILLIAM G. SEBOLD DIESEL ENG., the words painted on the door of 627. The setup was centered around a large desk that was expertly bugged and within a few feet of a silver-coated two-way wall mirror behind which a Bureau agent (usually Richard

L. Johnson) was operating a spring-wound motion-picture camera in a soundproofed space. "We just barely had enough light to make a picture, and it was necessary to slow the camera down as slow as it would go and open the lens wide-open in order to get a good picture," Johnson said. Positioned within his line of sight were a clock (encased within a wooden frame whittled by Agent Friedemann) and a flip-page calendar, both of which had numbers large enough to be readily viewable to future jurors. "Well, Sebold had his back turned to me at most times," said Johnson, "and at some times he had his face, the side of his face, turned to me. Of course, we were more interested in the other person." The conversations in the room were monitored by headphone-wearing, German-speaking agents (typically Friedemann and Fellner), who could take the stand as eyewitnesses to bolster Sebold's (likely voluminous) testimony, and recorded onto lacquered aluminum discs by the turntables of the state-of-the-art Presto recording system. By early December, a telephone had been installed (phone number BRyant 9-1609), business cards printed up, and $5,000 in Nazi money wired through Mexico to Sebold's new account at Chase National Bank, the first of three transfers sent via this method totaling $16,500.

The first visitor was the flight attendant on the Pan Am Clipper, who suspected nothing of the ruse, telling Sebold that he was "extremely careful" to ensure that the authorities "had never gotten anything on him." And he was "going to see to it that they never would." The second was Ed Roeder, who, now based at Sperry's Garden City laboratory in the suburbs, would become a less active producer in light of the worrying presence of the FBI around Sperry projects and his son's recent induction into the US Army. He told Sebold at one point that he only wanted to procure items that would hurt Great Britain and not the United States. But his inactivity was mostly due to money. The Abwehr was unwilling to pay for items that were often prevented by the FBI from reaching Germany. "Why does Carr want money?" according to one radio message. "We have lately received practically nothing from him." Roeder had to wait until early May to receive his next (and last) payment, a paltry $100. He couldn't understand why Ast Hamburg, which had once been so generous with him, wouldn't provide him with just compensation.

The third guest was Paul Fehse's young sidekick, Leo Waalen, an employee of a boat basin in the Bronx who, like his mentor, was always ready with richly detailed reports on shipping movements. Waalen came bearing a document received from "a girl who is connected with the German Consulate," probably Else Weustenfeld, which alleged that the Berlin office of an American newspaper syndicate was helping Jews obtain forged documents to flee from Germany.

On the same evening, Sebold welcomed the spymaster of *another* ring into the snare, Carl Reuper, a technician at an aircraft parts plant in New Jersey who had returned to the United States after graduating from Ast Hamburg's spy school in April 1940. Like Hermann Lang of Carl L. Norden Inc., Reuper was a member of the Nazi organization of industrial workers, the German-American Vocational League (DAB), which helped him establish a small spy organization that was populated by men with strong ties to ideological circles. His gang included a longstanding employee of the Nazi-centric Germania Book and Specialty in Yorkville; the onetime leader of the Staten Island *Ortsgruppe* of the German American Bund; a convicted counterfeiter from Düsseldorf with a Bronx apartment full of radio equipment; and the Hamburg-trained brother of one of Fritz Kuhn's top aides, whose coding system was based on the crime thriller *Halfway to Horror* by David Hume. It didn't much matter that Reuper refused Sebold's offer to join their operations together in common service to Hitler. "He wanted to keep the entire activity for himself because he was instructed by Germany to do that," Sebold said. "There was nothing personal against me." E. J. Connelly was free to assign agents to locate and tail the third ring's members without the double agent's active participation.

On December 29, 1940, the microphone in Fritz Duquesne's apartment on the Upper West Side picked up that he and girlfriend Evelyn Lewis were listening to the radio when President Roosevelt delivered the historic fireside declaring America as a "great arsenal of democracy" for the nations fighting Axis tyranny. He named China, Greece (which had been invaded by Italy), and, most especially, Great Britain, which, in addition to fending off Germany over the skies of Britain and in the waters of the Atlantic, was engaged in battles with Mussolini's forces in North Africa. The president pledged that US industry would produce "the implements of war, the planes, the tanks, the guns, the freighters, which will enable them to fight for their liberty and for our security." He said, "we must get these weapons to them, get them to them in sufficient volume and quickly enough, so that we and our children will be saved the agony and suffering of war, which others have had to endure." The talk served as a prelude to his grandiloquent State of the Union address on January 6, 1941, a statement of national purpose that dedicated the country to upholding four essential freedoms—of speech and worship, from want and fear—in the face of aggressive dictatorships and the "great numbers" of "secret agents and their dupes . . . already here, and in Latin America." He neglected to mention that he had granted Hoover the authority following the fall of France to dispatch FBI agents to Central and South American countries to uncover Nazi subterfuge. Or that the Centerport station had been put in contact with an Abwehr-operated radio outpost in Mexico (call letters GBO or Gustav Bruno Otto), which was discovered near the village of Coatepec by a Bureau agent who had been sent across the border with a backpack. "He told us later that it was a thrilling experience one night to take his equipment out a dirt road and when the broadcast began to follow the sound until looking through some brush across a field he could see an old farmhouse with a directional antenna which was the transmitter," wrote Ellsworth.

Four days after the speech, the Lend-Lease Act was introduced into Congress. It gave Roosevelt sweeping powers to provide American-produced aid to the now-broke British nation (or any country "whose defense the President deems vital to the defense of the United States") under the stipulation that the items (or something of equal value) would be returned at the end of the war, much as a man who borrows a neighbor's hose to put out a fire gives it back once the job is done, as he said in a much-quoted remark to the press. While the legislation eliminated the "cash" portion of cash-and-carry, it still required non-American ships to cart the goods across the Atlantic Ocean in the face of the U-boat threat. The isolationists were theatrically aghast at what was indeed an unprecedented power grab by the executive. Senator Wheeler likened Lend-Lease to the New Deal agricultural policy of reducing crop surpluses (and thus raising prices) by "plowing under" a certain proportion of the acreage, saying that the president sought to "plow under every fourth American boy," which became the title of an antiwar anthem written by the left-wing Almanac Singers of Woody Guthrie and Pete Seeger. Congressional opponents succeeded in attaching an amendment explicitly stating that "naval vessels of the United States" were not authorized by the legislation to protect the convoys of Allied merchant ships traveling across the Atlantic, an attempt to keep them from being fired upon and perhaps sunk, the quickest route to an American declaration of war. Hitler was also determined to avoid any action that would bring the Americans into the war before he could complete two quick campaigns scheduled for the spring of 1941. With Fascist Italy failing in its efforts to capture Greece and British possessions in North Africa, he'd decided to send troops to secure Germany's southern flank before turning against his truest enemy, the Soviet Union, which was under the misapprehension that the Hitler-Stalin Pact was binding. Once the Communist leviathan was easily overrun in a massive surprise attack, the Nazi regime would then have the material resources to fight against both Great Britain and the United States, according to the Führer's thinking. For now, he wanted to keep the Yanks out.

Among those sent south was Nikolaus Ritter, who no longer had day-to-day supervision of the ring that had been expanding ever since his peacetime trip to New York three years earlier. Fed up with Ast Hamburg's internecine conflict, he was glad to embark on a special mission to North Africa, where he commanded a unit that made a failed attempt to extract a pro-Nazi Egyptian general from behind British lines. During this novelistic interlude, Ritter enjoyed an alliance with the Hungarian aristocrat and adventurer László Almásy (the model for the lead character in the film *The English Patient*) and survived nine hours on a life raft after his Heinkel He 111 plunged into the Mediterranean off the Cyrenaican shore. But he couldn't help thinking about his spies in America and Great Britain. He wondered "if those behind could provide the personal control and contact on which the effectiveness of my ring of agents had thus far depended," he wrote of his Ast Hamburg replacements. "I only hoped the new officers maintained the standards we had established."

On the evening of Roosevelt's Four Freedoms address, the FBI recorded that Duquesne returned home "slightly drunk," which was an apt description of his current manner as an espionage agent. Over many get-togethers now often held in City Hall Park (La Guardia's Ranch, Duquesne named it) or a German restaurant called Van Axen's on Gold Street, he was supplying Sebold with ample evidence of his eccentricity. Duquesne wanted it passed along that American intelligence in Europe was sending information to the United States "by engraving messages on spoons, pots, pans, camera parts, etc." He asked Sebold to provide Germany with two articles written about him in 1925 ("Is Fritz Duquesne Alive?" and "Fritz Duquesne, the Sequel," both from *American Legion Weekly*), which Sebold did. Duquesne produced (fake) photographs of a special specimen of gas shell, which he said he obtained by sneaking into the Du Pont plant in Wilmington, Delaware, and described visits to Hyde Park, where he was somehow privy to conversations involving President Roosevelt. He would thenceforth sign his letters, he announced in February, with the ink stamp of a cat. "My pussy," he said. After complaining of gallstone trouble, he wondered if Germany still kept two beds at Lenox Hill Hospital for its stricken agents. (Er, no.) He declined Ast Hamburg's offer to go to Africa ("I will be put up against a wall and shot") and ignored its order to approach three high-society Nazi sympathizers (he said he was investigating them first). The FBI microphone in his apartment captured him more than once repeating the tall tale about how he was responsible for the death of Lord Kitchener, boasting to his girlfriend that he "was the unknown person who escaped on a raft" as the *Hampshire* was sinking. "The Duke was a very interesting talker but he always had to be the center of attention," wrote Agent Newkirk, who was listening in the upstairs apartment. In a message to Hamburg, Sebold said, "I have a feeling that Dunn is a dud." Yet he was regarded as astute enough in the ways of subterfuge to be kept away from the Forty-Second Street office, at least for the time being.

Not so Hermann Lang, who was invited up in early February and guided into a discussion of his 1938 trip to Germany. The FBI was still unsure exactly how he'd communicated the Norden data to the Germans.

"Must one take everything along in his head?" Sebold asked in German, referring to a previous hint from Lang that he passed along the bombsight details without the aid of blueprints.

Lang responded with a verbal shrug of his shoulders.

"Uh-huh," he said, according to Agent Fellner's testimony.

"You must be a master pirate," Sebold said. "Did you have everything in your head? The whole story, and over there put it together from memory?"

"Uh-huh," Lang repeated.

"Gee, that's something marvelous," Sebold said, before turning to other matters.

He was given one last try a month later when the two met for the final time. Sebold got him talking about his time in the Air Ministry in Berlin, which Lang described as "the most closely watched place in Germany." He said "a man had to be very important to get in there." Lang went on to praise Ernst Udet, whom he described as a "nice fellow" with an "excellent technical knowledge of airplanes." But that was about all that Sebold could get out of him. The bombsight wasn't mentioned.

With the overwhelming support of the American people, the Lend-Lease bill easily passed both houses of Congress by early March and was promptly signed into law by President Roosevelt. The initial shipments were funded with a $7 billion appropriation, the first installment of almost $50 billion in Lend-Lease aid that would be delivered, mostly to Great Britain, during World War II. "Our blessings from the whole of the British Empire go out to you and the American nation for this very present help in a time of trouble," Churchill said in a telegram to Roosevelt. The administration also asked for a vast increase in US military spending, which amounted to $13.7 billion for 1941, a figure that would only grow over the next four years as America mobilized itself out of the Depression. Two weeks after the enactment of Lend-Lease, Hitler sought to facilitate the invasion of Greece by coercing the leaders of Yugoslavia to join the Tripartite Pact, which, after they did, sparked a coup d'état in Belgrade that removed them from power. Enraged, Hitler ordered Yugoslavia to be destroyed with "unmerciful harshness." At dawn on Palm Sunday, April 6, German forces swept into Yugoslavia and Greece. Without the protection even of antiaircraft guns, Belgrade was subject to a vicious aerial assault from Luftwaffe bombers resulting in the deaths of an estimated seventeen thousand civilians. On the next day, the FBI recorded Else Weustenfeld telling Lilly Stein that "even though they may laugh at Hitler's invasion of Yugoslavia and Greece at this time, nevertheless in four weeks he will be master of those countries." Within three weeks, both countries had been conquered, which, coupled with General Erwin Rommel's successes in North Africa, left Hitler free to plan his invasion of the Soviet Union. On April 23, the day Greece signed an armistice with the Germans, Charles Lindbergh spoke before a raucous mass meeting of the America First Committee at the Manhattan Center on West Thirty-Fourth Street. "We have been led toward war by a minority of our people," he said. "This minority has power. It has influence. It has a loud voice. But it does not represent the American people." Among the ten thousand spectators in the hall—thousands more gathered outside in an atmosphere of vituperation that led to a few scuffles—were at least two of the Nazi agents under surveillance as part of the Sebold case.

In the midst of Hitler's call for a "merciless sea war" against British merchant shipping, the FBI was learning much from the leader of the marine spies, Paul Fehse, a determined soldier in the Kriegsmarine's campaign to strangle the UK into submission. During his first session in Room 627, he didn't deny a tale that Sebold had first heard from the butcher and the baker, the one about Fehse's mingling among British sailors in Oslo and picking up intelligence that resulted in the sinking of four ships during the Norway campaign, which would make him "quite a boy," said Sebold. ("Fehse replied that he would not lie to him," recorded the FBI.) On January 25, 1941, Fehse introduced Sebold to the head chef of the SS *America,* who produced the ship's blueprints and pointed out for the camera where the gun emplacements would be located when the liner was transferred to the US Navy, as was soon expected. On February 10, Fehse wondered if Sebold had ever heard of a courier named Walischefsky, which allowed agents to begin an investigation of one Adolf Henry August Walischewski, a steward on the SS *Uruguay* of the Moore-McCormack Shipping Line. On March 5, Fehse identified George Schuh, a Nazi ideologue who was a "commander" in the Hudson County, New Jersey, branch of the DAB. (He could be booked to give a talk titled "Cultural Decadence.") On March 12, Fehse arrived with Heinrich Clausing, a vegetable cook on the SS *Argentina*, who sent messages to Germany through a mail drop in Brazil, and spoke of Richard Eichenlaub, the owner of the Little Casino *Bierstube* on Sebold's block of East Eighty-Fifth Street, which turned out to be the rendezvous point for another ring of spies, the fourth. On March 19, Fehse went to Eichenlaub's bar and returned to Sebold's office with Heinz Stade, a cellist with a long-standing membership in the Bund who told Sebold he had been questioned in the World's Fair bombing. Stade bragged that he refused to talk even though the police broke three of his ribs and hung him out of a window. (He would later tell Sebold that a Jewish detective had hit him over the head with a typewriter.) Two days later, Fehse walked through the door with Max Blank, a bookstore clerk who was about to be hired by the German Library of Information, the Nazi government's propaganda publisher in New York. Speaking in German, Blank told Sebold that he had a "wonderful nose" for FBI men and Dies Committee investigators, able to "smell them right away." You "must have a marvelous knowledge of human nature to be able to do that," Sebold deadpanned.

But Fehse had been eager to return home since he'd first suspected that American investigators were on his trail. During an earlier meeting with Sebold, Fehse said that "he must have had an overdose of imagination in Germany when he accepted the job as a spy in America," pointing out that "the Americans are much tougher than the Germans indicated." On March 28, Fehse informed Sebold that he had signed on as a fry cook on the SS *Siboney* (which had replaced the SS *Exochorda* on the Lisbon run). He was planning to take the ship only as far as Portugal, from where he would jump ship and make his way back to the Reich. He couldn't be swayed by Sebold's comment that Fehse was "greatly needed here." On the following day, the FBI had no choice but to arrest Fehse before he had the opportunity to sail. To protect the Sebold operation from exposure, he was charged in connection with an unstamped letter of shipping information intended for a mail drop in Italy that the US Postal Service had passed along to the FBI. Quickly pleading guilty to a violation of the Foreign Agents Registration Act, Fehse was sentenced to one year and a day in the federal penitentiary in Atlanta. The *Times* noted that he "wept silently" when Judge Edward A. Conger rendered the judgment. "It stinks," said his loyal aide-de-camp, Leo Waalen, when he next visited the office, adding that he didn't believe Sebold had been exposed by Fehse's mishap.

Waalen, a thirty-four-year-old German national who lived over a pork store on Second Avenue in Yorkville, now moved to the top position, regularly offering leads on new contacts and delivering reports on ships moving in and out of the Manhattan, Brooklyn, and New Jersey docks. He became "Sebold's friend and messenger boy," a defense attorney later sneered. Waalen's work was of pressing consequence to the Nazi cause. In April 1941, U-boats sank 488,124 tons of Allied shipping, a 50 percent increase from the previous month. "A big British propaganda effort," Joseph Goebbels wrote in his dairy. "She is now forced to admit to 500,000 tons of shipping lost in April. The highest monthly total so far." Ast Hamburg was eager for information, complaining that Sebold's messages were not clear enough. They told him "only precise reports without the nonessentials are useful," unaware that the US government was doing *something* to protect the hardy British crews that were regularly departing from the port of New York to face what Churchill called a "shapeless, measureless peril." On April 28, Waalen brought up two items of nautical news that represented a typical haul for him. One was the arrival and departure information for eight ships. The notation for the last read "'*Robin Moor*' (Robin) Capetown, June 2, Lourenço Marques [Mozambique], June 10, from New York, May 3." His departure date was wrong by three days. The *Robin Moor*, a five-thousand-ton steamship under American registry with nine officers, twenty-nine crew members, eight passengers, and no war materials on board, left New York for Cape Town and Mozambique on May 6. The FBI had no intention of passing any of the details along to Germany.

While Fehse's arrest caused concern among the spies who worked with him, none of his circle seemed distrustful of Sebold until an Irish member of the Little Casino group made a stop at the *Newsweek* building. He had been recommended by the musician Heinz Stade as one of a number of "Irish insurgents" who "would be good workers for the German cause" (and were responsible for the World's Fair bombing, Stade claimed) and by bar owner Dick Eichenlaub as a maritime engineer who "used to turn in a lot of reports on ships which were very accurate" but lacked a means of getting the intelligence quickly across the ocean. On May 19, Sean Connolly settled into the visitor's chair in 627 and told Sebold that he was inspired to work for the Reich because the British had hanged his father. When Connolly asked for instructions and expense money, Sebold responded that he needed approval from Hamburg before he could welcome him into the organization. In the meantime, he asked Connolly to come up with a list of potential saboteurs, providing his latest PO box address.

A few days later, Sebold called up Eichenlaub at the Little Casino and learned that a rumor was going around that Sebold had a microphone hidden in the office. Suspicions had been raised by the way he kept glancing at a desk drawer.

On the evening of May 27, 65 million Americans (out of a population of 132 million) listened as President Roosevelt declared "an unlimited national emergency," which required the "military, naval, air, and civilian defenses be put on the basis of readiness to repel any and all acts or threats of aggression directed toward any part of the Western Hemisphere." Although he warned that U-boats were sinking merchant ships at more than three times the capacity of British shipyards to replace them, he did not announce the commencement of armed escorts. He merely said he was increasing "patrols" to alert British shipping to the presence of German warships. After the speech, Sebold visited the Little Casino, where he met with yet another conspirator, Paul Bante, a Bundist who had a cache of dynamite he was eager to deploy against the anti-Nazi congressman Samuel Dickstein and his supporters. Bante informed Sebold that the Irishman "started the rumpus" about the microphone, which led to a meeting attended by four of the spies to discuss the matter. Bante claimed he vouched for Sebold by noting his length of service to Germany and his strong relationship with the respected Paul Fehse.

On the next night, Sebold went to the bar and spoke with Stade, Eichenlaub, and Connolly, who was comfortable enough to provide the coordinates (which he wrote on the flap of an envelope) for Allied convoy routes in the North Atlantic. At the end of the discussion, Sebold brought up what he called the "microphone incident." Connolly said that Sebold asked "too many funny questions." Sebold countered that he "wants to know something about a man before he deals with him." Although the three seemed satisfied with his explanation, Sebold left the Little Casino feeling that the matter wasn't entirely resolved. He sensed that Eichenlaub, who spoke of connections to the Gestapo in Hamburg, was making an effort to report Sebold to the Nazi authorities.

On June 9, Stade and Connolly refused to meet Sebold at the Forty-Second Street office, instead asking him to come to the corner of Eighty-Sixth and Broadway on the Upper West Side, which he did. Connolly offered to hand over valuable details on convoy routes that he'd received from a Canadian who had made the crossing three or four times. The price was $200. Sebold said he would see what he could do. Later that evening, after receiving approval from Ellsworth to pay the money, Sebold met with Stade at the Little Casino. Sebold told him to send Connolly up to the office on the following day to receive payment. But the Irishman never showed.

On June 10, an Associated Press radiogram from Rio de Janeiro broke the news that the *Robin Moor*, which was clearly marked with Stars and Stripes insignia, had been sunk on May 21. A Brazilian steamship had picked up eleven survivors floating in one of the ship's four lifeboats. They described how the *Moor* had been stopped in neutral waters about four hundred miles south of the Cape Verde Islands in the Middle Atlantic by a German U-boat, whose commander gave the crew and passengers thirty minutes to abandon ship. Once they did, *U-69* sent a single torpedo into the *Moor*'s side, followed by a barrage of thirty-odd shells from the deck gun, a blatant violation of Hitler's order to avoid any contact with American maritime traffic. It took twenty-three minutes for the *Robin Moor* to become the first American-flagged vessel to be sunk by a U-boat during World War II. "Auf Wiedersehen!" the German sailors could be heard shouting. President Roosevelt asked for judgment to be suspended until the details could be confirmed.

On June 13, the papers announced the official word: "*Robin Moor* Sunk by a U-boat, U.S. Asserts; Nazis 'Undoubtedly' Knew It Was an American Ship," declared the front page of the *Herald Tribune*. The thirty-five passengers in the other three lifeboats were probably dead, said Undersecretary of State Sumner Welles. On June 14, FDR froze all German and Italian assets in the United States, including those of Nazi fronts such as the DAB and the German American Bund. On the same day, word arrived from Cape Town that a British ship had rescued the missing thirty-five. Everyone had survived. "I'm so elated," Alice Phillips of Bay Ridge, Brooklyn, the wife of the *Robin Moor*'s second assistant, told the *Post*. "I don't know what to say. It's such a pleasant shock." On June 16, FDR ordered Nazi Germany to close its consulates and affiliated agencies, giving the 171 "German agents" attached to the Nazi institutions until July 10 to leave the country. That evening, Leo Waalen walked into Sebold's office and asked about the arrest of Paul Fehse, apparently in the new-found belief that something other than Fehse's carelessness was to blame. Sebold brushed him off by saying "he was probably picked up as a result of one of the letters he was sending to Germany." Waalen mentioned nothing about the possibility that he had a role in the sinking of the *Robin Moor*.

The investigation was approaching its denouement. Two Justice Department officials arrived from Washington for a conference with Sebold to discuss the endgame. "Trouble was brewing everywhere," Ellsworth wrote. On June 20, the FBI was forced to arrest the butcher (Erwin Siegler) and the baker (Franz Stigler), both of whom had signed onto ships that were preparing to take them out of American jurisdiction for good. In an attempt to prevent the case from coming undone in its final moments, the two were booked on charges of attempting to leave the country without notifying their draft boards and, in a move of dubious legality approved by acting attorney general Francis Biddle, prevented from appearing before a federal magistrate to hear the charges against them. Later that evening, Sebold was walking past the Little Casino when he bumped into Eichenlaub, who told him that Stade and Connolly were expected at the bar later. Sebold told him he was only interested in business matters and "did not want to be bothered with their personal opinions" of him. He didn't go.

Then on June 22, Hitler launched the most spectacular invasion in the history of modern warfare. Three million German troops surged across a nineteen-hundred-mile front from the Baltic Sea to the Black Sea, overrunning an unprepared Red Army and quickly gaining control of eastern Poland, Belorussia, Latvia, Lithuania, and Ukraine, lands with huge Jewish populations that would be subject to the most ferocious phases of the

quest for an Aryan racial utopia. Hermann Göring had begged for a postponement to give his Luftwaffe a rest ("I've made up my mind!" Hitler responded), but at least his newest medium bombers could now conduct aerial bombardments equipped with their own Norden bombsight, the Lotfe 7D and its successor models, which the Germans would always claim was better than the American version. The Technical Office had finally succeeded in exploiting the technological innovations pioneered by Carl Norden to advance the regime's ignoble goals.

It is a consolation of history that the German air force was unable to install its new bombsights into a fleet of long-range bombers able to conduct sustained strikes at the heart of a distant enemy's strength. The simple bureaucratic failure to maintain sound and uninterrupted development of an aircraft such as the four-engine Heinkel He 177 meant that the Luftwaffe was unequipped to win a *world* war. Within months, Ernst Udet committed suicide with a gunshot to the head in the knowledge that the air fleet shaped to his technical specifications was doomed to failure. "In attacking the Soviet Union, the Luftwaffe left the relatively narrow confines of the European conflict and had to fight an intercontinental war against overwhelming material resources," wrote Ernst Heinkel. "It never had the ghost of a chance."

Fritz Duquesne could be invited to the office at last.

Sebold told him to stop by because "he might need his presence and assistance from time to time inasmuch as he was more experienced than he in spy matters," wrote the FBI. Making his entrance in the early evening of June 25, Duquesne conducted a minute examination of the interior that surely gave pause to the agents behind the two-way mirror. "Where are the mics?" he

asked. He "opened the towel chest and looked in all the corners," said the FBI. Sebold chattered about diesel motors for twenty or thirty minutes before his visitor was comfortable enough to talk. Like a real spy, Duquesne raised the leg of his trousers and pulled an envelope from his sock, a detail that would be much remembered in later years by the agents who worked the case. The package included seven items: a sketch and photograph of the M1 Garand automatic rifle; a sketch of an airplane described as a "new design accepted by government"; a drawing of a tank, the "latest model light tank for air transport"; a photograph of a model of a US Navy Mosquito boat; a photograph of a grenade projector; and a typed statement about Chrysler tanks he had observed "at West Point" and "Tennessee maneuvers."

As he often did in his conversations with Sebold, Duquesne spent much time musing about sabotage techniques, describing a method of starting fires by hiding phosphorus in pieces of chewing gum and dropping the "candy bombs," as the newspapers would later call them, at key points in a munitions factory through a hole in your pants' pocket. He told Sebold that he would like to have a piece of slow-burning fuse "because he might be able to make use of it at the General Electric Plant in Schenectady, N.Y." But before long, he was talking about his favorite subject, the old days. He (further) embellished the story about his 1902 escape from the Bermuda penal colony by claiming that he was transported from the scene "on the Vanderbilt yacht," which was apparently fancier than the Bromo-Seltzer King's vessel. He recalled an instance in prison when a German Canadian offered him 10 percent of $40 million to betray the Kaiser, a proposal he said he refused because he knew the man was a British counterspy. He would never turn his back on Germany, he vowed. And he devoted the requisite amount of time to complaining about poor pay. Back when he began working for the

Nazis in the late 1930s, he said, he was regularly given impressive sums by a cabin boy on the SS *Bremen*. The money enabled him to throw cocktail parties at the Roosevelt Hotel attended by aircraft-industry types who, once they were sufficiently inebriated, divulged valuable tips about the latest advancements. He used to wear finely tailored suits. Now he was forced to wear "John David $29.50 clothes."

The three-hour session ended with Duquesne reminding Sebold not to leave his sketches and photographs lying around to be discovered by the cleaning lady.

"The old devil sat there," said Agent Johnson, "and told us the story of his life."

CHAPTER TWELVE

THE TRUSTED MAN

Q: Would you lie under oath on this witness stand?
Sebold: I don't lie.
Q: You would not lie under any circumstance?
Sebold: No, sir. I don't lie.

—Brooklyn Federal Court,
September 10, 1941

On Friday, June 27, 1941, some 250 agents (about a fourth of the entire G-man corps in the country) gathered on the twenty-sixth floor of the federal building in Foley Square, where E. J. Connelly "outlined the squads, assigned the spies to be arrested, and gave detailed instructions about guards, searches, evidence, room assignments in the building," wrote Ellsworth in his diary on the next day. "Plans were to start the raids about supper time tonight, June 28, 1941, Saturday. They would all be held and questioned Saturday night and Sunday. I told Sebold nothing of these plans. Tonight I covered him at his office, 152 W. 42nd Street. No one showed up. I met Bill down on 42nd Street, and put him in my car and headed with him to the radio station at Centerport, L.I. I then told him that right at that moment raids were under way. He said he had a feeling it was breaking. We went to Centerport for the night, away from any possible reprisals."

Spies were pulled from ships, roused from beds, escorted out of bars. Erich Strunck (the waiter) was seized in a room in Milwaukee. Heinz Stade (the musician) was taken off the bandstand at Geide's Inn on Route 25A in Centerport, of all places. Lilly Stein was busy with a gentleman caller, who was permitted to complete his visit before the FBI entered her apartment. "Well, I'll say one thing, you sure got an earful," she said after learning that her place had been bugged. Later, she propositioned one of the agents. "A real Aryan type," said Agent Friedemann. "It was the great incident of the night." A party was going on at Ed Roeder's home at 210 Smith Street in Merrick to celebrate the upcoming marriage of his son when the FBI knocked on the door. Roeder "requested that nothing be done to disturb the said party and willingly signed a waiver permitting his home to be searched at a later time." *Newsday* reported that a hundred thousand rounds of ammunition were found in his basement.

Hermann Lang and his wife were spending the weekend at Bell's Wellington Farms Cabins, a summer gathering spot for members of the DAB located a few miles outside Coram, Long Island. "As we drove up, he came to an open window and asked who was there," testified Agent Reuben Peterson. "I approached the window and identified myself and asked him if he would come to the door. He opened the door, and I advised him that I had a warrant for his arrest, and he was taken into custody." Fritz Duquesne thought nothing of it when he answered the door and found Agent Newkirk standing in the hallway, believing him to be "Ray McManus," the upstairs neighbor he had spoken to a number of times over the past year. "Knowing me, Duquesne invited me in and I told him I had some friends with me and he said bring them on in," Newkirk wrote. "Although armed, none of us drew a gun. I informed Duquesne we were FBI agents and that he and Miss Lewis were under arrest. Two agents took Duquesne and another agent and I took Miss Lewis to FBI headquarters in separate cars for questioning. The Duke never spoke to me again."

Thirty men and three women were arrested. They were organized into roughly four separate rings—the original I-L spies (Duquesne, Lang, Roeder, and Stein); the marine division (composed of some fifteen stewards, cooks, waiters, etc.); the Carl Reuper group (whose leader only met with Sebold once); and the Little Casino faction. Of the few suspects who operated more or less as lone wolves, the most prominent was the Detroit-based agent ("Heinrich") who used Lilly Stein's East Fifty-Fourth Street address as a mail drop for letters crammed with aviation data, which were intercepted by agents before they could reach Germany. Edmund Carl Heine was a former executive with Ford and Chrysler who boasted of a ten-year friendship with Henry Ford, the automotive pioneer and celebrated author of *The International Jew: The World's Foremost Problem* (1920), a favorite tome of Nazi Germany. (While he was under FBI surveillance, Heine placed a phone call to Ford and asked to return to the company. "Mr. Ford told him that he could have a job in the factory, but that he believed that he was in the United States for no good and was, in fact, a spy," wrote the Bureau.) Only one suspect eluded capture, the wily Sean Connolly. At the request of the State Department, two Japanese agents identified by the investigation were not apprehended. (Both would be out of the country by August.) Of the thirty-three, twenty-eight were born in Germany, twenty-two of whom were naturalized citizens of the United States. Of the other naturalized Americans, one was born in Latvia, another in France, and a third in South Africa (Duquesne). Two of the accused were native-born Americans: Evelyn Lewis and Ed Roeder. Just six of the spies were *not* citizens of the United States. Meanwhile, the Bureau continued to investigate an entire constellation of other individuals uncovered by Sebold's efforts.

DOUBLE AGENT

On Sunday evening, June 29, J. Edgar Hoover allowed his pal Walter Winchell to break the story on his popular radio program ("Good evening, Mr. and Mrs. North and South America and all the ships and clippers at sea," he began in his rat-a-tat-tat style) while a press conference was held downtown to give the story to the rest of the media. Hoover described the investigation as "the greatest of its kind in the nation's history" and "the largest since the enactment" of the Espionage Act of 1917. Perhaps in a calculated attempt to draw attention away from Hermann Lang and the sensitive matter of his theft of the Norden, he described Fritz Duquesne as the most important member of the ring. "Under his direction the group paid particular attention to aircraft and tank work," Hoover said, even though Duquesne supervised no other operative but himself. Hoover revealed that Lilly Stein, an "artists' model," was the unnamed foreign agent whom press accounts had connected with the State Department's Ogden Hammond Jr. When sought for comment, Hammond, who failed in his legal attempt to be reinstated with the government, ungallantly called her "a pathetic little creature." Hoover said the Little Casino was the "principal" gathering spot for the spies, which sent reporters out to East Eighty-Fifth Street to detail its "bright German beer mugs and jukebox which plays German records," wrote the *Post*. Dick Eichenlaub's wife said, "Just friendly people come in here. I recognize the pictures of some of those arrested, but they looked so dumb. They couldn't be spies." Hoover mentioned nothing of the radio station, the Forty-Second Street office, or William Sebold.

It may have been the greatest moment of Hoover's career. In the afterglow of the triumph, the powerful Capitol Hill journalist Drew Pearson, who wrote the Washington Merry-Go-Round column for United Features Syndicate, celebrated the director's capture "of the biggest spy ring in our history" and lauded the democratic, humane, and discreet manner with which he was handling his new responsibilities as the nation's protector from foreign intrigue. Pearson's fantasy version of Hoover, so unrecognizable to even the most tendentious reading of the historical record, nabs malefactors without wiretaps in deference to the Supreme Court's rulings. He believes "there must be no politics in the FBI." He "will drop nothing because of political pressure. Nor will he investigate a Congressman, Senator or newspaperman without written orders from the Attorney General himself." Further: "No suspect gets his reputation ruined by having his name splashed in the headlines unless Hoover has the goods on him. There are no raids on the private or political files. Hoover is tough, but respects the rules—especially fundamental liberties." Pearson concluded, "The nation is lucky to have him on the job."

Yet the column, which included details about the case that were clearly leaked from deep within the FBI, was an obvious part of Hoover's campaign against his emerging rival for counter-espionage supremacy. William "Wild Bill" Donovan, the World War I hero and Wall Street lawyer who had been serving as a personal envoy for the president, had just been named to head the office of the Coordinator of Information (COI), which became the Office of Strategic Services (OSS) during the war and the Central Intelligence Agency (CIA) after it. The national-security state was in its foundational phase, with the FBI retaining the responsibility for enemy spies operating within the domestic sphere while the OSS/CIA was handed the task of combating them overseas.

The Germans were livid. The chargé d'affaires in Washington, Hans Thomsen, wrote a blistering telegram to the Foreign Ministry in Berlin on July 7: "Most, and probably all, of the persons involved in this affair were totally unqualified for operations of this kind, according to everything the Consulate General had heard about them. To give themselves importance, these people kept hinting all the time among their acquaintances that they had been given such missions and were carrying them out. It can be assumed that the American authorities had long known all about the network, which certainly would not have been any great feat, considering the naïve and sometimes downright stupid behavior of these people." Thomsen concluded, "Such poorly organized operations by irresponsible and incompetent agents, which most likely have not benefited our conduct of the war, may cost us the last remnants of sympathy which we can still muster here in circles, whose political opposition is of interest to us."

Thomsen's accusation that the spy ring had done nothing for Germany was passed through the bureaucracy to Admiral Canaris, who, on July 23, signed his name over a five-page response stamped *Geheime Reichssache* (or "secret Reich matter") that argued strenuously for the importance of several of the captured spies. Ed Roeder "delivered valuable technical material in the original, including remote-control machine-gun sight, bombsights, blind-flight instruments, Sperry's course indicator, speech scrambler, radio equipment on Guenn-Martin [*sic*] airplanes from Russia. Most items delivered were designated as 'valuable,' some as 'very valuable,' and 'of great importance.'" Since 1937, Fritz Duquesne "delivered valuable reports and important technical material in the original, including US gas masks, radio-control apparatus, leakproof fuel tanks, television instruments, small bombs for airplanes versus airplanes, air separator, and propeller-driving mechanism. Items delivered were labeled 'valuable,' and several 'good' and 'very good.'"

But Hermann Lang, described as *"sehr ruhig, verschwiegen, und zuverlässig"* (very quiet, discreet, and reliable), was given the highest honors. Since 1937, he had provided intelligence that was "important and decisive in the prosecution of the war." To support this weighty conclusion, the letter included two paragraphs submitted by Ernst Udet's Technical Office: "As a result of delivery by the *V.-Mannes* [*Vertrauensmann*, literally "trusted man"] of technical drawings and design elements of a bombsight accompanied by insightful explanations, it was possible to reconstruct the implement," the memo said, which confirmed that Lang did, in fact, convey blueprints to Germany. ". . . Considerable research expenses have been saved by the delivery of these items. In actual tests of the device it was revealed that the principle realized therein reacted favorably for the projected bomb drop. Accordingly, the items concerning the bombsight delivered from the USA by the Abwehr have successfully influenced the development of the German bombsight."

His crime was thus described: Hermann W. Lang had played a pivotal role in the creation of the new Luftwaffe bombsight that was then operational over the Soviet Union.

"The success of the secret military intelligence service which is confirmed again and again by our military offices," concluded Canaris, "sufficiently proves that the structure of the intelligence network or the selection of agents in and for USA have been necessary and correct."

Which was written before the regime knew about the treachery of Bill Sebold.

America was hovering between war and peace that summer. President Roosevelt sent four thousand troops to occupy Iceland, attempting to prevent the Nazis from gaining a stepping-stone on the way to the Western Hemisphere, but Congress barely passed an eighteen-month extension of the Selective Service Act. The count in the House of Representatives was 203–202, an indication of just how far federal legislators were from voting for a declaration of war. Roosevelt met with Churchill off the coast of Newfoundland to codify Anglo-American objectives for a postwar world after "the final destruction of Nazi tyranny," but FDR rebuffed the British leader's hope that the United States would immediately pick up arms and join the still-standing Soviet Union in the nascent Grand Alliance. Instead, "he would become more and more provocative," according to Churchill's account. "If the Germans did not like it, they could attack American forces. Everything was to be done to force an incident." FDR told Churchill (but not the American public) that US Navy vessels would begin escorting British merchant ships as far as Iceland on September 1, which was just the action that might instigate such an incident.

The double agent was safely ensconced in the bucolic isolation of Lake Ronkonkoma on Long Island. "Sebold wanted his wife with him in hiding out until the trial started and did not want her to be the only woman around," wrote Ellsworth. "He asked me to have my wife Nell with us. I took it up with Mr. Connelly who authorized the procedure." One cabin in the woods was for the Sebolds, one for the Ellsworths and their two children, and a third for a team of agents. "We lived well, close to the earth, had no bath but the lake, no toilet but the old style outhouse in back with its rank odors, and cooked on a kerosene burner," Ellsworth wrote. "But we loved it." In later years, he would recall how removed they were from the world's troubles: "At this location we had wild blueberries along the roadside and often would pick a bucket of berries, wash them, put them in a bowl covered with sugar and eat blueberries and cream." They tossed horseshoes and darts, listened to Brooklyn Dodgers games on the radio (a pennant year!), played cards, and went swimming in the lake. Home movies capture Ellsworth as a Clark Kent look-alike with ramrod posture and navel-level bathing trunks while Sebold is seen (literally) standing in the shadows, smoking a cigarette and chatting with his wife and his wife's sister, Rosie Wien.

In Brooklyn, where the case was to be tried, some of the spies began pleading guilty to the two-count indictment, which charged them with violating the Foreign Agents Registration Act (maximum penalty of two years) and the Espionage Act (up to twenty years). The latter outlawed the communication of "information respecting the national defense" to be "used to the injury of the United States or to the advantage of any foreign nation." Lilly Stein made no attempt to deny her guilt. "I have said all that I think is important in this whole case and only ask whom it may concern that they may have some mercy with me even if I have done things which I myself should have judged as wrong," she declared in the first of several statements to the FBI. "While she was in jail, she would often ask the warden to call us as she had some information for us," wrote Agent Newkirk. "All she actually wanted to do was to get out of jail for a few hours to vary the monotony. When we had time we would have her brought to our office and talk to her. Also, while she was in jail she knitted several hats which she gave to various agents she liked to give to their wives." Walter Winchell devoted an item in his newspaper column to the fears that her arrest had caused among the fashionable set. "Many New York men-about-town are quaking," he wrote.

With the newspapers publishing clarifying stories that described Hermann Lang of Norden and Everett Roeder of Sperry as the true "brains" of the outfit (rather than the more copy-worthy Fritz Duquesne), Roeder decided to give up the fight, pleading guilty to the Espionage Act count. "Compared with the other individuals involved in this investigation," wrote the FBI in a postwar summation, "Roeder was probably the greatest producer of detailed technical data relating to national defense materials and production." Winchell crowed that his oft-broadcast warnings about such nefarious figures lurking within Sperry Gyroscope Co. had been proven correct. "It has taken more than a year to confirm these allegations," he wrote. Roeder's conviction ensured that his son wouldn't be permitted to serve overseas with the US Army. His father, Carl Roeder, the esteemed Juilliard professor who saw himself as "a preacher of righteousness," made no comment on the family disgrace.

On Wednesday, September 3, 1941, a jury of nine men and three women was selected in three hours and twenty-five minutes to sit in judgment of the sixteen spies who had pleaded not guilty. (The number would drop to fourteen by the end of the trial.) "Any prejudice because defendant was born in Germany, became a naturalized citizen and is now charged with conspiring to convey defense secrets to the German Reich?" was one of the jury qualification questions. "Have any of you had relatives in European countries who have fled or become refugees from said country?" was another.

On the following day, the American destroyer *Greer* was traveling with mail and supplies to the new US Marine garrison in Iceland when a British plane alerted it to the presence of a U-boat in the vicinity. The *Greer* located *U-652* with the aid of sonar-detection equipment and passed along its location to the RAF, which flew to the spot and dropped depth charges at 10:32 a.m. "The *Greer* continued tracking the submarine until at 12:40 p.m., the U-boat ceased fleeing, turned on the *Greer,* and fired a torpedo that missed," according to the official account from the chief of naval operations. It was the first Nazi shot fired at the US military. "The *Greer* counterattacked with depth charges and the U-boat responded with torpedoes." Neither vessel was hit. Although the *Greer* was clearly the instigator of the confrontation, President Roosevelt was determined to tell a different story more in line with his foreign policy objectives. On Saturday, September 6, the White House announced that he would be delivering a speech of "major importance" on the following Monday. It would be broadcast on all three national networks and translated into fourteen languages for rebroadcast throughout the world. When the president's mother died on Sunday night at age eighty-six, the speech was postponed until Wednesday.

Early on the morning of Monday, September 8, Ellsworth and Sebold, accompanied by four agents, traveled from their temporary quarters in Brooklyn Heights to the courthouse on Washington Street for a final conference with the chief prosecutor, US Attorney Harold Kennedy. "Then I had the agents keep Sebold in the petit jury room just off the courtroom on the third floor," Ellsworth wrote. "I got Bill into the courtroom and let him try out the witness chair. He was very nervous and had given me a real scare recently when he refused to testify unless we guaranteed his people in Germany would not be endangered as a result and unless he had a status other than that of informer with us. I took him to Mr. Connelly who explained all we could do was help him get his folks to America after the war if they wanted to come. We also assured him that he is not an informer but a counterspy of the FBI. He agreed to go ahead with the trial."

At 10:30 a.m., the proceedings began, presided over by Judge Mortimer W. Byers, a silver-haired eminence with an officious manner who was eager to keep things moving. The German defendants mispronounced his name as "Judge Bias," which Duquesne decided was the perfect nickname for him. "A diagram has been prepared of the defendants as they are sitting in the courtroom," the judge said, "and copies will be submitted to the jury to simplify matters." Although the rumor mill was full of speculation about a surprise witness, Kennedy mentioned nothing during his forty-five-minute opening statement, which detailed how the spy plot relied on what the *Times* described as "such out-worn movie props as complicated radio codes, contained in the pages of best-seller novels; micro-photographs of documents and blueprints, telegraphy, and mail drops scattered from China to South America." Fritz Duquesne was characterized as a "spy for forty years" who was so brazen that he concluded a letter to the Chemical Warfare Service in Washington by writing, "Don't worry if this information is confidential, because it is in the hands of a good citizen." Hermann Lang "furnished the particulars about the design" of the Norden bombsight during his 1938 visit to Germany, Kennedy said, pointing to the $3,000 that had been placed in a German bank account as compensation. "Whether the motive of these men was money, hatred of one country, or love of another country, the fact is that they transmitted information which affected our national defense," he said.

After Kennedy was finished, each of the several defense attorneys delivered brief opening remarks. The most fiery was Duquesne's attorney, a Coughlinite activist named Frank Walsh, who made the (inaccurate) argument that the accused were within their rights to provide defense information to Germany "if it does no harm to America," as he said. "We were not at war with Germany in 1936 when this conspiracy allegedly began. We are not at war now. Nothing has been shown to indicate anything transmitted by these defendants affected the United States. They may have affected Britain and others, but not this country." He blamed the whole thing on an unnamed "informer" and "out-and-out double-crosser." This shadowy individual "was the one who schemed, he planned this, he developed, and when the situation became slow, he coerced, he coerced these individuals day by day. 'You have to go out and help Germany.' 'I want this, go and get me this, bring me that.'"

The first witness was a State Department official who testified that none of the sixteen had registered as agents of a foreign
government as required by the law.

The second was Bill Sebold, now revealed as an actor of
consummate skill who had been fooling them all along. The
Herald Tribune called him "a powerful six-footer who speaks
with a heavy German accent and wears an ominous expression."
A female court spectator complained to the *Brooklyn Eagle* that
he "never smiles and he looks and wears his good clothes kinda
sloppily, like my dad." Fritz Duquesne said that he and his fellow
spies "were just suckers for a German wharf rat."

Prosecutor Kennedy walked Sebold through the events of
his early life before turning to the main story, his journey to his
mother's house in Nazi Germany to recover from stomach surgery in early 1939, his coercion into the espionage service, his
training in Hamburg, and his departure for the United States
equipped with the tools to be a coordinating figure in Ast Hamburg's New York operation. "His testimony was a sensation,"
wrote Ellsworth. "The court was packed. The newspapers ate it
up. I have a full file of news clippings on the case. Bill was worn
out. I was proud of him." The *Times'* front-page story on the trial
was headlined, "U.S. Bomb Sight Sold to Germany, Spy Jury Is
Told." The *Herald Tribune's* headline was "Spy Trial Hears Nazis
Got Secret U.S. Bombsight." The *Daily News* wrote, "Trapped
by the Gestapo during a trip to his native Germany, a naturalized American citizen was forced under threat of death to act as
a Nazi spy in America." According to the *Eagle,* the "Gestapo"
employed "the gangster 'or else' threat," a nod perhaps to the
much-discussed murder trial of mobster Louis "Lepke" Buchal-
ter that was about to begin in nearby Kings County Courthouse.
"Hitler Couldn't Scare Sebold, Spy Trial Star," the *Boston Globe*
said. "So He Helped F.B.I. Round Up Nazi Agents in U.S.A."

Nikolaus Ritter was preparing to travel to a new assignment in Rio de Janeiro, from where he would continue his work against the United States, when he received a phone call ordering him to Berlin. Arriving at the Abwehr headquarters at Tirpitzufer 72–76, he says he was presented with a copy of the *Times*. " 'That sonofabitch,' I said. 'That traitor.'" His Abwehr superior, Hans Pickenbrock, responded, "But Ritter, according to your own rules, 'Tramp' was no traitor, not even a spy. He was a man who worked for his new Fatherland." Ritter's career as a spymaster was over.

Asked by the Foreign Office for explanation, Admiral Canaris claimed that suspicions had been aroused by some of Sebold's radio messages but emphasized that agents in the United States had been thwarted in their work by the German embassy and consulates, which provided "neither financial support nor the use of diplomatic couriers for transmittal of information." During a 1945 interrogation with American officials, General Erwin Lahousen, a senior Abwehr official tried at Nuremberg, described how Canaris would talk up "one man in the USA who apparently turned out well, and by whom bombsight was delivered," referring to Hermann Lang. "Canaris constantly emphasized this success particularly, especially in dealing with the *Luftwaffenführungsstab* [Air Force Operations Staff]," probably at a time when the Luftwaffe was losing the war and the spy chief was trying to prove that he was a faithful servant of the regime. He wasn't. He was executed at Flossenbürg concentration camp on April 9, 1945.

On September 9, Sebold continued his narrative up to the point when the Centerport radio station made contact with Hamburg, which dominated the coverage in the next day's papers. The *Times* called the communications link "probably the greatest hoax perpetrated on the vaunted Nazi military intelligence to date." The *Daily Mirror* said the FBI played "Nazi espionage heads in Germany for a bunch of suckers." A total of 468 messages—301 from Centerport to Hamburg; 167 from Hamburg to Centerport—were exchanged via a cipher system based on Rachel Field's novel that left everyone befuddled. "Neither the jury or the spectators seemed able to fully understand the code method after it was outlined," said the *Herald Tribune*.

During the afternoon session, the prosecutor paused in his questioning of Sebold to allow defense attorneys to begin cross-examination. Hermann Lang's counsel, George W. Herz, a German-speaking attorney based in Ridgewood, emerged as Sebold's principal antagonist. Herz went after him for initially entering the country illegally when he jumped ship at Galveston in 1922 ("Did the thought ever occur to you that perhaps you were violating the laws of the United States by remaining in the country without notifying some American immigration official?"); for once working at a Communist-affiliated summer camp in the Catskills ("Did you have to sign any pledge of allegiance to the Communist Party before you got the job?"); and for returning to Germany at a time when it was universally regarded as an outlaw nation ("And by that time you were able to read the New York newspapers and understand what was in them?"). Sebold grew angry when Herz asked for the "names and addresses" of his relatives back in Germany. "I do not think I have to tell that in the presence of all these people," he said. The judge agreed, eventually castigating Herz for persisting in a line of questioning that is "nothing more than an attempt to intimidate him by fear of reprisals." Ellsworth wrote, "Very trying day but Bill is over a bad hump."

Yet on the following day, the grilling continued. Herz made a point of noting that Sebold's wife did not travel with him to Germany in 1939, explaining to the judge, "I am interested in showing that this man did not lead a normal family life. I have that right. And if I can show that he went from place to place without his wife, the jury has a right to draw such inferences of the circumstances under which he lived as they may see fit." Herz brought up the time Sebold went to Bellevue Hospital complaining of stomach trouble and was admitted to the psych ward after arguing with a doctor, which was gleefully picked up by Duquesne's counsel, Frank Walsh. After a stay of "twenty-one days, two weeks, I don't remember," Sebold said, he was examined by "a big doctor there, from Brooklyn, Professor Dr. Koenig. He laid me out and touched my stomach and he said, 'That man has a terrific adhesion on the stomach, he has to be operated on immediately,' and I went up to the surgical ward."

"In the interest of clarity or accuracy," Walsh asked, "would you mind telling me how long you were in the psychiatric ward before you were released and declared not to be feebleminded?"

"I object on the ground that question is not proper," Kennedy interjected.

"The objection is sustained," responded Judge Byers. "And I warn you not to ask any such question as that."

But Herz was the instigator of one of the most dramatic moments of the trial.

"Did you say to me a minute ago, or did I misunderstand— did you say you agreed to become a spy because you had to give in?" he asked.

"Well, they had me in a corner," Sebold responded.

"You mean they threatened to use physical violence?"

"Well, they don't do such things," Sebold said. "They do that in a nice way." He explained that explicitly stated threats weren't necessary in a terror state such as Nazi Germany.

"But you did agree to become a spy?" Herz asked.

"Sure, wouldn't you?"

"No, I wouldn't."

"All right, then you lie down and die, or goose-step for the rest of your life," Sebold snapped.

It was Sebold at his best. "He gets really good under fire and his mind seems to work better," wrote Ellsworth. The defense attorneys "sought to belittle the former German army machine gunner with ridicule," wrote the *Mirror*. "They attacked his veracity. They engaged in sharp argument with the court while attempting to refute Sebold's claim to having been accepted by the Gestapo as an agent. But they failed to alter his story."

On September 11, President Roosevelt made maximum use of the *Greer* incident, announcing that the US military would now protect convoys of merchant ships bound for Great Britain and, more provocatively, be permitted to "shoot on sight" at any Axis submarines or raiders operating in "waters which we deem necessary for our defense." From this date forward, the United States and Nazi Germany engaged in what amounted to an undeclared war on the high seas of the Atlantic. Following FDR's address, Charles Lindbergh took the stage at an America First event in Des Moines, Iowa, and discredited himself and his cause by stating plainly what he had long implied. He said "the Jewish" were one of three groups (also "the British" and "the Roosevelt administration") pushing the country into war. He chillingly suggested that Jews would be subject to a violent backlash if the United States became involved, which can be heard as both a provocation and a threat. "Instead of agitating for war, the Jewish groups in this country should be opposing it in every possible way for they will be among the first to feel its consequences," he said. In addition to its anti-Semitism, Lindbergh's speech was noteworthy for its defeatism, its sense that America wasn't up to the task of confronting German industrial and military might. We are unprepared for a war "which cannot be won without sending our soldiers across the ocean to force a landing on a hostile coast against armies stronger than our own."

During the following week in Brooklyn, the nation was provided with a glimpse of the advanced techniques that were already being deployed against the enemy. After Agents Friedemann and Johnson testified about Duquesne's single visit to the Forty-Second Street office—sound recordings were not admissible—Judge Byers made the following announcement: "Members of the jury, I am going to ask you to come over to the other side of the courtroom. You will occupy the seats on this side. It may not be possible for some of you to see from the chairs, some of you may have to stand. If you do not observe everything, please interrupt and tell us." The courtroom was darkened and Johnson's film was projected onto a five-foot screen behind the jury box. The American relationship with the hidden surveillance camera was born as the rapt audience watched twelve soundless minutes of Fritz Duquesne glancing throughout Room 627, sitting down opposite a partially obscured Sebold, reaching into his sock for his spy secrets, and conversing animatedly. When the lights came up, reporters noted that Duquesne had a broad grin on his face. "All my life I wanted to be in the movies, and when I made it, what do I do?" he said, according to Agent Newkirk. "Sit there and scratch my ass and pick my nose." The *Times* scoffed at how the government "resorted" to "the use of motion pictures in open court." Wrote Ellsworth, "I think Duquesne is convicted now."

The only serious obstacle remaining for Sebold was Hermann Lang. He spent days going over the "Lang notes" with Ellsworth, attempting to get straight just what had happened during each of the nine meetings. "Up early and had Bill give me his testimony on Lang," Ellsworth wrote on September 23. "Seemed to be sure of himself." During that day's session, Sebold "did okay," he wrote. In describing a visit to Queens on July 11, 1940, Sebold recalled asking Lang if a cousin of his who had just left the apartment knew "anything about his transactions." Lang said the man didn't. Lang was "the only man who knows the American secret." Sebold had slightly flubbed the line. According to the FBI account, Lang had told Sebold of his exclusive knowledge of "the *great* American secret." On the following day, Sebold had more stumbles during Herz's cross-examination. "Bill did fairly well in the morning but got all mixed up on dates," Ellsworth wrote. "In view of his confused condition when court adjourned for lunch, I did not go near Bill during recess but ate lunch at Joe's Place with [Special Agent in Charge Thomas] Donegan and two Navy commanders. The first question Herz asked Bill at 2 p.m. was whether I had refreshed Sebold's mind, etc., during the recess. So we outsmarted them. Bill did a lot better in the afternoon and got in good evidence on the bombsight information, on bombsight production at Norden's factory, on new experiments, etc., which Lang had given him."

But did the Germans really have the Norden bombsight? In Washington that week, the US Navy's Bureau of Ordnance sent a confidential message to the undersecretary of the navy, "Necessity for Safeguarding Security of the Norden Bombsight," which delivered the official view of Lang's theft in its final paragraph: "The Bureau of Ordnance does not believe that Hermann Lang, the alleged spy now on trial in New York, was able to impart sufficient information to Germany when he visited that country on vacation from the Norden company in 1938, to enable the Germans to duplicate the bombsight. Supporting this belief are the fact that a German bombsight manufactured in 1939 and turned over to us by the British does not possess the features of the Norden sight, and the fact that German horizontal bombing of ships at sea is very poor and shows no improvement since the beginning of the war." During a press conference, Secretary of War Harry Stimson didn't help the prosecution when he said there was "no reason to believe" the Germans had obtained the details of the Norden, which led George Herz to raise a noise about calling Stimson to appear as a witness on behalf of Lang. "I think it would be an idle trip for me," Stimson told reporters, "and I hope I will not have to make it." He didn't. The accepted view among "authoritative" sources, according to the Associated Press reporter covering the trial, was that the Germans "weren't able to steal enough information about the Norden to manufacture it properly." After the trial, Norden president Ted Barth told the papers that Lang was a "fool" who was watched day and night and couldn't have snuck "so much as a piece of scrap paper" past plant security.

The United States would enter World War II with the myth of its secret bombsight fully intact.

On the evening of October 16/17, a U-boat fired three torpedoes at the USS *Kearny*, which was escorting a merchant convoy about 350 miles south and west of Iceland. This time one of them struck. Initial reports indicated no casualties. On the next day, the House of Representatives passed legislation that permitted US merchant ships to be outfitted with guns, which President Roosevelt hoped would be amended in the Senate to allow US merchant ships (thus armed) to transport war materials into combat zones and belligerent ports, ending the "carry" portion of the Neutrality Act. Then on October 19, the US Navy announced that eleven of the *Kearny*'s sailors were "missing." They would soon be confirmed as the first US combat deaths of the war. "America has been attacked," Roosevelt said in a radio address. "The USS *Kearny* is not just a Navy ship. She belongs to every man, woman, and child in this nation. Illinois, Alabama, California, North Carolina, Ohio, Louisiana, Texas, Pennsylvania, Georgia, Arkansas, New York, Virginia—those are the home states of the honored dead and wounded of the *Kearny*. Hitler's torpedo was directed at every American, whether he lives on our seacoasts or in the innermost part of the nation, far from the seas and far from the guns and tanks of the marching hordes of would-be conquerors of the world."

After another week of testimony and films focused on a parade of other spies, the prosecution began debating how to finish its part of the case. Charles Appel, a handwriting expert from the FBI Lab in Washington, suggested bringing up Leo Waalen's attempt to send information to Germany about the *Robin Moor*, which would be a convenient way to remind jurors that the defendants were in league with the U-boat assassins now openly warring with the US Navy. Later in the day, Waalen's list of eight sailings, given to Sebold in the Forty-Second Street office on April 28, was duly introduced into evidence. But the merchant ship was not mentioned until a defense attorney, David Kumble, picked up the document and began reading aloud from it. When he came to the words "S.S. *Robin Moor*," Harold Kennedy "could not contain himself and blurted out, 'What?'" wrote Ellsworth. The entire defense table jumped up and demanded a mistrial. "That was the boat that was torpedoed and sunk, and the jury knows it," one of the lawyers protested. "It was done intentionally by Mr. Kennedy to inflame the minds of the jurors." But the judge said he hadn't heard a thing. "There was a big scene," wrote Ellsworth. "Judge Byers refused a mistrial and we had our climax."

It was now time for Fritz Duquesne to perform one last strut on the public stage. "When were you born?" he was asked upon taking the stand in his own defense. "In 1877 or 1878," he responded, setting the tone. He spoke of matriculating at the elite École Spéciale Militaire de Saint-Cyr in France; visiting the battlefields of the Russo-Japanese War of 1904–5 as a cadet observer (not a combatant); receiving an appointment to the Belgian Congo Army by King Leopold; searching for rubber plantations in South America; attempting to convince Washington politicians to introduce hippos in the United States as a food source; working as publicity man for former ambassador Joseph Kennedy's film company, Robertson-Cole. He was not a spy, he said. He was an inventor—of "a vaginal device, a medical instrument, for the use of the natives in the Congo"; "a means of keeping airplane engines warm so they could make a quick take-off"; "a method of catching animals doing away with the cruelty in the way I saw them caught in my childhood"; "a submarine mine called a magnetic mine to use in war"; and a "float dock for pontoon airplanes." After his arrest by the FBI, he claimed he was "cross-questioned, bulldozed, and bully-razed"; examined by a doctor who "inserted a steel arrangement in me"; invited to commit suicide with a pistol; forced to drink washing soda that made him "so sick that I nearly went mad"; asked "all sorts of questions about my sexual relations"; marched naked past Sebold; required to read verses of Shakespeare; and accused of being "a leader of the German spies in America."

"I stayed there for some time," he said of the office where he was questioned. "I don't know how long because I was very sick. In the room was a mattress covered over with blood or excrement, sheets of hardness on it, and I stayed there, and these men returned later and they interrogated again along the same lines. It is hard for me to go on with this thing."

"It would be," said Kennedy.

Duquesne called Sebold a "very dangerous lunatic" who tried to convince him to contribute Nazi money (to be supplied by Sebold) to the America First Committee and plant dynamite (supplied by Sebold) in President Roosevelt's church in Hyde Park. He claimed that Sebold once flashed "French pornographic pictures" of Lilly Stein during a meeting in City Hall Park "and spoke in laudatory remarks about her capacity as a sweetheart."

Asked about the hard-to-refute footage from Forty-Second Street, this son of the nineteenth century had a difficult time coming up with an explanation. "They were not my activities," he claimed. "They were fake activities."

Of the famous sock incident, he said, "As I sat down the bandage on my leg slipped over my shoe and I pulled it up. While I was pulling it up a bunch of things I had in my pocket fell out of my pocket and I picked them up. The taking of anything out of my stocking never happened."

"There is no use saying anything to the witness or his lawyer," Kennedy told the judge at one point, "but it seems to me that the jury should be instructed that these picturesque words that he slips in are improper, and the jury should know it."

"His talks are so fantastic," wrote Ellsworth. "I hope the jury realizes he is a liar."

Hermann Lang left an entirely different impression during his turn in the witness chair. He spoke so softly that George Herz repeatedly asked him to speak up. "Will you please get— sort of mad and talk as loud as you can." The *Times* described Lang as "sad-faced." The AP said he was "mild and clerkish." In his demure manner, he denied participating in the Munich Beer Hall Putsch, knowing Adolf Hitler or Ernst Udet, or joining a pro-Nazi organization in the United States. (He told the FBI that the DAB "was just more for pastime, playing games, having parties.") His alibi was this: Yes, his Norden coworker Fritz "Pop" Sohn introduced him to Nikolaus Ritter during the latter's recruitment trip to the United States, which conforms with Ritter's postwar story, but Ritter never spoke to him about the Norden bombsight, which doesn't. Lang said he went to Germany in the summer of 1938 because of his wife's poor health and was horribly abused by Nazi officials upon his arrival at Hamburg. "When I got down from the steamer and went to the custom agent—(the witness at this point cried)," according to the transcript. Court was recessed for five minutes while he regained his composure. When he returned, he described how he and his wife were segregated from the other passengers, had their baggage closely checked, and were threatened with imprisonment in Dachau if they complained. Allowed to continue to Berlin, he registered with the authorities as required by the law. He soon received a letter from Ritter, who asked to meet him on a street corner. From there, the two went to the Air Ministry, where Lang was browbeaten for information about the Norden. He said that no amount of threatening would induce him to give up the great American secret.

But the story ran on page 27 in the *New York Times* ("Mechanic Denies Bombsight Sale") because of what happened in the North Atlantic in the hours before Lang took the stand. *U-552* delivered a single torpedo into the USS *Reuben James,* which was one of five American destroyers protecting a British merchant convoy of more than forty ships in the waters near Iceland. The old tin can sank within minutes, becoming the first US military vessel lost during the war. "Fear 'Heavy' Loss of Life on Destroyer," reported the *Daily News* on its front page. "Well, a hundred men went down in that dark watery grave," sang the Almanac Singers, who had been converted to the interventionist cause by Stalin's sudden alliance with the Western democracies. "When that good ship went down only forty-four were saved." A total of 115 sailors were killed in a blatant act of war, but the president didn't feel that public opinion was outraged enough to markedly alter American policy. Congress responded by barely passing the amended revision of the Neutrality Act that allowed armed merchant ships to carry munitions to combatant nations. In the Senate, the vote was 50–37; in the House, 212–194. Apparently only a truly spectacular act would jolt America into greater engagement. Few expected that it would come from the increasingly belligerent and expansionist Empire of Japan.

On the Monday following the *Reuben James* attack, Lang testified about his contacts with Sebold, saying he agreed to meet with him because he wanted to protect his family back in the Bavarian village of Schwarzenbach am Wald. "He said, 'Well, if you don't want to work, we know a nice way to make you work if I report it to the other side,'" Lang said. "And he told me, 'You have relatives out there. It will not be so good for you and for them.'" The plan was "to kid him along." Lang concocted a tale about Sebold's offering Lilly Stein up for Lang's carnal delectation. "He said, 'Are you interested? I could make an appointment for you. If you are interested and want to have a nice time, why, I could fix it up.' So I looked at him and said, 'What ideas you got? You know I am married and what I am interested in another girl?'"

Ellsworth admitted that Lang's previous testimony about his trip to Germany was somewhat convincing, "but he lied consistently today about his meetings with Sebold so now I can't believe any of his story. He must have been very deeply involved with Ritter and his crowd in Germany."

All that was left of the defense case, Ellsworth wrote, were "lies, lies, lies." Franz Stigler, the baker, repeated the popular story about Sebold's threatening behavior. "Look at the English Americans—they go up and down the street, doing everything for their side," he quoted Sebold as saying. "But you guys, when you get your citizenship papers, you'd go over to Germany and shoot your own mother." Leo Waalen said Sebold promised to "make it hard" for his parents in Danzig if he refused to provide intelligence on Allied ships. In fact, Sebold often made a point of warning the spies against participating in the conspiracy. "I said, 'You might go to jail for ten to twenty years, you better look out,'" Sebold said in reference to a conversation with Waalen. "He said, 'I am going up. I can paddle my own canoe.'" The other principal accusation was that Sebold was a Communist, which was presumably enough to sow doubts about his character. Duquesne said Sebold was a true believer who only agreed to work for the Nazi regime when "they poured hot water in his bowel through a funnel." A defense attorney suggested Sebold was once known in New York by a Russian name, Siebufsky. Erich Strunck, the waiter, said Sebold spoke to him about the glories of the workers' struggle as they listened to soapbox orators in Columbus Circle. "If you are interested in Communism, I can fix you up with the party," he claimed Sebold told him. "Whenever you lose your job on the ship, they take care of you. They give you a job and everything. I am an old-timer myself." In a postwar interview, Agent Johnson said the FBI never uncovered a bit of evidence that Sebold was a Red.

But occasionally the defendants let the truth slip out. Late in the trial, Paul Scholz, the salesman at Germania Book and Specialty who was part of Carl Reuper's ring, was called to the stand. "Scholz, when asked by the clerk Scotty to raise his hand to be sworn in, came to brisk attention and gave the Nazi salute, then realized what he had done and raised his hand high above his head and took the oath," wrote Ellsworth.

On Wednesday, December 3, the defense attorneys began their closing arguments. "The fact is that as much of an adventurer and as much as a wanderer Duquesne has been," said Frank Walsh, "so also has been Sebold. Sebold went from San Francisco to South America to Germany, and back and forth all his life. His family life, as far as it has been developed in this case, has been almost negative." Walsh argued that the German-born defendants were being targeted because they belonged to an ethnicity that was unfairly tarred by the broad brush of public opprobrium. "Where else as a German or German American living in New York, living in Manhattan, where else can he go when he has an hour off other than Yorkville? That is where they congregate. That is where they have these casinos and these *Bräus*, these beer places. That is the way these people enjoy themselves. Are you going to say merely because he lives in Yorkville, or he went to the German bookshop or some other place, that smacks of Hitler—Nazi? Why, that is not so."

Walsh concluded that Sebold was "a scoundrel."

Court adjourned for the weekend on Friday, December 5.

On Sunday, December 7, the debate over American neutrality ended. Pearl Harbor had been attacked.

That evening, President Roosevelt issued Proclamation 2525, which subjected Japanese nationals to the Alien Enemies Act of 1798, giving the FBI the power to summarily arrest and detain the "potentially dangerous" noncitizens on its Custodial Detention List.

On Monday at 12:30 p.m., FDR delivered his seven-minute "Day of Infamy" address to a joint session of Congress, asking for a declaration of war against Japan but making no mention of the other Axis nations. The vote was 82 to 0 in the Senate; 388 to 1 in the House. In the afternoon, he signed Proclamations 2526 and 2527, which extended the Alien Enemies Act to German and Italian nationals because of "threatened" invasion or "predatory incursion" from Germany and Italy. "I don't care much about the Italians," Roosevelt told Attorney General Biddle. "They are a lot of opera singers, but the Germans are different, they might be dangerous." Biddle telegraphed the news to J. Edgar Hoover, but the raids had already begun in German neighborhoods.

"With Your Honor's permission, Mr. Kennedy, Mr. Foreman, and ladies and gentlemen of the jury," began George Herz in Brooklyn federal court that morning. "There is almost a hushed silence that pervades our city and our country today, the silence that comes before a storm or before a hurricane. It seems as if a great deal has taken place since last weekend when we were here. There is a great deal on my mind today as an American besides the fate of Hermann Lang, and apparently there must be a great deal on your minds as Americans besides this case. But nevertheless, we as Americans are proud of our American heritage, as we have a duty here which we must face, and as Americans cannot shirk, and that duty, on my part, I propose to perform, and I know that you will also do your best.

"It would be an easy thing for you to leave this courtroom and to come back within five minutes and say, 'We find them all guilty,'" Herz continued. "That would be an easy thing. But that would not be the American thing to do, and that kind of act on your part would have a greater tendency to create hysteria throughout the country than anything else, because these men are entitled to their civil rights."

Herz attacked Sebold's "ridiculous story" of how he was induced to become a spy in Germany and described Lang "as a dumb-witted, shy working man" who was the true victim here. But Herz knew his effort was doomed. As he told an interviewer in 1973, "I could see the hatred in the jury's eyes. They were just literally manifesting their hatred for me because I had the nerve to get up there and speak on behalf of Lang."

After Herz finished on December 9, another of the defense attorneys rose to speak, Charles Oberwager, a German American civic leader who had advocated on behalf of the community during the bad old days of the Great War. He celebrated the patriotism of those "men of German flesh and German blood who helped lay the foundation of this country and who helped to defend it." He spoke of Peter Muhlenberg, the Revolutionary War–era clergyman who "wore his robe on a Sunday, and after he delivered his sermon, as you will recall, in Virginia, on Sunday, he took his robe off, and beneath the robe was the uniform for which Americans stand today and stood then." Oberwager likened the accused spies to "men like Carl Schurz, who after he was here eight or nine years became the American ambassador to Spain, sought a United States senatorship at Wisconsin, and became a major general in the Civil War—closely allied to that great president of blessed memory, Abraham Lincoln." Oberwager urged the jurors to remember that "the mere place of birth, the mere speaking of a language, or the reading of foreign newspapers is not in itself an indication of one being any less loyal as an American citizen." He sarcastically characterized Sebold as "the holy individual, the innocent man."

On December 10, Harold Kennedy began the prosecution's summation. He defended his star witness as a patriot who, after he was pressured into the service of the Nazi state, refused to commit a single act on its behalf. "Sebold said, 'They are getting me to do a dirty thing and I am going to get out of this country as quickly as I can, and when I get out, I am going to divulge it to the authorities.' . . . Now, isn't that the conduct of an honest man who is invited to stick a dagger in the back of his adopted country?" Kennedy pointed out that Sebold's experience in Germany closely mirrored the (made-up) tale Lang had told about how he was harassed by Nazi agents in Hamburg and Berlin. "Now isn't that so?" Kennedy said. "The only difference is this: that Sebold would not go along, and I will prove to you that Lang did. That is the difference."

Kennedy continued addressing the jury during the following day, December 11, as it was becoming known that Adolf Hitler had joined with his Japanese ally and declared war on the United States. Mussolini immediately followed the Führer's lead. At just after noon, President Roosevelt sent a written message to Congress seeking two additional declarations of war. Both were passed with no dissenting votes and signed by his hand at a few minutes after 3:00 p.m. "Generally, it seemed, Yorkville will remain loyal to the United States," wrote one of the reporters assigned to gauge the mood in the country's most famous German enclave. "Here and there on the street, men and women were outspoken on this point. In other places the men were silent and looked sullen." Employees at the two movie houses along Eighty-Sixth Street told the press that German-language films would no longer be shown. "Why do they stop the pictures?" a middle-aged woman wanted to know. "Let them take the Nazis, but not the pictures." The *Post* took a photograph of the new message on the marquee of the Garden Theater: CLOSED FOR ALTERATIONS. By this point, the FBI had seized 1,002 Reich citizens throughout the country.

"Just think of the effect," Kennedy told jurors of the possibility of acquittals. "Just think of the joy in Yorkville at what they can get away with on American jurors. You know, we haven't got them all. We will, I think. We will get many of them. But just think of the rest of them sitting around, using the tactics that these people have used, and excused their conduct as these people have attempted to excuse it."

Judge Byers began his charge to the jury at 10:30 a.m. on the next day, December 12. He pointed out that a man "is entitled to believe that the German race is a superior race and that the world was created in order that the Germans might dominate it . . . so long as he does nothing to carry those views into effect, to the detriment of the United States of America." Noting that twelve of the fourteen defendants were naturalized Americans, he remarked on the "sanctity of the citizenship oath, which requires that an alien forswear 'absolutely and forever' allegiances to all governments but that of the United States." The newly sworn American "does not agree that he will conduct himself as a hybrid citizen of two countries or more, nor does he, on taking the oath, agree to aid the country of his birth in its conduct of a war against another country while he poses as an American citizen." Judge Byers seemed to foreclose the last possibility of acquittal when he informed the jurors that "the safety of Great Britain became a matter of the national defense of the United States" when the president signed the Lend-Lease bill into law on March 11, 1941, which meant the defendants couldn't find succor in the claim that they were merely out to hurt the Brits.

The jury was given the case at 1:00 p.m. After a lunch break, deliberations began at 2:30 p.m., lasting for four hours until dinner. Resuming at 8:20 p.m., the jury reached a decision at just before midnight. The *Times* recorded that Hermann Lang's wife, Betty, was the only close relative of the accused in attendance. The verdict was never in doubt. They were all guilty. The United States had achieved its first success as a wartime power.

And Bill Sebold had already disappeared.

EPILOGUE

Yes, such are their laws; the man who fights, and kills, and plunders, is honored; but he who served his country as a spy, no matter how faithfully, no matter how honestly, lives to be reviled, or dies like the vilest criminal.

—James Fenimore Cooper
from *The Spy* (1821)

He'd always loved the town he called Frisco.

By the middle of November, with the trial entering its final weeks, Sebold was preparing to become the first participant in an early version of the witness protection program. With Hoover's approval, Ellsworth was assigned to pack up the Sebolds' belongings and escort them to a new life on the West Coast.

But first they had to travel to Washington to complete necessary paperwork for the move. On November 21, Ellsworth, another agent, and Bill and Helen were four of six passengers on an American Airlines flight from Newark to the just-opened National Airport. "That airport is a dream and beyond my powers of description," wrote Ellsworth in a letter to his wife and parents. "We took a cab into town and drove to the Dodge Hotel up near the Union Station and next to the Capitol grounds." After settling into connecting rooms on the third floor, the group walked down Pennsylvania Avenue to the Bureau offices. "Bill and Helen were all eyes at the immense government buildings all along the way." During a tour of the FBI facilities, Sebold was allowed the use of a Thompson submachine gun in the basement shooting range. "He was shaking all over with excitement when he had fired twenty shots," Ellsworth wrote. "Then in the gym I put him on an electric horse and shook the stuffings out of him, then put him on an electric bicycle which runs your legs and at the same time sways your body back and forth at the waist. He was worn out after that."

They devoted the following day, a Saturday, to sightseeing. "Bill was entranced with the quietness, the calmness of people while eating, the leisure of the waitresses, the clear air, the lack of elevated, street car, taxi, noises, etc., and started one of his health and good living lectures," Ellsworth wrote. They visited the new Supreme Court building and the US Capitol. "Congress was not in session but we enjoyed it all the same. Bill said he was beginning to understand America a little now. The history and art surprised him." Then they drove out to George Washington's estate in Mount Vernon. "Here was Bill's outstanding item of the trip," Ellsworth wrote. "He admired the simple mansion, the outhouse organization, that is a building for the kitchen, one for the spinning, one for the tools, one for the smoke house, the green house, the laundry, etc., each with its living quarters for the slaves doing the work there. We spent much time there and Bill said that was the kind of a life he wanted—a little kingdom not dependent on anyone for its existence."

After another day as tourists, they checked out of their hotel, returned to the airport, and took an 8:00 p.m. flight to La Guardia. The following week was full of downtime that allowed Ellsworth to spend two days escorting *Life* magazine photographer Ralph Morse to the principal locations of the story for the celebratory post-trial article. On Saturday, November 29, Ellsworth met with Harold Kennedy in Brooklyn. "He said he is through with Sebold and me so we can leave any time," he wrote. "I feel like a kid all of a sudden." On December 3, Ellsworth and the Sebolds boarded a train at Penn Station for a four-day journey to San Francisco. They arrived at 8:25 a.m. on December 7. "Bill is blooming like a flower with his freedom and lack of hiding attitude," Ellsworth wrote.

In the afternoon, they learned that the world had changed. "Went to FBI office at 1 p.m. for a car and found [Special Agent in Charge Nat] Pieper and all agents on duty," he wrote. "Japanese planes have just bombed our bases at Hawaii and at Philippine Islands and have sunk two battleships." Agents were being dispatched to seize Japanese enemy aliens. "Newspapers are screaming WAR. Radios are almost exclusively war talk. We seem to be suddenly a united people—Senator Wheeler has even declared we should now go to war in earnest.

"I step off the train expecting to be in a land of quiet rest and anticipate a vacation with my family and a couple of hours later we are at war."

On December 9, Ellsworth, his wife, Nell, and the Sebolds enjoyed a last meal together at a Chinatown nightclub with a floor show. On the next day, the two men parted. "Hard to realize I am leaving a man I have lived and worked with for nearly two years," Ellsworth wrote. "This seems to be about the final chapter in another phase of my life."

On January 3, 1942, Judge Byers sentenced the thirty-three convicted spies before a courtroom crowded with their friends and relatives. "On account of the war I expect the judge to be harsh," Duquesne had written to a friend. "I am innocent and that is what is driving me mad. I cannot believe it all and yet I *am* here."

Duquesne and Lang were each given eighteen years on the Espionage Act count and two years on the Foreign Agents Registration Act count, with the terms to be served concurrently. "He of all men knew the value of the Norden bombsight," the judge said of Lang. "He of all men knew to what use it might be put by the 'chivalrous' powers of the Axis in waging their war against civilization." Roeder got sixteen years on the Espionage Act violation; Stein received ten years for espionage and two on FARA. Franz "the baker" Stigler got sixteen and two; Paul "Fink" Fehse, fifteen and two; Leo Waalen, twelve and two; Erwin "the butcher" Siegler, ten and two; and Erich "the waiter" Strunck, ten and two. Of the less severe punishments, the DAB lecturer George Schuh, the bookstore clerk Max Blank, and the Little Casino owner Richard Eichenlaub each received eighteen months in prison and a $1,000 fine. "It was remarked by some of the court attachés who have followed the course of the long trial that the trip of the defendants across the Federal Building corridors last night did not reveal the jauntiness and confidence that marked their conduct throughout the trial," wrote one reporter.

With the assistance of the Bureau, the Sebolds moved into a small house in Walnut Creek, California, a short ride from San Francisco. "I am a mechanic in a tank shop," he wrote to Ellsworth on March 25, 1942. "I had my wish and I like it very much." Like many in wartime America, Sebold heeded the government's call to reduce pressure on food supplies. "I have everything planned and spaded for the Victory Garden," he wrote. "We planted all kinds of vegetables and also sweet corn. The trees are in bloom now. You should see the place. I feel like a sauerkraut baron. I have two dogs—a black pinscher and big Alaskan husky, a real dog. I did a lot of remodeling on my garage, the chicken house, and the house." He added, "When this emergency is over, I want to go into the ranching business."

EPILOGUE

For the rest of the war, German, Japanese, and Italian nationals (along with a few Hungarians and Romanians) were rounded up by the FBI on suspicion of retaining loyalty to the Axis regimes of their native lands. They were brought without the right of legal representation before an Alien Enemy Control Unit hearing board, which was established by the Justice Department to sift evidence (often hearsay from spiteful neighbors or business rivals) and determine whether the arrestee posed enough of a threat to be interned. Five such boards were established in Manhattan. Active members of the Bund and the DAB, both of which shuttered operations upon the American declaration of war, were automatically eligible for confinement. "33 Aliens Seized in Yorkville Raids," reported the *Times* in a story from March 5, 1942. Confiscated were "many cameras and short wave–equipped radios, one fine photographic enlarger, a modern, compact radio transmitting and receiving apparatus, sixteen rifles, five pistols, a blackjack, a vicious trench knife, a Sperry 'marching compass,' and chemicals capable of being compounded into explosives." The Bureau's sweeps increased in frequency following the capture of eight Nazi saboteurs who landed in two U-boats in Florida and Long Island in June 1942, a farcical mission that was made necessary by the convictions of so many potential bomb-planters in the Sebold case. During the month of July alone, 350 alleged Nazi supporters of Reich citizenship were arrested in the New York area.

In Los Angeles, Jim Ellsworth received a request from J. Edgar Hoover "to call on Bill Sebold at once and warn him to be very cautious as his life might be in danger as revealed to the Bureau by one of the eight saboteurs." Ellsworth took the train to San Francisco, caught a cab, and rode out to Walnut Creek, where he spotted Sebold walking on the street. "Went home with him to his little country place and Helen and had a big German supper, talked about the spy case and old times and I got acquainted with his ferocious watchdog," Ellsworth wrote in his diary. "I spent two days and nights with them and thoroughly enjoyed myself. They are being cautious and I hope no harm ever comes to them." After trial by military commission, six of the saboteurs were electrocuted in the District of Columbia jail on August 8, 1942. The two others were spared because of the cooperation they provided to the FBI. One of them, George Dasch, later wrote a memoir that detailed how he was given a file on Sebold during his training period in Germany. "What do you think of that son of a bitch?" the Abwehr organizer asked. "I tell you, there is no stone big enough for him to hide under. We will get him."

In total, 10,905 ethnic Germans were incarcerated in seven internment camps in five states during the war. Among them were a handful of the lesser spies from the Duquesne ring who, stripped of their US citizenship, needed somewhere to go following the completion of their terms. After fifteen months in the federal prison in Sandstone, Minnesota, Heinz Stade, the cellist in the Little Casino cabal who claimed to have knowledge of the (still-unsolved) World's Fair bombing, was transferred to the facility in Crystal City, Texas. He became a music instructor there.

The government also initiated several high-profile prosecutions of prominent Nazi agitators of American citizenship who, it was charged, maintained the movement under the guise of German singing societies and sports clubs. Dozens of top officials of the Bund and the DAB were charged with violations of the FARA, the Selective Service Act, or the Alien Registration Act. In late 1942, twenty-nine Bundists were targeted for conspiracy to counsel resistance to the draft. The following year, twenty-seven DABers were accused of acting as American representatives of the German Labor Front, the Nazi workers' organization. Prosecutors had little trouble in gaining convictions until the so-called Great Sedition Trial of 1944, which attempted to show that American rightists had joined with German Bundists in a Hitler-directed conspiracy "to interfere with, impair, and influence the loyalty, morale, and discipline" of the US armed forces and "to cause insubordination, mutiny, and refusal of duty." The trial dragged on for months until the presiding judge died of a heart attack and a mistrial was ordered. In 1946, a federal appeals judge dismissed the charges, saying a new trial would be a "travesty of justice."

In October 1943, when the federal prosecutor in Newark brought espionage charges against seven leaders of the DAB, he gave due credit to "Harry Sebold" for laying the groundwork. "For more than a year, the FBI knew of every move made by the enemy agents," said US Attorney Thorn Lord during a press conference. "As a result of this knowledge, the activities of most of the defendants named in yesterday's indictment came to the fore." The most prominent of the convicted was the national director of the DAB, a malign figure named Fritz Schroeder, who was described as a close friend of Hermann Lang's. "Now, Fritz Schroeder was not in the Duquesne case, was he?" a defense attorney asked an FBI agent during the trial. "He was under investigation at that time," the agent responded. Although the FBI uncovered a handful of Nazi spies operating under Reich direction in the United States during the war, the Sebold investigation "placed a decisive check on German espionage operations, from which it has found it difficult to recover," wrote the *Times* in February 1945. As early as October 1944, Hoover was boasting on CBS radio that "our Axis undercover enemies have been met and completely defeated."

German Americans were not subject to the virulent anti-Hun

prejudice that infected America during World War I. Instead, the Japanese suffered from the taint of collective guilt. Without the slightest evidence that they constituted a fifth column, 120,000 Japanese residents living on the Pacific Coast (78,000 of them US citizens) were forcibly evacuated to "planned communities" under War Department supervision in an initiative that existed outside of the Justice Department's Alien Enemy Control Unit. Hoover voiced his opposition, believing that the problem of treacherous foreign agents should be handled case by case. He told Attorney General Biddle there was no evidence that Japanese Americans "have been associated with any espionage activity ashore or that there has been any illicit shore-to-ship signaling, either by radio or lights." In 1988, the Congress issued a formal apology for actions that "were motivated largely by racial prejudice, wartime hysteria, and a failure of political leadership."

After working at the US Army's Benicia Arsenal from March to September 1942, Sebold received a two-month leave of absence for educational training that was extended when he ran into health problems. He told Agent E. F. McCarthy of the San Francisco FBI office that pills prescribed to treat a thyroid problem had revived an old shoulder injury. "It might be stated also that Sebold was found to be in a rather nervous condition and it was determined by Agent McCarthy that Sebold is worried because he has not been able to go to drafting school or engineering school as he had planned and he still is on leave from the Benicia Arsenal without pay," according to a report of November 10, 1942. "Sebold was advised by Agent McCarthy that he should cease worrying and that he should do everything possible to get himself into the proper frame of mind." He didn't go back to his job after his health improved because a copy of *Reader's*

Digest with an article that mentioned his name was being passed around the workplace. "The Bureau is of the opinion that in view of Sebold's hesitancy to return to his employment at the Benicia Arsenal in view of the fact that several employees know of his true identity, he should not be required to return to that plant," Hoover declared. On May 4, 1943, Sebold joined the staff of the Mare Island Naval Shipyard in Vallejo, California. He spent the remainder of World War II as a gauge repairman in the instrument department.

Unknown to his coworkers, he was the pseudonymous star of an FBI promotional newsreel about the case that was screened as a morale booster before spy movies across the country. "These pictures were taken at a busy New York street corner," Hoover intoned over grainy black-and-white footage of Forty-Second Street and Broadway. "The man walking up and down the street is 'Harry Sawyer,' a naturalized German American citizen. Sawyer visited Germany in 1939, where he was approached by the Gestapo, who urged him to return to the United States as a spy. Before leaving Germany, he sent word to us. A spy trap was set. Sawyer was working for the FBI." The bulk of the short feature was devoted to replaying portions of the Room 627 films that had so thrilled Judge Byers's courtroom. Special attention was paid to Fritz Duquesne's flamboyant visit. "He is describing to Sawyer the gas-operating principles of the M1 rifle," Hoover said over shots of the gesticulating colonel, "a secret that might've made a difference in the lives of a lot of Americans if it had reached Germany at that time." In light of the war in the Pacific, screen time is given to the Japanese agent Takeo Ezima, who made a single stop at the office and wasn't mentioned in the indictment or the trial. "All of these pictures you must remember were taken before Pearl Harbor," Hoover informs theatergoers. "But to the enemy the fighting in Asia and the fighting in France were already different fronts in a single war."

Omitted was any mention of Hermann Lang and the Norden bombsight, which was glorified in the early years of the war as our greatest advantage over the enemy. Hollywood played a leading role in the veneration. In *Joe Smith, American* (1942), Robert Young plays an employee of an armament factory who is assigned to work on "the only secret weapon in the world that this country has that no other country can get," as one character describes it. He is promptly kidnapped and tortured by Nazi agents ("You will either draw that bombsight installation for us or we will kill you") but escapes and contacts the FBI, which earns him a comparison with Nathan Hale. "Hero?" he responds. "Baloney. Nobody's a hero in this country. All of us guys are the same. We've got homes, and wives, and kids. . . . And we don't like people who push us around." *Bombardier* (1943), starring Pat O'Brien and Randolph Scott, hammered home the idea that a B-17 Flying Fortress or a B-24 Liberator equipped with the masterpiece could deposit a bomb in a pickle barrel from twenty thousand feet. "Through this secret bombsight the world's best bombardiers are aiming at Tokyo, Berlin, and all the Axis nerve-centers," shouted the film's trailer. "This is the story behind their deadly accuracy."

Stories spread that the bombsight's (etched-glass) crosshairs were made with either black-widow spiderwebs or the delicate blond hair of one Mary Babnick of Pueblo, Colorado. Photographs were published of armed guards carrying a canvas case containing what airmen called the Blue Ox, or the football, along the tarmac to the waiting planes. "It is never left unguarded for a moment," wrote John Steinbeck in his 1942 book about a bomber team, *Bombs Away*. "On the ground it is kept in a safe and under constant guard. It is taken out of its safe only by a bombardier on mission and he never leaves it. He is responsible not only for its safety but for its secrecy. And finally, should his ship be shot down, he has been instructed how quickly and effectively to destroy it." The recommended method was with two rounds from a .45-caliber service pistol into the rate-end mechanism and another round through the telescope. Some trainees were required to recite the so-called bombardier's oath, pledging to "keep inviolate the secrecy of any and all confidential information revealed to me, and in full knowledge that I am a guardian of one of my country's most priceless military assets, do further swear to protect the secrecy of the American bombsight, if need be, with my life itself."

"The more I found out about the bombsight," one of them told the *New Yorker* magazine, "the more ingenious and inhuman it seemed. It was something bigger, I kept thinking, than any one man was intended to comprehend. I ended up with a conviction, which I still have, that a bombardier can't help feeling inferior to his bombsight."

The United States went to war believing that its four-engine heavy bombers, equipped with the world's best bombsights (the Norden chiefly and the Sperry secondarily), could achieve victory by dropping relatively few bombs on a small number of high-value targets, a futuristic aerial assault conducted during daytime hours that would strike with pinpoint accuracy. *Collier's* magazine ran a cartoon of a bombardier turning to his pilot and asking, "Was that address 106 Leipzigerstrasse, or 107?" The American conception of "strategic" bombing (as opposed to the "tactical" support of ground forces) called for the *exclusive* targeting of "vital centers" or "choke points," which would sap the will of the enemy not by the incineration of its citizens but by the disabling of inanimate structures such as power stations and armament factories.

Which, of course, is not how the Allies emerged victorious. By the time the US Army Air Corps (renamed the US Army Air Forces) arrived in Europe, the RAF had determined that the best way to hasten the defeat of Germany was to pummel its cities under the cover of darkness. According to a British directive of February 14, 1942, the "area" (or terror) bombing of Germany "was focused on the morale of the enemy civil population and in particular of the industrial workers." The Allied plan was for the RAF to maintain its "city-busting" or "dehousing" assaults during the evenings while the USAAF conducted precision strikes against select targets during the day. "We should never allow the history of this war to convict us of throwing the strategic bomber at the man on the street," said Brigadier General Ira Eaker, commander of the Eighth Air Force. Let the Brits do the dirty work. US warplanes would spare average Germans.

But USAAF leaders quickly learned that theories formulated at the Air Corps Tactical School couldn't survive first contact with the enemy. The great bombers weren't able to soar above the Messerschmitt fighters and antiaircraft flak and penetrate without hindrance into German airspace, a problem that wasn't rectified until the introduction of long-range fighters such as the P-51 Mustang in January 1944 and the subsequent achievement of air superiority by the time of D-day in June 1944. (The frightful casualty rates for bomber crews proved that the loftiest modern aircraft weren't protected from the horrors of warfare.) Even if the planes remained unharried long enough for the bombsights to lock into the targets, bombardiers often couldn't see through the smoke, dust, and/or clouds, forcing the USAAF to order "blind bombing" or "overcast bombing technique," which guaranteed off-target strikes against civilians. The fatal flaw of the Norden bombsight was that it was a line-of-sight aiming instrument. "I could see bombs bursting ten miles behind American lines," said newsman Hughes Rudd of poor-visibility missions at the Battle of Monte Cassino during the Italian campaign. "They were dropping all over the fucking landscape. Maybe it was true that they could hit a pickle barrel with that Norden bombsight, but there were no pickle barrels in the Liri Valley that day."

By early 1945, the USAAF was continuing its attempts against the industrial and transportation hubs of Germany while also countenancing attacks on cities and towns in an attempt to demoralize the populace. Lieutenant General Jimmy Doolittle called the recourse to terror bombing a violation of "the basic American principle of precision bombing of targets of strictly military significance for which our tactics were designed and our crews trained and indoctrinated." Although historians have long debated how essential the British-American air campaign was to Nazi Germany's defeat, which was only achieved with the arrival of ground forces in Berlin, the material fact is that Allied raids struck more than a hundred towns and cities, destroyed 3.5 million homes, and killed 600,000 civilians. The industrial Ruhr Valley, the home region of Bill Sebold, was targeted mercilessly.

On May 13, five days after V-E Day, Sebold wrote a note to Ellsworth that seemed to commemorate the end of hostilities in the European theater. "Today is Sunday morning. I am all by myself and Helen is still snoring. And feel like writing to you." Sebold said he was no longer working at the naval shipyard. He'd had it with the long commute and "sitting in one place all day." Instead, he had "remodeled the place in the back" and was now in the chicken business "up to my neck." He had joined the Poultry Producers of Central California. "I am in the egg business, too, but in a moderate way. . . . I am not making a big profit. But I am breaking even and that is a very good thing for a beginner like me." He said he was getting "a tremendous kick out of all this and this reminds me of my father's business and his struggles."

Helen, he said, has a "Park Avenue complex." Every so often she "kicks like a mule and wants to go back to New York. And I cannot see anything in it. I don't want to see the smelly place again."

Then he turned to the headlines. "I certainly feel better since the war is over in Germany now. I only hope my people are still there. I would like to get them over here so we could all live and work together. What do you think about fat Goering, you know old Hermann? The guy has a lot of nerve. I hope we turn him over to the Russians. Wouldn't it be a thrill if I could see my dear 'Uncle Hugo' and some of his companions in this country? Well, I got my satisfaction in one way, although it is not very nice to think that way, but justice is justice."

Sebold signed off by acknowledging that the war wasn't yet over. After victory in the Pacific, he promised, he'd visit the Ellsworth home in Los Angeles. "You can count on that."

The USAAF had even less use for the Norden bombsight during its final-stage assault on Japan. (The US Navy, with its wartime emphasis on dive-bombing, even lesser still.) After the capture of the Mariana Islands in November 1944, formations of the new B-29 Superfortress began high-altitude daylight missions against the Japanese home islands. But after four months of indifferent results, the decision was made to lay waste to Japan's wood-constructed cities with low-altitude firebombing attacks at nighttime. On the evening of March 9, 1945, nearly three hundred B-29s dropped two thousand tons of jelled-gasoline incendiaries into the center of Tokyo, setting an inferno that killed upward of a hundred thousand people. By summer 1945, more than 150 square miles of Japanese cities had been decimated by fire without any indication that the Imperial command was ready to capitulate. With US leaders forced to contemplate the unpleasant prospect of a land invasion, the decision was made to deploy the newest wonder weapon, the one that would cause everyone to forget all about the purported glories of the Norden bombsight. On August 6, 1945, a single B-29, the *Enola Gay*, dropped the atomic bomb on Hiroshima. Three days later, another B-29, *Bock's Car*, released a second bomb over Nagasaki. Carl Norden's son said his father never knew that both planes discharged their cargo with assistance of the Norden bombsight, which he had spent more than two decades developing in the utopian belief that victory could be achieved without the massive loss of life. "It would have destroyed him," his son said. On August 15, Emperor Hirohito announced Japan's unconditional surrender in a radio address, the first time his subjects had heard his voice.

Within six weeks of V-J Day, Twentieth Century–Fox presented J. Edgar Hoover and his G-men with Hollywood's version of a Medal of Honor. "Vigilant. Tireless. Implacable," begins the voice-over for *The House on 92nd Street*, released in late September with the Bureau's full cooperation. "The most silent service of the United States in peace or war is the Federal Bureau of Investigation. The Bureau went to war with Germany long before hostilities began. No word or picture could then make public the crucial war service of the FBI. But now it can be told." The film tells the story of William Dietrich (William Eythe), the American-born son of German parents who is studying diesel engineering at "a Midwestern university not far from Columbus, Ohio," a white-bread version of Sebold without a hint of foreignness. Emissaries from the Nazi regime approach him during a break from his training with the track team. He immediately informs the FBI. "When the meaning of the German invitation was explained to him, Dietrich offered his services to the Bureau," according to the voice-over.

"Dietrich" travels to Germany, is trained (rather than merely lodged) at the Pension Klopstock and sent to New York with microfilm instructions. Under the guidance of the FBI, Dietrich meets Elsa Gebhardt (a chaste Lilly Stein with a snarl and the unlikely code name of Mr. Christopher), Colonel Hammersohn (who turns Duquesne into a slow-witted English butler), and Charles Ogden Roper (an amalgam of Everett Minster Roeder and Hermann Lang with the brainpower to play "fourteen games of chess at the same time"). Our hero is portrayed as a handsome naïf who would be lost without Bureau guidance while faceless FBI men are seen dutifully operating a gadget-filled radio station in the wilds of New Jersey and making movies from behind a two-way mirror in Dietrich's Columbus Circle office. After a shoot-out at the titular residence in Yorkville, the spy headquarters, the Bureau and its ur–double agent succeed in preventing the Germans from stealing the US military's greatest treasure, Process 97. As Dietrich nurses a bruised jaw suffered in the climactic battle, the narrator delivers the conclusion: "Elsa Gebhardt, alias Mr. Christopher, was no more successful than other foreign espionage agents. Process 97, the atomic bomb, America's top war secret, remains a secret."

In the years following the war, it would be revealed that the FBI had not prevented Communist spies from infiltrating the Manhattan Project, which developed the real-life Process 97. With secrets gathered from the likes of Klaus Fuchs, a wartime employee of the Los Alamos Laboratory who confessed to his crimes in 1950, the Soviet Union of Joseph Stalin was able to develop a successful atomic bomb much sooner than otherwise would have been possible.

Two months after the film opened, Sebold wrote a Christmas letter to Jim Ellsworth that mentioned nothing of the screen portrayal. "I had some spell with my shoulder again. But through the [FBI] office in San Francisco, I was recommended to some of the best doctors in S.F. The man took x-rays and found a broken right shoulder and a piece of bone that was broken off a long time ago. And surprisingly the man fixed me up and neck and shoulder pain are gone." Sebold described his pleasure in decorating the couple's small Christmas tree. "I get quite a kick out of doing this. That's the second tree in Walnut Creek." He was also full of enthusiasm for the poultry business. "The chickens are still laying and that means a lot. I improved the place some more. I bought the land which lays in back of the garage— about one acre with a lot of pine and almond trees. Now all I need is a horse to get around my place."

At Bureau headquarters in Washington, memos were circulating about the necessity of learning the fate of Sebold's mother, sister, and two brothers. "You will recall that just prior to the trial in this case some discussion was had as to whether William Sebold, the informant, would testify in view of the fact that to do so would in all probability endanger the position of his family still residing in Germany," wrote assistant director D. M. Ladd. "Notwithstanding the safety of himself, he volunteered to testify and did a remarkably good job."

In a letter to J. Edgar Hoover on December 17, 1945, Ladd delivered the FBI's most explicit statement on Sebold's achievement: "As you know, Sebold gave us the most outstanding case in the Bureau's history. The 'Ducase' has been the basis for a terrific amount of publicity dealing with the Bureau's success prior to and during World War II. This case opened the door to real knowledge of German espionage activities and it is impossible to describe the situation in which we might have found ourselves had not Sebold turned against the Germans in our favor. It is to be pointed out that unlike many other double agents Sebold turned against the Germans from a patriotic love for the United States and conducted himself always in absolute accord with the Bureau's wishes. He has not sought personal notoriety and has never placed his personal wishes or fortune above the Bureau's interests."

Sebold's next letter to Ellsworth, not written until the following summer, July 6, 1946, brought good news. He had independently learned that no retribution had been meted out against his family. "My mother is still alive, 74 years old. She was the only one left in the house during the war. Everyone else went to the country. She gave me quite a humorous story about it, and I had to laugh despite the drama. She went through plenty." He said his sister Maria and brother Karl also survived. But his other brother, Hermann, and his wife were killed in an automobile accident. "They were buried on Christmas Day 1945. My Hermann was always a reckless wild boy but in a good way, a regular sportsman. I am sort of glad he was instantly killed and not crippled for the rest of his life." Sebold told Ellsworth that he was thinking of leasing the chicken farm and going to Germany to see his mother, who was now living in the basement of her bomb-damaged home. "Besides I'm too young to bury myself in the country among a bunch of cackling chickens and griping mossbacks. It's a nice life for a guy about 80 years old with gout in one foot," but not for a healthy forty-seven-year-old such as him.

A month later, he wrote again, on August 9, the one-year anniversary of the Nagasaki bombing: "A couple days ago, I received another letter from Germany and my mother says she is ill. She grieves too much for her Hermann and she wants to see me." Sebold told Ellsworth that he was considering a job with the US occupation forces. "I have the paper filled out on my desk. But I cannot come to a decision. I have everything I ever wished for, and Germany doesn't appeal to me a bit. If only my mother wasn't there." He then wondered if the FBI could facilitate her relocation to the United States. "Since my doings were not recognized by the government I have no right to ask any special favors, otherwise I would write direct to Mr. Hoover or the president of the country. Now I am asking you if that would be the right thing to do. I never asked for anything. My mother could make the trip by plane at my expense. That would take only a couple of days in this advanced age. They would give her a sedative and before she knows what happens, she would land in Concord, only ten miles from Walnut Creek." He said he was willing to "bite the sour apple" and return to Germany himself, but "if there is a remote chance to do it the other way, I would be very happy. I am only afraid that my mother can't hack the wintertime in her weakened condition. And if she could come over here, that would give her a different outlook on life after all that misery in Germany."

Nearly two months later, on October 1, 1946, Sebold penned his last letter to Ellsworth that survives. He acknowledged "all the trouble you went through in account of my mother," but "things took a different turn." He was having health problems. His stomach ulcer had recurred. "They gave me five blood trans-fusions, and now I cannot have my mother here. On top of that I face another operation. They discovered a broken vertebra in my spine and that has to be fixed by grafting a piece of shinbone in it. I am not able to work any more, have to be very careful." He showed a hint of impatience with the Bureau, the first instance of it in his letters to Ellsworth. He wanted to know why note-books taken from him during the trial hadn't been returned. "I don't see why the government has any more use for them and, if you think they do, they can make a Photostat of it and send the originals back to me. I waited all these years to have them returned. If I don't get them back, I'd like to know the reason why. This is my personal property." The correspondence ended on a warmer note: "Hoping you and your loved ones are well settled in the new house now. If you ever come this way again, Helen will cook you your favored dish."

Over the next several years, he continued to suffer physical debilitation, which led the FBI to provide him with financial assistance that he never requested. The files also indicate that five or six agents from the San Francisco office donated blood to assist in his ulcer recovery. In order to supplement his limited income from the chicken business, Sebold rented out three apartments on his property and took occasional jobs, working as a janitor at the Walnut Creek Post Office and "as a clean-up man at the rest room and bar of the Club Diablo." He left the first position because of a disagreement with the postmaster and quit the second because he "found this job of the very lowest type." Although he succeeded in patenting his own invention, an air-conditioning unit that kept eggs from reaching the germinating temperature of 68° Fahrenheit, Sebold failed in his attempts to make much money from what he called the Eggmaster.

During a talk with an agent in May 1949, Sebold "mentioned in passing that the motion picture company which produced *The House on 92nd Street*, which was based on his experiences, no doubt realized a good profit from this film. He felt that this was excellent publicity for the Bureau and was glad they could have it, but mentioned that while he did not know whether the Bureau received any revenue from this film, someone certainly did."

In January 1950, he quit poultry farming because "it has developed that the bottom has literally dropped out of the chicken business in California which has left the informant in an unfortunate position," according to the Bureau.

Two months later, he told the San Francisco office about a letter he received from his brother in Mülheim. "I will not neglect to inform you that you must be careful," wrote Karl Sebold. "About a year ago a customer said to me, 'We will dispose of him.' What this means I do not know." Bill Sebold "felt in reading between the lines that the Nazis were still interested in finding him for the purpose of revenge. He indicated that he would be careful in his dealings with any strangers."

Within just a few years of the end of the war, the leading spies started to leave prison. After serving her sentence in the women's facility in Alderson, West Virginia, Lilly Stein was deported back to Austria, a survivor of the Holocaust who owed her life to the power of her sexual allure. According to the story told by her American relatives, she was last heard from working at a luxury resort near Strasbourg. "Maybe in charge of men's special entertainment," quipped one of her cousins.

During his first years behind bars, Ed Roeder requested an information bulletin from the US government, "How Inventors Can Aid National Defense." He sent along a number of ideas, some of which bore a close resemblance to what he'd delivered to the Germans, but none were ever accepted. He also authored a book, *Formulas in Plane Triangles,* which contains little prose and is impenetrable to anyone but a specialist. Released on July 6, 1950, he lived in Milwaukee and then Peoria, Illinois, working as an engineer and firing recreational weapons until his death in 1955. When the Justice Department asked him in a 1952 questionnaire to name his former espionage supervisor, his response was "William Sebold."

Fritz Duquesne spent World War II in Leavenworth, composing letters to the newspapers about how he was "framed up by a dirty German punk that got $20,000 for the job." His attempts to establish contact with his girlfriend Evelyn Lewis, who was released from custody in 1942, were rebuffed. "The tragedy and suffering which his activities and connections in this war have brought upon me and my family have been almost beyond repair," Lewis wrote to the authorities, "and any thought of any future connection is quite impossible." By early 1945, the once-dashing soldier of fortune was suffering from such mental and physical debilitation that he was transferred to the Medical Center for Federal Prisoners in Springfield, Missouri. Yet the old charm remained. "I would certainly like to know more of the details of this man's life," wrote a prison official to the warden in 1952. "If you can encourage him to write his exploits and adventures, I wish you would do so." After Duquesne was released in 1954, he returned to New York. He died an indigent at City Hospital on Welfare Island a few years later, but not before giving one last lecture to the Adventurers Club. The title was "My Life—in and out of Prison."

Initially incarcerated at Leavenworth, Hermann Lang was transferred to the federal prison at Milan, Michigan. As part of his efforts to win early release, he sent a handwritten letter to Senator William Langer of North Dakota on April 2, 1948, describing "the irresponsibility and untrustworthiness" of "this man Sebold," who threatened to "bring harm to my relatives in Germany" unless Lang revealed the Norden secret, which he refused to do. Lang told the staunchly anti-Communist senator that Judge Byers had barred a witness who knew of Sebold's "Communistic activities" from testifying. It isn't "a pleasant thought to consider" that he was sitting in jail "on the basis of evidence given by a person whose political ideas and allegiance run so completely counter to the established principles of our government—a man of the political ideology which today is the subject of penetrating inquiries." Lang was playing to his audience. The House Un-American Activities Committee was entering its second, more famous phase of its existence. Joseph McCarthy had just been elected the junior senator from Wisconsin. And J. Edgar Hoover was utilizing powers granted to him during the Nazi scare to become a colossus in the fight against the subversive ideology he always loathed above any other.

Since his US citizenship had been revoked back in 1943, Lang was deported to (West) Germany following his release on July 25, 1950, which meant that he served less than half of his eighteen-year sentence. Three years later, he was hailed in the pages of Germany's popular newsweekly *Stern,* which presented the Sebold investigation as a morality tale in which Lang was a national hero who suffered the Wagnerian stab in the back, the *Dolchstoss,* from a perfidious turncoat who was only pretending to love the fatherland. Lang "accomplished something tremendous for Germany, which would secure him a place of honor in the history of the Luftwaffe," the story said. But along came Sebold, who used "tricks and deceptions" to lure loyal servants of the German state into the clutches of the FBI. Tried in an atmosphere of "hatred and contempt," Lang maintained his innocence even after serving hard time in prison, where he was forced to perform chores "that the negroes refused to do." To this day, the magazine wrote, he wouldn't confess to his role. "I was sentenced without being guilty," Lang was quoted as saying.

A principal source for *Stern* was Nikolaus Ritter, who left the Abwehr following the revelations of the spy trial in 1941 and spent the remainder of the war on active duty with the Wehrmacht, concluding his service as a brigade commander in the Harz Mountains. After the Nazi surrender, he was imprisoned by the British military at Bad Nenndorf, where he underwent extensive interrogation about his espionage activities. In reference to Ritter's spy work during 1940 and 1941, the British War Office's Combined Services Detailed Interrogation Centre concluded that his "activity and ability in that period earned him not only notoriety, but also a certain respect." Following his release in 1947, Ritter returned to Hamburg, where he eventually found work as an export merchant. It took *Stern*'s reporters "several exciting weeks" to locate him. "He was not a spy within the meaning of this unsavory word," Ritter told them of his greatest recruit, Hermann Lang. "He was a German who selflessly wanted to serve his homeland. Nothing else." Ritter, who would die in 1974, reported in his memoir that Lang "initially found it difficult to get settled. With the help of other comrades and some connections, I was able to help him get recognized as a returnee." Lang found a good position in industry and lived out his years in southern Germany.

Sebold was appalled by the magazine's attack on his integrity. On July 22, 1953, he wrote to the San Francisco office, describing the articles as "completely distorted in favor of Ritter and Lang and G. W. Herz, Lang's defense lawyer, a resident of New York." The letter reflected the fact that Sebold had rebounded from his difficulties and found a good job as a criminal investigator at the Benicia Arsenal, where he was responsible for looking into such matters as the disappearance of a pair of binoculars. "The motive of publishing the story could be as follows," he wrote as if filing an assessment for a law enforcement agency. "A: Smear propaganda against the judicial branch of the United States. B: An effort by certain clique (Nazis) to whitewash themselves before the German people and C: As a side issue to ruin my people socially and economically." He said he was contemplating writing an article for the *Frankfurter Illustrierte*, a magazine for "thinking Germans," which he would submit free of charge under the stipulation that the issue's proceeds be donated to the German Red Cross. "Since everybody had his say about me, I think the time has come that I will tell my story also, and in the place where it hurts most—in Germany."

On August 4, 1953, he wrote a second letter to the Bureau

about the *Stern* article. He had learned from his mother that his brother Karl had twice "received visitors from Hamburg, who demanded to see her for the purpose of obtaining a photograph of me. My brother refused to give them a picture and showed them the door." Since the magazine's characterization of him as a disloyal German "had caused a lot of bad reflections on my relatives," he was thinking of providing *Stern* with a copy of his US citizenship papers, which would prove that he was not a Reich subject at the time he was forced into the Abwehr. "The German people will then understand my loyalty to America, and by exposing the real Ritter as a liar and opportunist, I would make him one of the most ridiculed men in present Germany."

But Sebold did not write the article for the Frankfurt magazine nor contact *Stern*'s reporter. While the Bureau initially agreed to assist him in his campaign of vindication, it soon recommended that he ignore the matter altogether. He complied.

By the end of 1953, he'd lost his job at the arsenal. "It is noted that while Mr. Sebold is sincere and conscientious, he seems to have the faculty of being a little overbearing at times and may have not followed instructions given him by his superiors as they would have him do," the Bureau reported. He again complained of stomach problems but his doctor testified that he was largely free of physical ailments. "The whole picture as to Sebold is related to tension," said Dr. Frederick Pellegrin. "He has a tendency to brood over lack of work or other inactivity." And Helen's "constant nagging" didn't help, Sebold complained. Playing marriage counselor, an agent "suggested to Mrs. Sebold that at the present time Sebold needs her encouragement and that any cheerfulness and encouragement on her part would be appreciated by him."

On September 22, 1954, Sebold summoned an agent from the San Francisco office and told him about a sleeping pill–induced haze that led him to imagine he had gotten out of bed and driven toward the Benicia Arsenal to see his former boss. "He thought perhaps in his subconscious mind he had been headed for Mr. Walter C. Roy and intended to harm him," wrote the agent. Later in the discussion, Sebold brought up the spy case. "It appeared that Sebold just wanted to talk to someone. He explained that he did what he did for the country rather than for the FBI. He pointed out that following the trial he did not take advantage of making money from his story or from radio or movie because he felt he had done what he did for the good of the country."

In January 1955, the San Francisco office conducted a comprehensive evaluation of Sebold's status and determined that he "apparently cannot or will not work" and "appears on the verge of becoming a mental case." Sebold "has complained of the pressure under which he is forced to live, stating that 'the Gestapo would eventually liquidate him.'" The memo wondered if his future livelihood could be provided for by some form of congressional appropriation or perhaps by a book written "in a manner that would meet with the approval" of the Bureau. "While it is realized that Sebold has been and is a problem, that he is a hypochondriac and has developed a persecution complex, nevertheless the fact remains that this man has performed outstanding service to the Bureau and to this country. Everything considered, he was one of the most important factors in enhancing the Bureau's reputation in the security field." The Washington headquarters could find no outside funding for him and decided against putting him in touch with a writer.

In May 1955, Sebold was so fearful of Nazi reprisals that he was thinking of procuring a handgun. He told Agent Richard Nichols that "he had received telephone calls, one within the past two weeks, in which the caller asked, 'Are you still there, Harry?' which he implied referred to his former name of Harry

Sawyer, which he used when he was an informant. He further pointed out that this name should not be known to anyone in this area. Sebold continued that within the recent past he had observed an individual loitering near his automobile and that upon seeing Sebold approach, the person had run away. Sebold stated that these incidents greatly perturbed him and that he had difficulty sleeping nights." Agent Nichols told him that "he has no concrete basis to believe that any of the things which caused his fear are in fact related with the Nazis and that he might be building these incidents up in his own mind." Nichols advised him against obtaining a firearm.

In July 1956, Sebold lost his job as a night watchman at the Vallejo docks after he became dizzy and slipped on a deck. The company doctor wouldn't certify him for work because "he frequently had fainting spells and he might fall off the ship or down one of the holds and kill himself." During the same month, Sebold revealed that Nazi phantoms were still chasing him. "He stated he went down to the Howard Terminal in Oakland, California, and studied the itinerary of ships of the North German Lloyd company; that while one ship from this company was in port, he received a threatening call and told the caller 'to go back to his ship.' Sebold stated that he has not since been bothered and mentioned this shows he was not just imagining things." By January 1959, he appeared to be doing better, performing occasional jobs as a handyman and securing a position as a workman with the mothballed fleet of merchant and military ships at Suisun Bay. "Sebold seemed to be in excellent spirits and stated his health had improved and attributed this to the fact that he had recently had twenty-two teeth extracted." But it wasn't long before he stopped working altogether.

Sebold doesn't appear in the files again until four years later. Now sixty-three, he "shows some of the effects of his many past illnesses," wrote Agent Spencer after a visit to Walnut Creek on March 7, 1963. "He lives in his memories and appeared to be a bit unstable." A month later, Sebold sent a short handwritten letter to Spencer. "After your last visit here something happened inside my neck: Later I remembered that since 1940 in New York I was asked by the government lawyers if I was willing to go through with them things and I agreed to everything. And [I] came to the conclusion that I have been a plain nuisance to pester anybody with my affairs."

In September 1963, Sebold called the office to complain about *The FBI Story* by Don Whitehead, which was published by Random House seven years earlier, with a foreword written by J. Edgar Hoover. He said the author inaccurately reported that he agreed to work for the Abwehr because he had a Jewish grandfather and was thus especially vulnerable to Nazi blackmail. "He continued that the book has a red, white, and blue cover, which gives it an appearance of being highly official. He added that the book makes him out as a 'louse,' whereas all he did was his duty, according to his beliefs." In April 1964, he called about another volume that mentioned his name, *Spy and Counterspy* by Phil Hirsch. "He stated that he considers this bad publicity for him because he likes to get jobs house painting and he feels he cannot advertise nor get a painter's license because of his reputation, and this means he has difficulty getting painting jobs. One lady mentioned to him that after reading this book and seeing what he did for the country, she thought someone ought to write to Congress because it is a shame that Mrs. Sebold still has to scrub floors to maintain their living. Mr. Sebold had no further comment to make and just wanted to bring this to the attention of the Bureau."

During late 1964 and early 1965, the San Francisco office attempted to determine whether Sebold, now "financially destitute," could receive assistance from "the new anti-poverty program of President Johnson" or the Interagency Defector Committee, which provided support to Soviet émigrés. He was found ineligible for both. He was surviving on $37.50 a month from Social Security "plus a small income from his rental properties which are old and which he cannot afford to improve."

On October 14, 1965, Helen Sebold called the office and "advised that her husband, William Sebold, was mentally ill; that he ran up a bill of $800.00 at a hardware store, ordered a fence for the home property costing $2,000.00, purchased a tape recorder for $226.00, an electric stove for $229.00 and numerous other items; and that he has no money to pay for these items. Mrs. Sebold stated that she canceled the order for the fence and returned most of the other items."

The report continues:

"According to Mrs. Sebold, she had her husband committed to the Martinez County Hospital, Martinez, California, for observation and hearing to determine if he should be committed to a state mental institution." The hearing was scheduled for the following morning at 10 a.m. "Mrs. Sebold related that her husband had informed the Contra Costa County Sheriff's Office of his past cooperation with the FBI and, therefore, she desired to have someone from the FBI present at the hearing." The agent declined to attend "but told Mrs. Sebold that if the sheriff's office or the doctor desired a verification of Mr. Sebold's cooperation with the FBI they should feel free to contact the FBI."

Eight days later, Mrs. Sebold reported that her husband had been committed to Napa State Hospital "for an indefinite period of time."

"The San Francisco office has maintained close contact with the Sebolds," according to a memo from October 29, 1965, which effectively closed the case. "For a number of years he has been in dire financial straits with very little income. Every feasible effort was made to find him employment and to assist him in receiving increased retirement income. In view of his commitment, there appears to be little possibility of rendering him assistance at this time."

Sebold spent the last five years of his life at Napa. "My dad and mom often went to visit him on Sundays," said one of his nieces, Christel Little. "Sometimes my dad picked him up and brought him to our house for Sunday dinner and then took him back." Another niece, Shirley Camerer, recalls him as "a silent man with deep grunts to acknowledge you" who "usually had a warm look in his eyes so you knew he was teasing." The young relatives would've never imagined that their Uncle Bill was a man of formidable moral and physical courage who led one of the great spy missions of American history, a landmark figure deserving of a place among the nation's most honored war heroes. "When I first heard about it, I was totally shocked," said Little. "I believed that there had to be another William/Wilhelm Sebold from Mülheim, Germany. That is what I thought for years." During an interview in 2011, Sebold's ninety-seven-year-old sister-in-law suggested that his accomplishment was a family secret because of a belief that he'd caused harm to fellow Germans. In her thick accent, she spoke of how Sebold "did things bad for the German people and good for the American people."

Sebold died of a heart attack at Napa State Hospital in the early hours of February 16, 1970. His death certificate says he suffered from manic depression. "We went to the cemetery after the services in the mortuary chapel," said Camerer. "There were some old friends there, not many and I can't remember who. Afterwards we went to Aunt Helen Sebold's house. After a meal we all went home. Very quiet and very nice service." Mrs. Sebold picked out a gray-black headstone that left space for a second inscription. IN GOD'S CARE was the simple message along the lower border. The local press made no mention of his passing.

Jim Ellsworth, who'd left the FBI sixteen years earlier to join the banking business, had fallen out of touch. He wasn't among the small group gathered at the graveside in the Queen of Heaven Cemetery in Lafayette. But he never forgot his old friend. When his daughter moved to Walnut Creek seven years later, he asked her to look up Sebold's name in the telephone book. "I doubt he is alive," he wrote on July 25, 1977. On a subsequent visit, Ellsworth placed a call to Helen, who told him the news. "I listened to the conversation and, of course, don't remember it all," said Mary Pletsch, the youngest of the Ellsworths' five children. "But I remember Dad's voice being very friendly like he was talking with someone familiar."

Ellsworth never sought public acclaim for his part in the historic case, but he could be persuaded to tell the story before community and church groups, where he displayed a remarkable memory for the smallest of details. He wrote about Bill Sebold one last time in a postretirement journal, narrating the tale of an immigrant who so honored the democratic ideals of his adopted homeland that he was prepared to stand in its defense. "He told me that he had found everything in this country wonderful," Ellsworth recalled. "He could go from city to city without registering with the police as he had to in Germany. He could follow any occupation that he pleased. He had all the personal liberties which he had missed in Germany. And so when he took the oath of allegiance, he really meant it and made up his mind that if ever he could prove his devotion to the country he would do so."

ACKNOWLEDGMENTS

This book could not have been written without the generous assistance of Christel Little, Shirley Camerer, and the late Helen Büchner (Bill Sebold's sister-in-law); the family of the late James C. Ellsworth, in particular Thomas Ellsworth and Mary Pletsch; Katharine R. Wallace; Ray Batvinis; Art Ronnie; Joni Newkirk; Jim Millen; Diana "Dee" Schumann; Patrick Connelly and Trina Yeckley at the National Archives branch in New York City; Amy Reytar and Britney Crawford at the National Archives in College Park, Maryland; John F. Fox of the FBI; and translator Barbara Serfozo. Praise is due to the staffs of the FDR Library at Hyde Park, the Library of Congress, the New York Public Library, the Brooklyn Public Library, the New-York Historical Society, the Hagley Library and Museum, the Museum of the City of New York, Kulturbetrieb Mülheim an der Ruhr, Contra Costa County Genealogical Society, and Politisches Archiv des Auswärtiges Amt in Berlin. Thanks also to George Spitz, Brian Hollstein, Kathy Jolowicz, Arthur Jacobs, Steve Landrigan, Peg Hoversten, Hal Shevers, Alice Ra'anan, Carolinda Witt, Ed Appel, Jeff Cuyubamba, John Driscoll, Janon Fisher, Corey Kilgannon, Patrick Weaver, Thomas Buechner, Alan Goldberg, Leo Jakobson, Gene Fein, Robert Shapiro, Nancy Ellen Goldsmith, Joe Fodor, Michael Skakun, Dennis Heaphy, L. G. Khambache Sherpa, Steve Chiu, George Miller, Ran Graff, Nat A. Pinkston, Daniel Stein, Paul Kerzner, Charles Donaldson, and Laura Harris of the *New York Post* photo library. I am the lucky beneficiary of the skill and

ACKNOWLEDGMENTS

professionalism of my editor, Colin Harrison, and his outstanding assistant, Katrina Diaz. The sound advice and spirited advocacy of my agent, Mary Evans, have been invaluable. Without the love and support of my wife, Laura, and daughter, Eleanor, I would've been nowhere.

NOTES

PROLOGUE

1 *"I have everything I ever"*: The quotation is taken from one of six surviving letters written from William Sebold to Jim Ellsworth generously provided to the author by the Ellsworth family.

2 *"lapsed into an obscurity which"*: Henry Lee, "Smashing the Biggest Spy Ring," *Coronet*, December 1951.

3 *"those who reflect in their"*: George McJimsey, ed., *Documentary History of the Franklin D. Roosevelt Presidency,* 40 vols. (Bethesda, MD: University Publications of America, 2001–8), 32: 34–41.

4 *"knowing that he would never"*: FBI File 100.HQ.373899, Sections 1 and 2, Record Group 65, National Archives, College Park, MD. Hereafter cited as Sebold personal FBI file.

5 *"elimination of this organization, which"*: Samuel A. Tower, "FBI's Hidden Struggle Against Spies Continues," *New York Times,* February 11, 1945.

5 *"a sacred thing"*: Sebold personal FBI file.

5 *"This Sebold is the kind"*: U.S. v. Hermann Lang, et al., United States District Court for the Eastern District of New York, Case 16000, Record Group 21, National Archives at New York City. Hereafter cited as trial transcript.

6 *"as you know"*: Sebold personal FBI file.

CHAPTER ONE: THE OBJECT OF THE BOMBARDMENT

7 *"It is only a question"*: Richard Suchenwirth, "Command and Leadership in the German Air Force," *United States Air Force Historical Studies* 174 (Aerospace Studies Institute, 1969), 8.

7 *"not for an adjustment of"*: On general rearmament, Richard J. Evans, *The Third Reich in Power* (New York: Penguin Press, 2005), 337, 615.

7 *Even though only about eight:* Edward L. Homze, *Arming the Luftwaffe: The Reich Air Ministry and the German Aircraft Industry, 1919–39* (Lincoln: University of Nebraska Press, 1976), 98.

9 *"fifth column" within, "men now":* Paul Preston, *The Spanish Civil War: Reaction, Revolution, and Revenge* (New York and London: W. W. Norton, 2009), 181; and Louis De Jong, *The German Fifth Column in the Second World War* (Chicago: University of Chicago Press, 1956), 4.

9 *Over one month:* Antony Beevor, *The Battle for Spain: The Spanish Civil War, 1936–1939* (London: Penguin Books, 2006), 173.

10 *At about 4:40 p.m. on:* Herbert Rutledge Southworth, *Guernica! Guernica! A Study of Journalism, Propaganda and History* (Berkeley: University of California Press, 1977), 240–41, 245, 277.

11 *"Guernica has taught us what":* Ibid., 231.

11 *the "complete annihilation":* R. Chickering and S. Forster, eds., *The Shadows of Total War: Europe, East Asia, and the United States, 1919–1939* (Cambridge University Press, 2003), 288.

12 *"Germany did not possess a":* Ernst Heinkel, *Stormy Life: Memoirs of a Pioneer of the Air Age* (New York: E. P. Dutton, 1956), 162.

12 *"only in closely limited areas":* Richard Suchenwirth, "Historical Turning Points in the German Air Force War Effort," *United States Air Force Historical Studies* 189 (Aerospace Studies Institute, 1969), 28.

12 *The Air Ministry's Technical Office:* James Corum, *The Luftwaffe: Creating the Operational Air War, 1918–1940* (Lawrence: University Press of Kansas, 1997), 200.

CHAPTER TWO: THE HIGHEST HUMANITY

13 *"everything that could be procured":* Nikolaus Ritter, *Deckname Dr. Rantzau: Die Aufzeichnungen des Nikolaus Ritter, Offizier im Geheimen Nachrichtendienst* (Hamburg: Hoffman und Campe, 1972). The book was written with an uncredited ghostwriter, American author Beth Day. I rely on two main sources for Ritter's recollections: an English-language translation of *Deckname* generously provided by Ritter's daughter, Katharine R. Wallace, and Ritter's interrogation at the hands of British intelligence immediately following the war. Since the Ritter-related information in Ladislas Farago's *Game of the Foxes* (New York: David McKay, 1971) is often at variance with Ritter's own account, I have avoided Mr. Farago's version. (Mr. Farago

is equally unreliable in his presentation of William Sebold's story.)
In addition, I have gained insights on Mr. Ritter through interviews
and correspondence with Mrs. Wallace, who authored a book on the
wartime experiences of her family: KF Ritter, *Aurora: An Alabama
School Teacher in Germany Struggles to Keep Her Children During WW II
after She Discovers Her Husband Is a German Spy* (Xlibris, 2006).

15 *On or about February 1, 1937:* The British investigation and interrogation of "Nikolaus Adolf Fritz Ritter, alias REINHARDT, alias VON
RANTZAU: based mainly in Hamburg," can be found in files KV2–
87 and KV2–88, British Archives, Records of the Security Service,
Kew, London. Thanks to Carolinda Witt for providing the author
with copies of the documents.

18 *"The essential thing for a":* John Rodden and Ethan Goffman, eds., *Politics and the Intellectual: Conversations with Irving Howe* (West Lafayette,
IN: Purdue University Press, 2010), 315.

19 *the picturesque activities of the pro-Nazi Amerikadeutscher Volksbund*:
Following Adolf Hitler's ascension to power in 1933, Heinz Spanknoebel, a Reich citizen who had been active in Nazi circles in Detroit
in the 1920s, was assigned by high officials including Rudolf Hess,
Hitler's deputy, to consolidate all local German groups in America
into a national movement that could serve as an advertisement for
the regime's objectives. Within months, his Bund der Freunde des
Neuen Deutschlands or Association of the Friends of the New Germany had organized more than twenty locals in German neighborhoods throughout the United States, a clutch of ideology-spreading
newspapers for regional distribution, an elite Ordnungsdienst or
Order Force with paramilitary uniforms and a spy branch that sought
a reliable "young lady of good appearance" who would "come over
on the *Europa* or *Bremen* as a hairdresser" to conduct espionage,
according to a letter intercepted by the Communist *Daily Worker*, the
New York newspaper dedicated like no other to smoking out the Fascist enemy.

With a mustache trimmed in the Hitler fashion, Spanknoebel
stormed into the offices of the daily newspaper *New Yorker Staats-
Zeitung und Herold* and demanded, on authority from Berlin, that the
publication cease printing "pro-Jewish articles," even though it carried no criticisms of Nazism. Bernard Ridder, who was copublisher
of the newspaper with his brother Victor, said he told the visitor,
"All I can tell you, Spanknoebel, is to get the hell out and stay out."

Spanknoebel had greater success forcing his way onto the board of directors of the United German Societies of Greater New York, which included seventy organizations that represented the breadth of German life in New York, everything from Alte Bronxer Carneval Ritterschafter (the Old Order of Bronx Carnival Knights) to the Bund der Sudeten-Deutschen in Amerika (Association of Sudeten Germans in America), from the Damenchor des Baeckermeister Gesangvereins (Ladies Choir of the Bakers' Singing Society) to the German-American Athletic Club of East Eighty-Second Street. He promised that the Nazi regime would bring punishment on the "parents or other relatives" of anyone in the group who stood in the way of his plan of Nazification, a boast that carried significant weight coming from a credentialed agent of the Reich. The story broke into the open when Mayor John P. O'Brien, a Tammany hack in the midst of a reelection campaign, said he would refuse to allow German Day festivities starring Spanknoebel to be held at a city-owned armory. He said the "occasion would be utilized by aliens to sow seeds of Hitler's intolerant and intolerable religious prejudices in New York, where we have no room for the bigotry of anti-Semites, Ku Kluxers, or other principles of spite and hatred." Carefully crafted to appeal to Jewish, Irish Catholic, and black voters, the message didn't prevent Mayor O'Brien's loss to the reformist energy of Fiorello La Guardia, the half-Jewish Italian Episcopalian with a fed-up-with-it bravado and visceral hatred for Hitler (a "perverted maniac," "the brown-shirt fanatic") who was destined to become the colorful personification of New York's civic life in the 1930s, the inimitable "Little Flower."

Within days, the US Attorney for the Southern District of New York announced he was conducting an investigation into Spanknoebel for violating a federal law passed in 1917 that required representatives of foreign governments to register with the State Department. At this point, Hitler's conservative diplomatic corps, which wanted above all to *improve* the image of the Reich in America, distanced itself from the whole affair, and some Nazi officials began considering the need for more subtle methods of persuasion in a country like the United States, where "the opposing elements are in every respect all-powerful." His assignment canceled, Spanknoebel was confronted by an operative from Berlin in an apartment just off Park Avenue where he was hiding from a US arrest warrant. The man put a gun to Spanknoebel's chest and escorted him to the waiting *Europa*, which carried him back to Germany and, according to one story, a successful career with the SS.

In the meantime, Samuel Untermyer, a seventy-five-year-old Wall Street lawyer and Jewish civic leader, was gaining notice for his call to "undermine the Hitler regime and bring the German people to their senses by destroying their export trade on which their very existence depends," a resonant issue in a city that was populated with 2 million of the world's 15 million Jews. During an address over WABC radio, Untermyer said his boycott campaign (opposed by some Jewish organizations as too provocative) targeted "German-made goods" and "German ships or shipping" but also "any merchant or shopkeeper who sells any German-made goods or who patronizes German ships or shipping," which located the matter directly on the streets of New York. Noisy sidewalk demonstrations soon convinced major department stores such as Saks, Hearns, Straus, Gimbels, and Woolworth to drop their business with Hitler's Germany.

The "jüdischen Boykott" would be the rallying cry in a renewed effort to bring German America under the umbrella of the Friends of the New Germany. The vehicle would be an auxiliary organization called the German-American Business Committee, known by its German-language acronym of DAWA, launched to "boycott the boycotters" by urging adherents to "buy German" and "patronize Aryan stores only," according to the language of its handouts. Within a month of its formation in early 1934, the DAWA published a "trade guide" that listed 750 member businesses, including more than 200 in Yorkville, each of which paid a sliding-scale registration fee for the privilege of placing a blue eagle sticker in their window, a physical mark on the city's landscape that denoted either support, acquiescence, or fear of Nazism. The *New York Times* reported that "several large establishments" in Yorkville didn't display the eagle and only joined DAWA "in order not to offend the Friends of the New Germany" but that the proprietors of "delicatessens, groceries, and fish markets" were "enthusiastic about the blue DAWA eagle," saying it increased business, which was probably what really interested them about it. The next step could've been predicted: in short order, "dozens" of Jewish businesses in the neighborhood "had their front windows marked with large swastikas," including an optical company, a cut-rate drugstore, a bakery, and two furniture stores, according to a Jewish newspaper. Some Jewish merchants in Yorkville were so fearful that they sought membership in DAWA in order to save businesses dependent upon German patronage. "I sent two letters, one of them registered, to the DAWA offices," said one. "They did not respond."

Anti-boycott sentiment appears to have done wonders for Nazi recruitment efforts by stoking the same resentments that had enabled Hitler to gain popular support back home. In a scene that was replicated in all the major German American auditoriums in the metropolitan area, more than two thousand people gathered on March 17 at the rustic Schwaben Halle on the Brooklyn side of Ridgewood, located in what today would be referred to as the Bushwick neighborhood. In between bursts of martial music, a succession of speakers demanded support for the DAWA campaign by shouting that "Jewish economic masters" were seeking the impoverishment of all German Americans. A reporter for a Jewish newspaper noted that only a dozen hands were raised in stiff-armed salute as the first notes were struck of "Deutschland über Alles." "After one verse it swung into the *Horst Wessel Lied*, the Hitlerite marching anthem, and half the audience saluted," he wrote. "When the band began the fourth and last verse of the song, every hand in the house (with one exception) was raised. And as the music mounted higher in the closing bars, Nazis besought a unanimous salute to Hitler. 'Hoch mit den Haenden,' they urged." High with the hands. Three weeks later, and several blocks to the east over the Queens line, six thousand Germans jammed into the Ridgewood Grove arena for a similar evening of obloquy and song while a few thousand more gathered outside on Palmetto Street and St. Nicholas Avenue. To make the scene a near replica of what was happening in Germany, the Nazis engaged in "eighteen brawls," according to the careful accounting of one reporter, with their political foes, in this case hundreds from the "Anti-Fascist League of Brooklyn, the Blue Shirt Minute Men of Brownsville, and the Jewish War Veterans League," according to the papers. The Ordnungsdienst used billy clubs to attack those who stuck around after the cops left. Then on May 17, 1934, more than twenty thousand gathered at Madison Square Garden, which was decorated with swastikas, American flags, and English- and German-language banners, including one near the speaker's rostrum that urged German Americans to "Erwache!" Awake! Protected by seven hundred and fifty officers of the NYPD outside and eight hundred Ordnungsdienst men inside, the speakers said that the DAWA was a "defensive measure against the reign of terror foisted upon the United States and especially the City of New York by certain professional Jews and their Bolshevist confederates," according to a featured orator. "We give you warning today for the last time," said another. "Stop the incitement. Stop the boycott and we too shall be silent and we too shall then devote ourselves to our special task. But if you continue the battle, you shall find us fully armed and then you will have to bear the consequences."

By 1935, Nazi Germany and its outspoken representatives were not particularly popular in the United States, even if many Americans believed, as FDR did, that most Germans were blameless victims of a pitiless tyranny. A call to boycott the Olympics scheduled there for 1936 was joined by organizations as varied as the National Council of the Methodist Church, the Catholic War Veterans, and the American Federation of Labor. A Gallup poll revealed 43 percent of the country felt strongly enough about the Nazi regime to support boycotting the games, which the US team wound up attending after a long and bitter debate. A respected elder of the US Senate, William King of Utah, proposed that a committee look into Nazi persecution of Jews and Catholics to determine whether the United States should sever diplomatic relations. Matters were compounded by the conviction of Bruno Richard Hauptmann, a Reich citizen living illegally in the Bronx, for kidnapping and murdering Charles Lindbergh's infant child after a lurid trial-of-the-century across the river in New Jersey. Vilified by the nation at large, the "former German machine gunner," as the papers called him in reference to his World War I service, found succor within a German American community willing to give him the benefit of the doubt. The Bruno Hauptmann Defense Committee, which hosted rallies and raised funds, was headquartered on the block of East Eighty-Sixth Street between Second and Third Avenues, its geographical dead-center. "And Hauptmann is a hero/ And Lindbergh is a swine/In Yorkville, in Yorkville/In Yorkville on the Rhine," wrote Walter Winchell in his gossip column syndicated to two thousand newspapers. Joseph Goebbels's grand plan to have millions of German Americans arise with one voice in compelling defense of the Fatherland was proving a failure, Nazi diplomats were telling its superiors back home.

The regime decided to make a public show of severing ties with the Friends of the New Germany, which had been so racked by internecine conflict that it failed to participate in German Day festivities in

October 1935, in the hope that vehicles more palatable to the American commonweal could be used to spread the word, as Goebbels had put it, that "a lasting prosperity in the United States is dependent on a reorganization of Europe." The connection with German America would be maintained under the cover of cultural organizations like the Verein für das Deutschtum im Ausland (League for Germans Abroad or VDA), the Volksdeutsche Mittelstelle (Ethnic Germans' Liaison Office or VOMI), and the Deutsche Ausland Institut (German Foreign Institute or DAI). Ever-greater funding would be given to the German consulate in downtown Manhattan to disseminate propaganda through new initiatives like the German Library of Information, which published English-language periodicals and books on the latest in Nazi thinking. So on December 27, 1935, Rudolf Hess released a statement to the Associated Press declaring that all German citizens (even those who had taken out "first papers" indicating their formal intention to become naturalized Americans) were forbidden from membership in groups with explicitly political aims. (The Friends of the New Germany was not named.) With about 60 percent of its estimated ten thousand members covered by the order (including senior leadership), the Bund der Freunde des Neuen Deutschlands was effectively shuttered. Or it would've been if the most politically committed element of German America hadn't already dedicated itself to the toilsome advance of National Socialism in a style that looked a lot like the version back home. These ideologues were inherently suspicious of any statement from the Reich government that denied them the opportunity to carry out their sacred calling, especially one issued to an American news agency.

Clicking his heels to lead this community of souls was Fritz Kuhn, a chemical engineer from Munich who, as a fast-rising figure in the movement with his citizenship papers freshly stamped, was christened as the Friends' new national director after word of Hess's intentions reached America. Kuhn was a quintessential member of the front-fighter generation of German rightists, a lieutenant in the machine gun detachment of the Alps Corps who had earned an Iron Cross during his four years on the Western Front, one of the "princes of the trenches, with their hard-set faces, brave to madness, tough and agile to leap forward or back, with keen bloodthirsty nerves, whom no despatch ever mentions," as author Ernst Jünger characterized those patriots ennobled by the experience of the war.

Kuhn returned from the front to take up arms against Marxist insurrectionists during the short-lived German Revolution of 1918–19. "I fight the Communists there," Kuhn later told Congress of the battle against the Bavarian Soviet Republic, which was overthrown after hundreds of German Communists were killed by right-wing forces that included many future Nazis. "I was in that revolution in Munich, active, of course, with officers of my old regiment." He would later claim that he decided to emigrate in the early 1920s because of difficulties in finding employment. "There was not any work in Germany at all," he explained. "Every second one was out of work. And if a man had a job he got a salary he could not live on. I had to go somewhere." Unable to enter the United States because the quota for German refugees had been filled, he and his wife, Elsa, lived in Mexico for four years until they were permitted entry. In 1928, Kuhn arrived in Detroit, finding employment as a chemist first at the Henry Ford Hospital (where he was "laid off due to the fact that he was too familiar with the female employees," according to a later FBI report) and then at the laboratory of the Ford Motor Company (where he was once caught practicing speeches in the darkroom). Soon after Kuhn joined the Detroit branch of the Friends in the summer of 1934, he was elevated to be its leader. Within a year and a half, he was running the nationwide organization, a "well-built, square-jawed aggressive Aryan, more than six feet tall and over two hundred pounds," wrote an observer. "When he stands erect in his storm troop uniform with grey officer's coat, his paunch is not so very noticeable. He is hard-faced and stern when reviewing his troops, issuing orders, or making a fighting speech; but he can relax, laugh, and drink beer with his fellows in *Gemütlichkeit*."

In late March 1936, Kuhn brought together the leading activists from across the country at the Hotel Statler in Buffalo. It was a heady time for Nazi Germany, just a few weeks after the Wehrmacht marched into the demilitarized Rhineland in blatant violation of the terms of Versailles, fortifying the country's borders with France and Belgium and bringing a surge of pride to nationalists everywhere. After being reelected as Bundesführer, Kuhn announced he was changing the name of the organization to the Amerikadeutscher Volksbund or German American Bund, part of a stepped-up plan to advertise the Americanism of the "new" group with frequent calls to "uphold and defend the Constitution and the law of the United

States," as the first item of the new Bund charter had it. Realizing he had to defy Hess's decree in order to keep the group viable, Kuhn determined that German nationals could remain in the new Bund if they began the naturalization process and joined its "Prospective Citizens' League," which meant that less than 10 percent of the membership actually departed (some back to Germany) and the Friends' institutions could remain in place. He ensured that his subtle defiance of Berlin's will wouldn't be challenged when he assumed the mantle of tyranny: "The Amerikadeutscher Volksbund is conducted upon the führer principle," he wrote. "Consequently there are no elections or majority decisions."

Setting up his national offices on the second floor of a three-story building hard by the rattling Third Avenue El at 178 East Eighty-Fifth Street in Yorkville—it also included a beauty parlor, dress shop, dental supply company, and insurance office—he moved quickly to quell dissension within the ranks and bring order to the Friends' disparate holdings. But Kuhn had ambitious plans to create a multi-institutional entity that could contain the whole of the German American community, his own mini-Reich at the center of the American republic. He spent the spring and early summer of 1936 speaking at German American meeting halls in and around New York, announcing plans to train orators, expand the would-be shock troops of the Ordnungsdienst, enhance Hitler Youth–style indoctrination for boys and girls, involve the women's auxiliary in social-service projects, and leap unapologetically into American politics. He turned the DAWA, the boycott subsidiary that had been so successful in marking territory with its storefront stickers, into the German-American Business League or DKV, which continued boycott efforts while also hosting exhibits of German goods and participating in local trade conferences. He established the AV Publishing Company, which churned out the Bund's newspapers (including its flagship, the *Deutscher Weckruf und Beobachter*), magazines (a monthly youth publication called *Junges Volk*), and pamphlets ("Communism with the Mask Off," "The Riddle of the Jew's Success," etc.). He incorporated the German-American Settlement League, which purchased a picnic grounds along the banks of the Mill River in Yaphank, Long Island, a bucolic spot of forty-two acres renamed Camp Siegfried where Hitlerite families could "leave the pavements, the crowded thoroughfares, the dust, the noise of the city behind," and enjoy fellowship with "people that think as you do . . . cheerful people, honest and sincere, law-abiding!" The highlight of that summer was a festival of marching, singing, and drinking that attracted at least fifteen thousand German Americans, many of them delivered out from the city via a "Camp Siegfried Special" provided by the Long Island Rail Road. The remembered sight of uniformed Nazis in garrison caps, jackboots, and Sam Browne belts marching through the rural burgs of eastern Long Island would become an indelible part of local folklore.

Kuhn hoped all his good work would impress Reich officials, who would have no choice but to restore formal support to the most powerful expression of Nazism in the United States. With two hundred other Bundists, he set out for Germany aboard the Hamburg America liner *New York*, arriving in early July to a country seeking to remake itself for the Olympic games scheduled for the first two weeks of August. The Kuhnites traveled up and down the country, participating in Nazi functions and meeting with representatives of Reich agencies. But the highlight of the trip—and surely the highlight of Fritz Kuhn's stormy life—happened on August 2, when Kuhn and four of his lieutenants were granted an audience with their Führer, who was meeting with a number of visiting delegations at the Reich chancellery. Kuhn presented Hitler with a donation for a German relief agency and a leather-bound *Goldene Buch* detailing the history of Nazism in America signed by six thousand supporters. According to one of Kuhn's aides, "He asked us about our comrades of German blood across the sea, thanked us for our strong opposition to the immoral press and its infamous lies, and inquired in detail about the future plans of our Bund and our excursion through Germany." As they were leaving, Hitler urged the men to "go over there and continue the fight." Although Kuhn didn't receive the official sanction he was hoping for, he arrived in New York Harbor with something perhaps as valuable: A photograph of himself standing in the presence of the mystical embodiment of the German people. It would be widely published as obvious proof that Fritz Kuhn was Hitler's man in America.

On October 4, 1936, he made his triumphant return during the annual German Day celebration at Madison Square Garden, now back in the control of the Bundists and packed with more than twenty thousand men, women, and children. It certainly looked as if Kuhn was an official representative of the Reich: He shared the stage with Mayor Karl Stroehlin of Stuttgart and the German Ambassador to the United States, Hans Luther. The highlight of the evening was the address (in English) by Avery Brundage, chairman of the United States Olympic Committee, who was an example of a native-born American who *got* Nazi Germany. "We can learn much from Germany," he said to thunderous applause. "We, too, if we wish to preserve our institutions, must stamp out Communism. We, too, must take steps to arrest the decline of patriotism." A few days later, Kuhn made the strategic error of pledging the Bund's purported fifty thousand nationwide members to Alf Landon's run for the presidency, which forced the Republican candidate to endure embarrassing headlines about "Nazis to Get Out Votes for Landon" and "Vote for Landon, Nazis Here Told" and required the German embassy to deny that Hitler had made an endorsement in the presidential race. It couldn't have helped the anti-Roosevelt cause. On November 2, President Roosevelt won a massive landslide on the back of the rejuvenated New Deal. In an editorial for his house organ, Kuhn muttered about FDR's "mandate for dictatorship," expressing his wish that the president "find the physical and spiritual strength to resist the onslaughts of the vermin that is undermining our American institutions and putting the axe to the very roots of our foundations."

19 *In September, the* Chicago Daily: John C. Metcalfe, "I Am a U.S. Nazi Storm Trooper," and numerous accompanying articles, *Chicago Daily Times,* beginning September 9, 1937, and running through September 24, 1937.

20 *East Eighty-Sixth Street, the bustling:* In those days, the neighborhood's Germanic boundaries spread roughly east from Lexington Avenue to the East River and north from East Seventy-Ninth Street to East Ninety-Sixth Street, although it is impossible to draw precise lines in a metropolis as diverse and ever changing as New York. To the south was a Hungarian section, followed by a Czech quarter; to the north were the Italian and Puerto Rican divisions of East Harlem; to the west toward Central Park resided the wealthy denizens of Park, Madison, and Fifth Avenues, the "Silk Stocking" district. Scattered within were Irish and Jews, many of whom were enmeshed in the commercial, if not cultural, life of the community.

The story goes that the Germanization of Yorkville didn't begin until 1904, when the steamship *General Slocum* caught fire and sank in

NOTES

the East River, killing a thousand German immigrants on their way to a church picnic on Long Island and casting a kind of curse on the old neighborhood, Kleindeutschland, in what is today the East Village/Lower East Side. But the flight to the rapidly urbanizing quadrant of northern Manhattan was in full progress by the 1880s, aided by the construction of the elevated subway lines above Second and Third Avenues that allowed the four-mile journey to be completed in minutes. Jobs could be had in the breweries founded by German immigrants that occupied a large swath of Yorkville's northern section, including George Ehret's Hell Gate Brewery, which was the country's greatest producer of beer in 1877. Spiritual comfort was on offer in the Teutonic churches constructed in the final decades of the nineteenth century—Immanuel Evangelical Lutheran on East Eighty-Eighth Street at Lexington Avenue with its three bronze bells donated by Augusta, empress of Germany, the larger of two German Lutheran congregations in the neighborhood; St. Joseph's on East Eighty-Seventh Street, a German national Catholic parish in a "handsome brick building with a steeple that could have been lifted right out of the Black Forest," according to a church history; and, most spectacularly, the Episcopal Church of the Holy Trinity on East Eighty-Eighth Street near Second Avenue with a church, bell tower, rectory, and parish house built in French Gothic and Renaissance Revival styles to recall the ambience of the Loire Valley. Less architecturally striking were the rows of standard brownstones and brick tenements that were being thrown up to house the growing population.

Still, it's true that Yorkville didn't become America's Little Berlin until the early twentieth century, when secular shrines were erected to serve the innumerable benevolent associations, singing societies, home-region guilds, reading circles, women's auxiliaries, shooting clubs, etc., that were an indelible part of the German immigrant experience. "The first thing that two Germans do when they meet abroad is to found three associations" went the quip. The Yorkville Casino, which would remain the anchor of the main block of Eighty-Sixth Street until the 1960s, opened during the same year as the *Slocum* disaster, 1904. Built by a musicians' union, the six-story building had meeting rooms and performance spaces (including one of fifteen thousand square feet) that were used for political rallies, gala banquets, Bach recitals, theatrical performances, and, soon, first-

NOTES

run German-language motion pictures. The Casino was far from the only *large* gathering spot to welcome the *Vereine*. The multilevel Kreutzer Hall was opened just a few steps to the east to catch any overflow business. Two blocks south, the Labor Temple was established as a center for the Socialist and trade-union crowd, but before long it became a "funny, musty" place where "everything in the world goes on"—including singing-canary competitions hosted by "strange, little old people" who gather "around like gnomes listening eagerly to the silvery liquid notes of their birds," wrote a visitor. The New York Turnhalle at the corner of Eighty-Fifth and Lexington had a fourth-floor gymnasium among its assembly spaces, making it the natural headquarters for German sporting organizations, but it was better recognized around town for the ground-level restaurant, Adolph Suesskind's, which became Hans Jaeger's, which attracted sophisticated diners over from Park Avenue for its lamb chops and roast pork.

By the early 1920s, Yorkville was seen as "a quiet German colony, with German theaters, the occasional beer garden or two, an epidemic of delicatessen stores, pork stores and bird stores—active by day and wholly out of it by night," which is only partially true. A strip of vaudeville and movie houses lined the block of Eighty-Sixth between Lexington and Third, establishing what a magazine writer called "an important amusement center" that surely functioned after dark. Yet it was the appearance of a theme bar called Maxl's, which specialized in creatively flaunting the Prohibition laws, that inaugurated Yorkville as a nightlife hot spot listed in all the visitors' guides. In 1925, Maxl Harder opened a restaurant/tavern on the bottom half of a brownstone on the north side of Eighty-Sixth Street near Second Avenue that was remodeled (both exterior and interior) to evoke a *ye olde* cottage right out of *Grimm's Fairy Tales*, perhaps the first act in the Disneyfication of Manhattan. The scene inside was raucous. "There is a stringy three-piece orchestra, which stops every other moment to drink and sing a toast to each newcomer," according to one guidebook. The boozy highlight of the evening was the singing of "The Schnitzelbank Song," a number traditionally used to teach children the German language. Hilarity ensued as the conductor pointed with a "schoolmarm's rod" at "a huge poster bearing the words in German illustrated by quaint little drawings," while the orchestra squawked along in accompaniment. The place grew so popular and spawned so many imitators that it was required to call itself The Original Maxl's. Another guidebook described the genre: "A Brau Haus (86th Street version) is a place in which all the waiters wear short, corduroy pants, Alpine hats, socks that cover only the calves of their legs, and funny suspenders," wrote Rian James in 1934. "The gentlemen are engaged (1) because they have grand German accents; (2) because, even if they can't sing, at least they know all the words to the popular old-school German *Bräustüberl* ditties; and (3) because they have learned to transport successfully sixteen steins of beers in one hand, while they write out and incorrectly add a patron's check with the other!" It was suggested that people avoid visiting during college football season, when "the teams and cheering sections are in town" from Syracuse, New Haven, or Pittsburgh, which makes it "a little bit strenuous for anyone who isn't up on forward-passing a frankfurter."

Although the Yorkville beer gardens survived Prohibition largely unmolested for reasons that might've had to do with the respected US senator who lived at 244 East Eighty-Sixth Street (the German-born Robert F. Wagner Sr.), Harder sold out for big money in 1929 and opened a classier joint across the street that was not reliant on the ostentatious consumption of vats of Bavarian lager. The Café Hindenburg featured dancing to the big-band sounds of Maria Wadynski and her orchestra in an upstairs ballroom and chocolates and pralines over quiet conversation in the downstairs lounge. Even with the onset of the Depression, the Hindenburg faced strong competition from along the boulevard and up and down the side streets, which only increased after Prohibition's repeal in 1933 removed any worries about the open consumption of spirits. The Gloria Palast (in the lower level of the Yorkville Casino building) described itself as "Yorkville's leading cabaret restaurant," with three large dining and fox-trotting spaces that could hold upward of two thousand people. Directly across the street, the Corso also went for the sleek look of a Fred Astaire–Ginger Rogers picture ("a futuristic stairway"), but boasted that its two orchestras could be enjoyed without a minimum-drink requirement. A few strides to the east, Restaurant Platzl employed the "famous" Willie Schiesser to direct its orchestra for nightly dancing, while the Café Mozart (249 East Eighty-Sixth Street) had Franze Deutschmann and his men render the romantic waltz beneath a bust of Wolfgang Amadeus with pfeffernüsse, anise, marzipan, and *Apfelstrudel* served till dawn. "A broad, bustling cross-

way, where you will find diversion good and plenty," wrote a nightlife author of New York's version of Unter den Linden. "Picture and
four-a-day vaudeville halls. Beer dens with yodeling waiters. Roof
gardens echoing guttural song. Fox trots at ten cents a dance. Plain,
unpretentious haunts, on the whole, with a sympathetic air. And
even if evening togs be few, the laughter is real and spontaneous."

    Charles Shaw, *Nightlife* (New York: John Day, 1931), 139–43;
Helen Worden, *The Real New York: A Guide for the Adventurous Shop-
per, the Exploratory Eater, and the Know-It-All Sightseer Who Ain't Seen
Nothin' Yet* (Indianapolis: Bobbs-Merrill, 1932), 338–49; "Yorkville,
Where Beer Never Ceased to Flow, Will Celebrate Return of Legal-
ity Tonight," *New York Times*, April 7, 1933; James Rian, *Dining in New
York, an Intimate Guide* (New York: John Day, 1934), 127–29, 241–44;
Scudder Middleton, *Dining, Wining, and Dancing in New York* (New
York: Dodge Publishing, 1938), 82–85; and "News and Gossip of
Night Clubs," *New York Times*, May 1, 1938.

20 *237,588 German-born and 127,169 Austrian-born:* According to the 1930
census. Ira Rosenwaike, *Population History of New York City* (Syracuse,
NY: Syracuse University Press, 1972), 205.

21 *"comes from pride in the":* New York Post, April 30, 1938.

22 *"We called them undercover men":* US Congress, House Special Committee on Un-American Activities, *Investigation of Un-American Propaganda Activities in the U.S.*, vol. 6, 1st sess., testimony of Helen Vooros,
August 18, 1939.

22 *J. Edgar Hoover, then forty-two:* Raymond J. Batvinis, *The Origins of
FBI Counterintelligence* (Lawrence: University Press of Kansas, 2007),
34–35, 48; Curt Gentry, *J. Edgar Hoover: The Man and the Secrets* (New
York: W. W. Norton, 1991), 207–9; and "Spy Quiz Shows U.S. Has
None of Its Own," *New York Daily News*, June 21, 1938. Mr. Batvinis
provides a comprehensive account of the FBI's counterintelligence
creation story in his important book. A scholar and former FBI special agent, he was most generous in offering his insights and research
assistance to the author.

25 *creation of Carl Lukas Norden:* The institutional history of Carl L.
Norden Inc. is explored in Stephen L. McFarland, *America's Pursuit
of Precision Bombing, 1910–1945* (Washington, DC: Smithsonian Institution Press, 1995).

25 *According to an internal history:* "Story of Norden Bombsight
Released," *Norden Insight* newsletter, December 1944.

26 *"My dear, we are a":* Ibid.

26 *in the living room of his Queens apartment:* In his book, Ritter writes that Pop Sohn lived at 248 Monitor Street, which is located in the Greenpoint neighborhood of Brooklyn. Public records reveal that Pop Sohn lived at 70-12 Sixty-Sixth Street in Glendale on the Queens-Brooklyn border, demonstrating Ritter's tendency to add dubious color to incidents that we know from other sources did actually occur.

27 *"technicians occupying responsible posts, many":* United States v. German-American Vocational League, Inc., et al., Case Files 2017C–2018C, Selected Case Files, 1929–ca. 1980, Office of the US Attorney for the Judicial District of New Jersey, Record Group 118, National Archives at New York City.

29 *Frederick "Fritz" Joubert Duquesne was:* Art Ronnie, *Counterfeit Hero: Fritz Duquesne, Adventurer and Spy* (Annapolis, MD: Naval Institute Press, 1995), 211. Mr. Ronnie's rollicking and well-researched biography goes a long way toward separating fact from fiction in Duquesne's story. "He was no hero," the author concludes, "but his was an incredible life encompassing bizarre exploits of drama, danger, and adventure few people are privileged to live." Mr. Ronnie was the picture of collegiality in providing archival materials to the author.

30 *"superlative gift of oriental storytelling":* Ibid., 102.

30 *"Suppose an elephant charges me":* "Get Tip on Big Game: President Learns How to Shoot Beasts of the Jungle," *Washington Post*, January 20, 1909.

31 *"directed all operations connected with":* Fritz Joubert Duquesne file, KV2/1955, British Archives, Records of the Security Service, Kew, London.

32 *"Speculation would suggest that he":* Ronnie, *Counterfeit Hero*, 136.

33 *"infinitely truer than any bald:"* Clement Wood, *The Man Who Killed Kitchener: The Life of Fritz Joubert Duquesne* (New York: W. Faro, 1932), 13.

35 *"all information possible about the":* Ritter's British interrogation.

CHAPTER THREE: ALMOST SINGLE-HANDED

38 *"in immediate proximity to the":* William L. Shirer, *The Rise and Fall of the Third Reich: A History of Nazi Germany* (New York: Simon and Schuster, 1960), 307.

40 *The supervisor answering the call:* Smelling a rat, Ira F. Hoyt, the office's supervisor, asked Rumrich if he could call him back to confirm his identity. Rumrich said, "unfortunately I could not reach him as he was at the Waldorf Astoria incognito and that no one must know that he is in the city; that this was all very secret and that the press must positively not get a word," Hoyt wrote. "He said that he felt sure I understood the meaning and his mission." Realizing the call was a fake, Hoyt agreed to send the passports to the Taft Hotel as instructed, estimating that it would take about an hour for them to arrive. After hanging up, he called Washington to confirm that Secretary Hull wasn't in New York and then made arrangements with a special agent of the State Department and two detectives from the NYPD's Alien Squad to meet in front of the Taft, located just north of Times Square. The officers would arrest the mysterious caller when he appeared in the lobby to receive a package of dummy passports from Mr. Hoyt. (Hoyt's statement, File 862.20211/1760, Box 6773, Record Group 59, General Records of the State Department, National Archives, College Park, MD.)

As Rumrich later admitted to authorities, he hung up the pay phone "almost certain" that Mr. Hoyt "knew he had not spoken to the Secretary of State." Despite his trepidation, he hopped the uptown IRT to Grand Central Station, found a phone booth, and placed a call to the Taft, asking if a package had arrived for Edward Weston. He was told it hadn't. He then dialed the Western Union office within the terminal and asked the dispatcher to send a messenger—"a boy," he called him—to pick up a package expected shortly at the Taft. After waiting for what must've been upward of a half hour to forty-five minutes, Rumrich called Western Union, asked if the package from the Taft had been retrieved, and was told the messenger had come and gone without finding it. Rumrich then slumped his shoulders and took the train back to the Bronx, "almost certain that the whole thing was off."

When Mr. Hoyt arrived at the Taft, he discovered that he had missed the connection with the messenger. He milled about the ornate lobby, which featured a woman in a glass booth under an ASK MISS ALLEN sign who distributed tourist maps and cut-rate Broadway tickets, while his police backup kept a covert watch on the door. "After waiting about forty-five minutes I went to the washroom after giving Mr. Tubbs [the State Department special agent] the wink and a little while after he followed to the washroom and we discussed procedure from then on," Mr. Hoyt wrote. Alas, Mr. Hoyt's brief career in counterespionage was over. He handed the envelope of fake passports over to a Mr. Robbins of the Package Room, spoke with the detectives outside on Fifty-First Street about his capitulation, and took the train back downtown with Mr. Tubbs. When the Western Union messenger showed up again to pick up the passports, the two NYPD detectives tailed him across midtown traffic to Grand Central Station, where they "will remain on duty until that package is picked up whether it is tonight or tomorrow or when," Hoyt told Washington.

Next morning, Rumrich reported for work as usual at his chemical company job at 163 Varick Street, where he was employed as a translator for $22.50 a week. At 12:15 p.m., he thought he'd give another try to the Western Union office at Grand Central. "I inquired whether the package had been called for from the Taft Hotel," he said. "The man answering the telephone said 'yes,' the package was being held there for me. He spoke so resolutely that I dismissed my doubts of the previous day." Rumrich asked for the package to be delivered to the Western Union office at 200 Varick Street, then went downstairs, posting himself across the street "to see if a package was being brought from the subway." But when nothing showed up by one minute to 1:00 p.m., he returned to his job.

After turning it over in his head for much of the early afternoon, Rumrich called the Kings Castle Tavern, where he sometimes lunched, and asked the proprietor's daughter if she would accept a delivery on his behalf, with the promise that he would reimburse the costs when he was able to come by. She agreed. Leaving the office again, he parked himself in a cigar store on Varick, used its phone to confirm that the Weston materials had arrived, and asked for the package to be rerouted to the tavern. He watched as the uniformed messenger walked half a block south and turned right on King Street. Rumrich took a parallel street, Houston, in the same (westerly) direction, turning south onto Hudson Street after one block and reaching the northwest corner of King and Hudson in time to see the messenger enter the tavern. Allowing sufficient time to lapse, Rumrich went in and ordered a beer from the bar. But something didn't feel right. "The place was rather dark," he said. He left without requesting the package.

Once outside, he asked a boy to do him a favor, explaining that he wanted to avoid the bartender at the Kings Castle because he owed him money. The boy agreed. Rumrich handed over two $1 bills and scurried to the other side of the street in his nervousness. When the boy returned to the original spot with the package in his hand, Rumrich whistled him across the street. But there was a problem. The boy wanted additional compensation for his labors, and Rumrich had "altogether 10 cents in my possession." As the argument escalated, detectives John Murray and Arthur Silk of the NYPD's Alien Squad broke in on the scene and took "Gus" Rumrich into custody.

40 *"much harder than the life"*: Statement of Guenther Rumrich, File 862.20211/1763, Box 6773, Record Group 59, General Records of the State Department, National Archives, College Park, MD.

40 *Dr. Ignatz Griebl, a Nazi*: Griebl was briefly president of the Friends of the New Germany, the pro-Nazi organization that became the German American Bund. During the organization's German Day celebration in October 1934, held on the grand stage of Madison Square Garden, he announced that anyone "who fights us must perish—socially as well as economically—because of our determination to destroy our enemies completely and without any consideration whatever." He was also the author of a seventy-one-page exercise in anti-Semitica called *Salute the Jew!,* which he wrote under a pseudonym, William Hamilton. He explained that he feared the Jews would destroy him if they knew he wrote it. "They are everywhere and at all times prepared to deliver a serious blow or declare an economic war on any people of different blood or of white origin," he wrote, noting that "Jews should never be regarded as a white race" because "their origin is as black as that of their brothers of common race and blood, the Syrians, Arabs, and Abyssinians of Asia and Africa."

Dr. Griebl's medical practice and residence was located in the beaux arts building at 56 East Eighty-Seventh Street next door to the ornate side entrance of the Park Avenue Synagogue. The waiting room of his office was graced with a large portrait of Field Marshal Paul von Hindenberg and typically filled with the higher class of German women, drawn by his specialties in gynecology and varicose veins. It was from among this population that he selected his mistresses, which caused considerable pain to his otherwise formidable partner in Hitlerism, Mrs. Griebl, who initially refused to swear on the "old Jewish Testament" or respond to questions from "Jewish judges and a Jewish district attorney" when she appeared before a federal grand jury investigating a Nazi comrade.

The FBI discovered that he kept an extensive library of files on prominent Jews in New York, cataloging their "birthplaces, schooling, and residences at all stages of their careers, their social, business, fraternal, and political connections, their estimated wealth, their friendships with non-Jews of note, the offices they held," Leon Turrou wrote. "It made, apparently, no difference whether they were professing Jews or not, as long as they had Jewish blood. I noted names which surprised me. All notes were interlarded with scurrilous, often obscene, remarks."

41 *"We handled him with gloves"*: Leon Turrou, *Nazi Spies in America* (New York: Random House, 1938), 136.

41 *"In every strategic point in"*: Ibid., 12.

42 *"partly false, partly exaggerated remarks"*: Nest Bremen's *Leiter* was Erich Pheiffer. His extensive interrogation is available in file KV2/267, British Archives, Records of the Security Service, Kew, London.

42 *According to Griebl's later statement*: Statement of Ignatz T. Griebl, File 862.20211/1850, Box 6773, Record Group 59, General Records of the State Department, National Archives, College Park, MD.

43 *J. Edgar Hoover was incensed*: "Hoover and Hardy Clash in Spy Case: FBI Holds Prosecutor Responsible for Escapes—Official Here Denies It," *New York Times*, June 2, 1938.

44 *"Nazi Gestapo men saw him"*: Turrou, *Nazi Spies in America*, 282.

48 *"mammoth bureaucracy, composed of mediocrities"*: Heinkel, *Stormy Life*, 187.

48 *"If we win the fight"*: David Irving, *The Rise and Fall of the Luftwaffe: The Life of Field Marshal Erhard Milch* (Boston: Little, Brown, 1974), 61.

50 the *Daily News* mused that: "Can Anything Be Done for the Austrian Jews?," *New York Daily News*, March 15, 1938.

50 *He penned two long memos*: Documents on German Foreign Policy, series D (Washington, DC: US Government Printing Office, 1951), 1:635–39, 1:664–77.

50 *a directive of two sentences*: Ibid., 1:691.

51 *Special Committee on Un-American Activities*: The congressional experience with un-American investigations can be traced to the efforts of one Congressman Samuel Dickstein. A Vilnius-born cantor's son who represented the Lower East Side, he convened informal hearings in late 1933, "Nazi Propaganda Activities by Aliens in the U.S.," under

the auspices of his Committee on Immigration and Naturalization. The impetus was the negative publicity surrounding the Friends of the New Germany. During five sessions in November and December, customs guards, journalists, seamen, and union officials detailed how German sailors were delivering printed matter, military garb, propaganda films, and spy directives to pro-Nazi operatives in the United States, particularly in the oft-mentioned Yorkville. In executive session, a witness described how two sailors of Nazi affiliation asked him if he would "represent them here as American agent" during a meeting at the Café Hindenburg on Eighty-Sixth Street. Another requested anonymity because "I am well-known in Yorkville and New York City, and they will make it very hard for me, as there are too many of them; they will make it so very hard for me that I will probably have to leave New York."

When Congress reconvened in January 1934, Congressman Dickstein pushed for a new, wider inquiry into what he described as an effort to undermine the foundations of our democratic system. He claimed on the House floor, "We have dozens of spies coming to America as sailors on German boats . . . trying to spread hate among our people," which caused the *New York Herald Tribune* to scoff that since the spies "had failed completely in this, Mr. Dickstein will organize a first-class heresy hunt to spread it for them." In the spring, the House of Representatives voted 168–31 to create the Special Committee on Un-American Activities Authorized to Investigate Nazi Propaganda and Certain Other Propaganda Activities, the "certain other" designation a concession to legislators, including those with large German American constituencies, more interested in examining the threat from Communist infiltration.

The McCormack-Dickstein Committee—it was chaired by the Irish Catholic representative John W. McCormack of South Boston to prevent "unkind criticism by certain persons or organizations," Dickstein said—heard testimony from an array of Nazi-sympathetic organizations and individuals, amplifying the message that *German-sponsored* Hitlerism was establishing a beachhead in America. Prominent figures in the public relations field, including "Poison" Ivy Lee (a well-known mouthpiece for John D. Rockefeller's Standard Oil) and Carl Byoir (whose PR firm was among the biggest in the country), were shown to have received Joseph Goebbels's money to burnish National Socialism's image in the

United States. Connections were drawn between German American supporters of Hitler and native-led Fascist groups such as William Dudley Pelley's Silver Legion of America (the so-called Silver Shirts), which promulgated the idea that President Roosevelt was descended from a Dutch Jewish family and his real name was Rosenfeld. Testimony revealed that New York–based members of the Stahlhelm (or Steel Helmets), a paramilitary clique of war veterans that conducted bloody battles with Communists during the Weimar years, had become integral members of the Nazi movement in the city. "No," said Bertha Ziegler, the proprietor of the F. X. Mittemeier bookshop at 229 East Eighty-Sixth Street when asked if she read the Nazi books, magazines, and newspapers she stocked in her store. "I just sell them." Several officers of the Friends of the New Germany testified without qualm about how membership lists had grown tenfold since the beginning of the year with fifteen locals now in operation in New York City and its suburbs alone. A Friends' turncoat told the committee that transatlantic couriers on the German liners were utilized to send messages to the Reich about those in Yorkville or Ridgewood who were unwilling to honor the legitimacy of the Hitlerites' claim on German American loyalty, an assertion that resulted in headlines about a "Nazi spy system" operating in New York. ("Nazi Spy System Is Reported Here," *New York Times,* October 17, 1934.)

"You do know of instances, however, where they have taken it out on relatives in Germany of people here who have not obeyed orders?" asked Thomas Hardwick, the committee's counsel and a former governor of Georgia.

"Of course, it is an official order," the witness responded.

"What do they do to these relatives?"

"They are immediately put in a concentration camp, if there are no reasons to be found, and they are investigated."

"They are put on suspicion and sometimes put in a concentration camp?" Mr. Hardwick asked.

"Yes."

"You know that to be true?"

"Absolutely."

When the Dies Committee was created as an explicit extension of McCormack-Dickstein in 1938, Congressman Dickstein wasn't appointed as a member, which had the effect of neutering his career as a Hitler scourge and ending the secret payments he had just started receiving from the Soviet Union: the opening of the KGB archives in the 1990s revealed that he had been in the employ of the Soviet Secret Service. His code name was Crook for his incessant demands for money. John Earl Haynes and Alexander Vassiliev, *Spies: The Rise and Fall of the KGB in America* (New Haven, CT: Yale University Press, 2009), 285–87.

55 *"Any comment you care to": Press Conferences of President Franklin D. Roosevelt, 1933–1945*, vol. 11 (New York: DaCapo Press, 1972), 488–90.

CHAPTER FOUR: TRUE FAITH AND ALLEGIANCE

59 *"What is America but millionaires":* Ernst Hanfstaengl, *Hitler: The Missing Years* (New York: Arcade, 1994), 222.

59 *"a sanctuary for those whom":* Thomas Jefferson, *The Writings of Thomas Jefferson: Being his autobiography, correspondence, reports, messages, addresses, and other writings, official and private* (New York: J. C. Riker, 1853–55), 7:84.

59 *"Don't you talk to me":* All the Sebold quotations from this chapter are from the trial transcript.

61 *August Thyssen, the steel magnate:* Jeffrey Fear, *Organizing Control: August Thyssen and the Construction of German Corporate Management* (Cambridge, MA: Harvard University Press, 2005), 396–411.

64 *Sebold hopped from job to:* Personal Employment Record, W. G. Sebold, property of Sebold family.

CHAPTER FIVE: WITH THE RESOURCES WE HAVE ON HAND

67 *"The techniques of advanced scientific":* The editors of *Look* magazine, *The Story of the FBI* (New York: E. P. Dutton, 1947), 21.

68 *"here was a man who":* Winston S. Churchill, *The Second World War, Vol. 1, the Gathering Storm* (Boston: Houghton Mifflin, 1948), 269.

69 *Flying back to London:* Michael Burleigh, *Moral Combat: Good and Evil in World War II* (New York: Harper, 2011), 37.

69 *"German air strength is greater":* Max Wallace, *The American Axis: Henry Ford, Charles Lindbergh, and the Rise of the Third Reich* (New York: St. Martin's Press, 2003), 174.

NOTES

70 *"A war of destruction against"*: Corum, *Luftwaffe*, 256–57.

70 *The Luftwaffe had about*: Wesley K. Wark, *The Ultimate Enemy: British Intelligence and Nazi Germany, 1933–1939* (Ithaca, NY: Cornell University Press, 1985), 245.

70 *Luftwaffe's medium bombers had no*: Irving, *Rise and Fall of the Luftwaffe*, 64.

72 *"execute a gigantic production program"*: Ibid., 67.

72 *mass production of two planes*: The two planes were the Heinkel He 177 and the Junkers Ju 88 "wonder bomber."

72 *Yet Ernst Udet insisted that*: Irving, *Rise and Fall of the Luftwaffe*, 65.

72 *Orders were issued to develop*: McFarland, *America's Pursuit of Precision Bombing*, 82.

72 *"It is comparatively easy to"*: "Norden Aide Says Nazi Bombsight Is 'Cumbersome,'" *Chicago Tribune*, April 13, 1943.

73 *When asked by reporters about*: *Press Conferences of President Roosevelt*, 12:145–47.

75 *espionage report to President Roosevelt*: Homer S. Cummings to President Roosevelt, Memorandum, October 20, 1938, Box 100, Attorney General Personal File, Homer S. Cummings Papers, Alderman Library, University of Virginia.

75 *"special legislation which would draw"*: "An Analysis of FBI Domestic Security Intelligence Investigations: Authority, Official Attitudes, and Activities in Historical Perspective," October 26, 1975, an FBI-prepared report submitted to the Senate Select Committee to Study Governmental Operations with Respect to Intelligence Activities (known as the Church Committee), 563–66; and Batvinis, *Origins of FBI Counterintelligence*, 56–57.

78 *According to a memo Hoover*: "Analysis of FBI Domestic Security Intelligence Investigations," 566–67.

79 *"to serve the American Public"*: *U.S. v. Karl Schleuter, et al.*, US District Court for the Southern District of New York, Record Group 21, National Archives at New York City.

81 *"The foreign press is very"*: Saul Friedlander, *Nazi Germany and the Jews* (New York: HarperCollins, 1997), 1:298–99.

81 *"a vote of condemnation so"*: Maria Mazzenga, ed., *American Religious Responses to Kristallnacht* (New York: Palgrave Macmillan, 2009), 2.

82 *"A new regiment of field"*: John Buckley, *Air Power in the Age of Total War* (Bloomington: Indiana University Press, 1999), 122.

83 *"A battle was won in"*: H. H. Arnold, *Global Mission* (New York: Harper and Brothers, 1949), 177.

84 *"perfectly amazing job in this"*: Press Conferences of President Roosevelt, 12:288–90.

CHAPTER SIX: TO LEAD AN ORGANIZATION THERE

85 *According to his service:* Personal Employment Record, W. G. Sebold.

87 *"all possible preferential treatment such"*: Documents on German Foreign Policy, series D, 4:651–52.

89 *"It is not a question"*: Keith D. McFarland, *Harry H. Woodring: A Political Biography of FDR's Controversial Secretary of War* (Lawrence: University Press of Kansas, 1975), 189.

90 *"international spy ring story you"*: Michael E. Birdwell, *Celluloid Soldiers: The Warner Bros. Campaign Against Nazism* (New York and London: New York University Press, 1999), 70.

94 *After a handful of NYPD officers carried:* Izzy Greenbaum's beating at the hands of Bundist thugs was the highlight of newsreel footage, which was pulled from movie theaters after two days because of the commotion it caused. "You say many women and children might have been killed or injured," Greenbaum told a city magistrate who gave him the choice of spending ten days in jail or paying a $25 fine for disorderly conduct. "Your honor, do you know how many children and innocent persons will be killed if the persecution they were speaking of last night were kept up?" He was freed after a Yiddish-language newspaper, *Der Tog*, offered to pay his penalty. "With him in court were his baby son and wife, Gertrude, who said her husband is 'kind and gentle' and 'no troublemaker' for all his clambering on to the speaker's platform in the middle of the tense rally," the *Brooklyn Eagle* wrote of the hometown hero. "He is all a person could wish to find in another," young Mrs. Greenbaum told the paper. "He is strong-willed, determined, proud. Didn't he work days as a plumber and nights waiting tables when the baby was born so that I could have everything?"

During an interview in 2011, one of Greenbaum's children, Bobbi Ott, said her father attended the rally with no intention of causing trouble. "He never planned anything in his life," she explained. Overcome by the moment, he rushed the stage not to injure Fritz Kuhn but to snatch his microphone, she said.

"He told me he actually got more hurt from the German doctor in the emergency room who, my grandpa told me, intentionally poked a needle in his back when he heard what my grandfather did," said Mr. Greenbaum's grandson, Brett Siciliano. "The needle incident hurt him for many years after."

Greenbaum moved to California in 1970 and became a fixture at the Newport Beach Pier, where he was known as "Pops." His fishing spot was called "Pops' Corner." According to the *Los Angeles Times* obituary published upon his death in 1997, "Along with his bait and tackle, Greenbaum decorated his corner every day with an American flag and photos of himself with people he met on the pier." Said another obit: "Near his displays he kept fishing poles with fish on them—if passersby picked them up, he'd take their photo and send it to them in the mail." The articles made no mention of his flamboyant act of anti-Nazi resistance.

"They show the clip on the History Channel," said Ms. Ott of the Madison Square Garden moment. "My mother would call me and say, 'Your crazy father is on TV again.'"

96 *the pages of* Musical America: *Musical America*, May 22, 1915.

96 *Elmer Sperry, who had founded:* Thomas Parke Hughes, *Elmer Sperry: Inventor and Engineer* (Baltimore and London: Johns Hopkins University Press, 1971).

99 *"my robot," which was "uncanny":* "Wiley Post Tells of Faith in Robot," *New York Times*, July 16, 1933.

99 *most advanced versions of each:* "Sperry: The Corporation," *Fortune*, May 1940.

99 *an antiaircraft-gun-directing system:* David A. Mindell, *Between Human and Machine: Feedback, Control, and Computing Before Cybernetics* (Baltimore: Johns Hopkins University Press, 2002), 88.

100 *Nazi Germany's highest-paid agent:* These details are gleaned from the voluminous FBI file on the Duquesne case, or, as it was known to the Bureau, the Ducase. The file is 65-1819. Hereafter cited as Duquesne case FBI file. In his 1953 interview with the German newsweekly *Stern*, Nikolaus Ritter says that during his 1937 visit to the United States he met with Everett Roeder. At that point, Roeder had been supplying materials to "Sanders" at Ast Hamburg for more than a year. In his memoir, Ritter doesn't mention Roeder but tells a fanciful tale about meeting with a Sperry employee he calls Burger, who was married to a "hotblooded and domineering" Puerto Rican intent on having Ritter arrested. ("'You damned German,' she hissed at me and did not even try to get herself under control," Ritter wrote. "'I hate

you. I hate you all. My husband told me everything, and he was stupid enough to think that I would help. Anybody else, yes—but never a German! You—*spy!*'") In fact, Ed Roeder was married to a Sullinger from the Bronx who never made an attempt to inform on him. Following Ritter's visit, Roeder began sending intelligence to "Dr. Leonhardt," one of Ritter's aliases, at Rothenbaumchaussee 135, Nikolaus Ritter's new address in Hamburg.

103 *"Well, when I arrived at"*: The diary of Special Agent James C. Ellsworth, courtesy of the Ellsworth family.

CHAPTER SEVEN: IN THIS SOLEMN HOUR

105 *"The Führer had to come"*: Marvin D. Miller, *Wunderlich's Salute: The Interrelationship of the German-American Bund, Camp Siegfried, Yaphank, Long Island, and the Young Siegfrieds and Their Relationship with American and Nazi Institutions* (Smithtown, NY: Malamud-Rose, 1983), 134.

106 *"frontiers we had proposed to"*: Churchill, *Gathering Storm*, 307.

109 *"The first B-17 was due"*: David Zimmerman, *Top Secret Exchange: The Tizard Mission and the Scientific War* (Montreal: McGill-Queen's University Press, 1996), 36–38.

110 *"In times like these, there"*: New York Times, March 24, 1939.

110 *"Where does he get his"*: Bernard F. Dick, *The Star-Spangled Screen: The American World War II Film* (Lexington: University Press of Kentucky, 1985), 51.

111 *"into cases involving actually or:"* "Analysis of FBI Domestic Security Intelligence Investigations," 568–69.

111 *"Anti-Spy Work Centered Under"*: Also: "1,000 Spy Cases Under FBI Scrutiny," *Washington Post*, June 16, 1939.

111 *"no investigations should be"*: "Analysis of FBI Domestic Security Intelligence Investigations," 570.

112 *"document identification, electrical equipment and"*: FBI file of Special Agent James C. Ellsworth, 317.

112 *"The contents of the letter"*: Details of Sebold's coercion into the service of the Abwehr come from the Duquesne FBI case file and the trial transcript.

115 *"German houses broken into with"*: Evans, *Third Reich in Power*, 696.

117 *"My Dear Mr. President"*: PREM 4/25/1. British Archives, Records of the Prime Minister's Office, Kew, London.

119 *scored direct hits on a blasting device:* Cajus Bekker, *The Luftwaffe War Diaries: The German Air Force in World War II* (Edinburgh: Birlinn, 2001), 26–27.

119 *Yet the most lethal of:* Timothy Snyder, *Bloodlands: Europe Between Hitler and Stalin* (London: Vintage, 2011), 119.

121 *"all local law enforcement officers":* "Analysis of FBI Domestic Security Intelligence Investigations," 571–72.

121 *"to protect this country against":* Tim Weiner, *Enemies: A History of the FBI* (New York: Random House, 2012), 83.

121 *Nearly two hundred acts:* Jules Witcover, *Sabotage at Black Tom: Imperial Germany's Secret War in America, 1914–1917* (Chapel Hill, NC: Algonquin Books of Chapel Hill, 1989), 321.

122 *"apprehended plotters and prevented consummation":* Emerson Hough, *The Web: A Revelation of Patriotism* (Chicago: Reilly and Lee, 1919), 59.

The other great explosion of the violent campaign occurred on January 11, 1917, when four hours of blasts destroyed the Canadian Car and Foundry Company plant in Kingsland, New Jersey, which manufactured artillery shells for Britain and Russia. One man perished in an attempt to escape from the chaos.

The American decision to join the war as a combatant nation on April 6, 1917, was made in response to unrestricted submarine warfare against American shipping in the Atlantic Ocean and the publication of the so-called Zimmerman Telegram, which revealed a German government attempt to persuade the Mexicans to invade the Southwestern United States with the help of the Japanese. But President Woodrow Wilson explicitly pointed to German-sponsored actions within the boundaries of the United States, and conducted with the assistance of some of its residents, as one of the "extraordinary insults and aggressions of the Imperial German government" that "left us no self-respecting choice but to take up arms in defense of our rights as a free people and of our honor as a sovereign government." In his Flag Day speech of June 14, 1917, Wilson said that Germany had "filled our unsuspecting communities with vicious spies and conspirators" and "sought by violence to destroy our industries and arrest our commerce."

Upon American entry into the war, the government acted quickly to impose what President Wilson called "a firm hand of stern repression" against anyone deemed too sympathetic to the other side. Most German saboteurs took this opportunity to flee to Mexico or farther south of the border. The president issued two executive orders that sought to restrict the activities of "enemy aliens," noncitizens born in the Central Powers nations, with the second requiring them to register with federal authorities or face imprisonment (as sixty-three hundred eventually did), a process overseen by a Justice Department law clerk who was always willing to work late, John Edgar Hoover. Within nine weeks of the war declaration, Congress passed the Espionage Act of 1917 and strengthened it the following year with the Sedition Act of 1918, which abridged the First Amendment by making it a crime to "utter, print, write, or publish any disloyal, profane, scurrilous, or abusive language about the form of government of the United States, or the Constitution of the United States, or the military or naval forces of the United States."

Gripped by a wartime panic of such determined ferocity, the nation sought to purge itself of anything that smacked of Germanness. Town and street names were changed (out with Berlin or Germantown, in with Lincoln and Pershing); Beethoven, Wagner, and Strauss were stricken from the repertories of symphony orchestras; German-language books were burned during patriotic rallies; the frankfurter became known in common parlance as the hot dog, inaugurating its journey to the quintessence of American cuisine. The same state legislatures that were passing laws that sought to ban the speaking of the German language in public were also voting in favor of the proposed Eighteenth Amendment to the US Constitution, which, when ratified in 1919 and adopted into law in 1920, prohibited just the sort of "intoxicating liquors" that were being produced in large quantities by German Americans with names such as Pabst, Miller, Anheuser, and Busch.

124 *Sebold made a "nationalistic impression":* "Jürgen Thorwald: Die unsichtbare Front. Das Tagebuch von OKW/Abwehr enthüllt den Einsatz des deutschen Geheimdienstes," *Stern,* March 15, 1953. Thorwald was assisted in his reporting by *Stern* reporter Günter Peis.

126 *Hitler was reviewing his triumphant:* Max Hastings, *Inferno: The World at War, 1939–1945* (New York: Alfred A. Knopf, 2011), 23.

127 *Klieforth offered his version in:* William Sebold, 10/26/39, Confidential File 862.20211/2249, Surveillance of William Sebold by Agents of the German Government, and William Sebold, 11/6/39, File

NOTES

340.1115/8207, Welfare and Whereabouts of American Citizen in Europe, Record Group 59, General Records of the State Department, National Archives, College Park, MD.

128 *"These wars in Europe are":* Leonard Mosley, *Lindbergh: A Biography* (Garden City, NY: Doubleday, 1976), 259.

129 *"will not evaporate into thin":* Quotations from La Follette's speech, *Daily Worker,* October 13, 1939.

129 *"driving Judaism out of government":* "Guardsmen Accuse Capt. Prout in Plot," *New York Times,* May 7, 1940.

130 *more than two hundred of:* Nathan Miller, *War at Sea: A Naval History of World War II* (New York: Scribner, 1995), 534.

130 *FDR was so fearful of:* Robert Dallek, *Franklin D. Roosevelt and American Foreign Policy, 1932–1945* (New York: Oxford University Press, 1979), 203.

130 *The US Navy was mostly:* Robert W. Love Jr., *History of the U.S. Navy* (Harrisburg, PA: Stackpole Books, 1992), 1:616.

130 *Of the Air Corps' more:* Bernard C. Nalty, general ed., *Winged Shield, Winged Sword: A History of the United States Air Force* (Washington, DC: Air Force History and Museums Program, 1997), 1:162.

130 *A bare fourteen of the:* Thomas H. Greer, *The Development of Air Doctrine in the Army Air Arm, 1917–1941* (Washington, DC: Office of Air Force History, US Air Force, 1985), 101.

131 *"only makes foreign agents try":* Zimmerman, *Top Secret Exchange,* 45.

132 *pledging to continue cultivating the:* Sander A. Diamond, *The Nazi Movement in the United States, 1924–1941* (Ithaca, NY: Cornell University Press, 1974), 333.

132 *"Every time a Pole appeared":* Nicholas Jenkins, "Goodbye, 1939," *New Yorker,* April 1, 1996.

137 *On the next morning, Sebold:* James C. Ellsworth diary.

CHAPTER EIGHT: "YOU ARE HARRY SAWYER"

140 *Sebold was escorted unnoticed past:* From an interview with former special agent William G. Friedemann conducted by author Art Ronnie, November 29, 1974. Special thanks to Mr. Ronnie for providing a copy of the interview notes. The principal sources for the narrative of the investigation are the Duquesne case FBI file and the trial transcript.

140 *Newkirk, in his unpublished memoirs:* Agent Newkirk's unpublished memoir was provided to the author courtesy of the Newkirk family.

141 *after once drinking from:* From a privately published booklet entitled "Memories of Jim and Nell Ellsworth," 17.

142 *dinner guests of the Vetterlis:* "That night Nell and I were dinner guests of the Vetterlis in their apartment and Reed of course was still very upset," Jim Ellsworth wrote in a postretirement journal. "During the evening he took me aside and said, 'Jim, I have been in 3 shooting scrapes now and have had men knocked down all around me but I have never been touched. I attribute this to the fact that I always wear my garments. You would never catch me day or night without my garments on. I have every faith in their protective power.'" Vetterli was referring to a type of underwear worn by Mormons.

142 *"alert, intelligent, well-acquainted with":* James C. Ellsworth FBI file.

143 *his diary of the case:* The diary was provided to the author courtesy of the Ellsworth family.

143 *"He at this time feels":* Sebold personal FBI file.

146 *"he would not go through":* Ibid.

151 *both of her late parents:* Stein family genealogy provided to the author by a distant relation of Ms. Stein's, Alice Ra'anan.

152 *"official Washington's first fascist family":* "Official Washington's First Fascist Family," *Friday* magazine, March 21, 1941.

153 *in a memo he sent:* J. E. Hoover memo to Brigadier General Watson, OF 10-b, Justice Department, FBI Reports, 1939–40, 34, FDR Library, Hyde Park, NY.

157 *workforce that had doubled in:* Sperry Gyroscope Company Papers, Series II, Box 35, Hagley Museum and Library, Wilmington, DE.

157 Time *magazine in article upon:* "Profits and Secrets," *Time*, September 4, 1939.

157 *he later wrote from prison:* Copies of Everett Roeder's prison writings were provided to the author courtesy of the Roeder family.

CHAPTER NINE: A VILE RACE OF QUISLINGS

163 *"Knox brought up the question":* Henry L. Stimson Diaries, vols. 29–34, 1939–41, Reel 6, entry for July 16, 1940, 14–15, Sterling Memorial Library, Yale University.

163 *"No one outside the FBI":* Gentry, *J. Edgar Hoover,* 212.

164 *The* New Republic *wondered if:* Francis MacDonnell, *Insidious Foes: The Axis Fifth Column and the American Home Front* (Guilford, CT: Lyons Press, 2004), 172.

167 *"what appears definitely to be":* Regin Schmidt, *Red Scare: FBI and the Origins of Anticommunism in the United States, 1919–1943* (Copenhagen: Museum Tusculanum Press, University of Copenhagen, 2000), 357.

169 *$2.2 billion for the year:* Laurence S. Seidman, *Automatic Fiscal Policies to Combat Recessions* (Armonk, NY: M. E. Sharpe, 2003), 212.

169 *"authorize the necessary investigative agencies":* Weiner, *Enemies: A History of the FBI*, 87–88.

171 *"to have more guts":* Organization—German American Bund, Fiorello La Guardia Papers, Municipal Archives of New York City, Roll 0150.

172 *"so unbelievable as to be":* Julian Jackson, *The Fall of France: The Nazi Invasion of 1940* (Oxford and New York: Oxford University Press, 2003), 3.

175 *wrote Richard L. Millen, a:* Agent Millen's essay on the establishment of the radio station was provided to the author courtesy of Mr. Millen's son, Jim.

180 *"the same old song and":* Joseph E. Persico, *Roosevelt's Secret War: FDR and World War II Espionage* (New York: Random House, 2001), 52.

181 *"the article mentioned might fall":* Franklin D. Roosevelt, *F.D.R.: His Personal Letters* (New York: Duell, Sloan, and Pearce, 1947–50), 2:1036–37.

182 *"Without making any specific admission":* J. E. Hoover memo to Brigadier General Watson, OF 10-b, Justice Department, FBI Reports, 1939–40, 153, FDR Library, Hyde Park, NY.

183 *"is not adapted for high":* Sperry Gyroscope Company Papers, Series III, Box 32, Hagley Museum and Library, Wilmington, DE.

183 *"Knox brought up the question":* Stimson Diaries, previously cited.

183 *the revelation that he had handed:* Tizard Diary, August 25, 1940, entry, Papers of Sir Henry Tizard, Imperial War Museum, London. "The President was very nice, a most attractive personality," wrote Sir Henry. "He said he was going to get his draft bill for conscription through Congress but it would probably lose him the election in November. However that 'didn't matter.' He talked generalities, except that he explained that the withholding of the Nordem ?? [sic] bombsight was largely political and that if he could get any evidence that the Germans had it, or something like it, he would release it to us."

NOTES

184 *that Churchill approved a plan:* Zimmerman, *Top Secret Exchange*, 70, 82.

184 *the resonant cavity magnetron tube:* Jennet Conant, *Tuxedo Park: A Wall Street Tycoon and the Secret Palace of Science That Changed the Course of World War II* (New York: Simon and Schuster, 2002), 182.

CHAPTER TEN: AND YOU BE CAREFUL

185 *"has undercover agents actually participating":* McJimsey, *Documentary History of Roosevelt Presidency*, 32:112–20.

186 *"What do you fellows suggest?":* Friedemann quote from Art Ronnie interview, November 29, 1974.

190 *The months-long bombardment campaign:* Irving, *Rise and Fall of the Luftwaffe*, 106–7; and Richard Overy, *The Battle of Britain: The Myth and the Reality* (New York: W. W. Norton, 2000), 95.

192 *"This is nasty business," Berle:* Odgen Hammond folder, Box 57, Adolf Berle Papers, FDR Library, Hyde Park, NY.

192 *Hans Ritter, the affable younger:* Hans Ritter would flee the United States before the FBI had gathered enough evidence to hold him.

CHAPTER ELEVEN: ROOM 627

200 *via this method totaling $16,500:* All told, Sebold received some $22,000 from Ast Hamburg.

200 *The first visitor was the:* It was the first of eighty-one meetings hosted by Sebold in Room 627. Batvinis, *Origins of FBI Counterintelligence*, 249.

201 *His gang included:* Among the German-born aircraft technicians that Carl Reuper sought to recruit was Walter Nipkin, who promptly informed the FBI and became the second double agent in the case (and in the history of the Bureau). As it happens, Nipkin was a native of Mülheim, Germany. Asked at the trial if he had met Sebold, he said he had. They had played together as children but hadn't seen each other since.

202 *He neglected to mention that:* Batvinis, *Origins of FBI Counterintelligence*, 207–25.

204 *Fed up with Ast Hamburg's:* Saul Kelly, *The Lost Oasis: The Desert War and the Hunt for Zerzura—The True Story Behind* The English Patient (Boulder, CO: Westview Books, 2002), 160–74.

204 *in America and Great Britain:* Of his spies in Great Britain, the record was not good. Operation Lena, Ast Hamburg's attempt to insert agents in preparation for Sea Lion, was an unmitigated disaster. "Of the twenty-five German spies sent to Britain between September 3 and November 12, 1940, all but one was caught (the lone evader shot himself); five were executed; fifteen were imprisoned; and four became double agents, the first recruits of what would grow into a substantial army of deceivers." Ben Macintyre, *Double Cross: The True Story of the D-Day Spies* (New York: Crown, 2012), 36.

206 *"Our blessings from the whole":* David M. Kennedy, *Freedom from Fear: The American People in Depression and War, 1929–1945* (New York and Oxford: Oxford University Press, 2004), 476.

214 *prevented from appearing before a:* Batvinis, *Origins of FBI Counterintelligence,* 252–53.

215 *at least his newest medium bombers:* Corum, *Luftwaffe,* 269; and Horst Boog, "German Air Intelligence in the Second World War," in *Intelligence and Miltary Operations,* ed. Michael Handel (London and Portland, OR: F. Cass, 1990).

215 *"In attacking the Soviet Union":* Heinkel, *Stormy Life,* 200.

217 *"The old devil sat there":* From an interview with former special agent Richard L. Johnson conducted by Art Ronnie, November 25, 1974.

CHAPTER TWELVE: THE TRUSTED MAN

222 *"of the biggest spy ring":* Published in the *Daily Mirror* on July 12, 1941.

223 *Thomsen, wrote a blistering telegram: Documents on German Foreign Policy,* series D, 8:98–99.

224 *a five-page response stamped:* Document #270473-77, Politisches Archiv des Auswärtiges Amt, Berlin.

225 *Lang had played a pivotal:* In his memoir, Ernst Heinkel writes that the problem of German horizontal bombers' hitting "the target with any degree of accuracy" was "solved only in 1938–39 when a German fitter who worked for the Norden factory in New York betrayed the secret of the bombsight to the Luftwaffe." Heinkel, *Stormy Life,* 162

On May 9, 1945, the day after Nazi Germany's unconditional surrender, US occupation forces interviewed Herbert Kortum, the chief bombsight engineer for the Carl Zeiss company, which provided precision instruments for the Luftwaffe. "He answered the questions put to him but actually volunteered very little information of his own accord," wrote a Captain James Harris. Kortum, an ideological Nazi who was a member of the SS for a time, denied any knowledge of a German effort to duplicate the Norden bombsight. Headquarters Air Technical Service Command in Europe, Director of Technical Services, APO 633, report of visit to the Carl Zeiss Factory at Jena, Germany, May 9, 1945, submitted by Captain James Harris to the Director of Intelligence, Headquarters USSTAF; Dolores L. Augustine, *Red Prometheus: Engineering and Dictatorship in East Germany, 1945–1990* (Cambridge: The MIT Press, 2007), 134.

228   *"The* Greer *continued tracking the":* Donald E. Schmidt, *The Folly of War: American Foreign Policy, 1898–2005* (New York: Algora Publishing, 2005), 174.

231   *"were just suckers for a":* Ronnie, *Counterfeit Hero,* 308.

232   *"one man in the USA":* Statement by General Major Lahousen, 109/51, Record Group 226, National Archives, College Park, MD.

237   *"Necessity for Safeguarding Security":* General Records of the Department of the Navy, Secretary of the Navy/CNO Formerly Classified Correspondence, Box 254, Record Group 80, National Archives, College Park, MD.

244   *Agent Johnson said the FBI:* From an interview with former special agent Richard L. Johnson conducted by Art Ronnie, November 25, 1974.

245   *"I don't care much about":* Arnold Krammer, *Undue Process: The Untold Story of America's German Alien Internees* (London; Boulder, CO; and Lanham, MD: Rowman and Littlefield, 1997), 32.

EPILOGUE

253   *"On account of the war":* Ronnie, *Counterfeit Hero,* 308.

255   *Alien Enemy Control Unit hearing:* Krammer, *Undue Process,* 31–37.

256   *In total, 10,905 ethnic Germans:* Ibid., 34.

257   *"Now, Fritz Schroeder was not":* Case File 2017C: *U.S. v. Fritz Schroeder, et. al.,* Criminal Case Files, US District Court for the District of New Jersey, Newark Term, Record Group 21, National Archives at New York City.

257   *Although the FBI uncovered:* See David Kahn, *Hitler's Spies: German Military Intelligence in World War II* (New York: Macmillan, 1978).

257   *"our Axis undercover enemies have":* MacDonnell, *Insidious Foes,* 182.

258   *"have been associated with any"*: Charles McClain, ed., *The Mass Internment of Japanese Americans and the Quest for Legal Redress* (New York: Garland, 1994), 39.

258   *After working at the US Army's*: Sebold personal FBI file.

260   *Stories spread that the bombsight's*: Albert L. Pardini, *The Legendary Secret Norden Bombsight* (Atglen, PA: Schiffer Military History, 1999), 274–79.

261   *The recommended method was with*: McFarland, *America's Pursuit of Precision Bombing*, 155.

261   Collier's *magazine ran*: Stephen Budiansky, *Air Power: The Men, Machines, and Ideas That Revolutionized War, from Kitty Hawk to Gulf War II* (New York: Viking, 2004), 286.

262   *"We should never allow the"*: McFarland, *America's Pursuit of Precision Bombing*, 168.

263   *"the basic American principle of"*: Ibid., 184.

265   *"It would have destroyed him"*: Ibid., 209.

266   *the likes of Klaus Fuchs*: John Earl Haynes and Harvey Klehr, *Venona: Decoding Soviet Espionage in America* (New Haven, CT: Yale University Press, 1999), 333.

271   *"framed up by a dirty"*: Ronnie, *Counterfeit Hero*, 313.

271   *"the tragedy and suffering which"*: Ibid., 316.

272   *"I would certainly like to"*: Ibid., 320, 325.

272   *"the irresponsibility and untrustworthiness"* of: Folder 16, Box 423, William Langer Papers, Chester Fritz Library, University of North Dakota.

273   *of Germany's popular newsweekly* Stern: One of the reporters on the *Stern* piece was Günter Peis, who published a chapter about the Sebold case in *Hitler's Spies and Saboteurs: Based on the German Secret Service War Diary of General Lahousen* (New York: Henry Holt, 1958), 19–41. The book was cowritten with Charles Wighton. The authors claim that Canaris and Lahousen were summoned to Hitler's side following the announcement of the arrests in the Duquesne case. "There was the usual preliminary shouting and weeping," they write. "Then Hitler, working up to the climax of his rage, demanded to know how Canaris 'explained this treachery of a German-American.'"
    "How is it possible, Herr Admiral?" screamed Hitler, the authors claimed. "How could it occur? I demand an explanation."

274   *Sebold was appalled*: The Bureau quotations for the remainder of this chapter come from Sebold personal FBI file.

PHOTO CREDITS

INDEX

INDEX

bombsights
films and novels on, 260–61
Lang's spying involving, 3, 27–28,
44, 48, 72, 137, 160–61, 182, 183,
206, 222, 225, 230, 232, 237–38,
241–42, 254, 260, 272
Luftwaffe's need for improvements
to, 12, 37, 38–39, 44, 48, 118–19,
137, 183, 225
from Norden , 26, 28, 37, 44, 48, 109,
118, 137, 157, 180, 181–84, 187,
197, 206, 215, 222, 225, 230, 231,
237–38, 241–42, 254, 260, 261–62,
272, 317n, 319–20n
Sebold's knowledge of, 137–38
from Sperry, 99–100, 157, 184, 188,
197, 224, 261
trial testimony on, 230, 237–38, 241–
42, 254, 260
wartime use of, 261–63
Borah, William, 108
Borchers, Hans, 94
boycotts, 289–91n, 294n
Bremen (ship), 17, 42, 81, 116–17, 217, 287n
Bridges, Styles, 181
Brooklyn Eagle, 231, 310n
Bruder, Gallus, 64
Brundage, Avery, 296n
Büchner, Lorenz, 65
Bund der Freunde des Neuen
Deutschlands (Association of the
Friends of the New Germany),
287n, 289n, 291–93n, 304n, 306n,
307n
Burke, John W., 54
Busch, Kate Moog, 42, 76–78
Byers, Mortimer W., 2, 5–6, 229, 234,
236, 239, 248–49, 253, 259, 272
Byoir, Carl, 306n

Camerer, Shirley, 280
Camp, Florence, 131
Camp Siegfried, Yaphank, Long Island,
19, 294–95,
Canaris, Wilhelm, 22, 95, 224, 225, 232,
321n

Carl Norden Inc. *See* Norden Inc.
Centerport, Long Island, radio station,
175, 197, 202–3, 219, 232, 233
Central Intelligence Agency (CIA), 223
Chamberlain, Neville, 68–72, 106, 107,
115, 117, 120, 124, 168
Chicago Daily Times, 19, 21, 296n
Christian Front, 91, 129, 140, 167, 172, 187
Churchill, Winston, 71, 166, 168, 171,
183, 184, 207, 210, 226
Clausing, Heinrich, 208
Cogswell, Virginia, 131
Collier's magazine, 130, 261
Confessions of a Nazi Spy (film), 90
Conger, Edward A., 209
Connelly, Earl J., 186, 202, 219, 226, 229
Connolly, Sean, 211, 212, 214, 221
Consolidated Aircraft Corporation, 85,
103
Coughlin, Father Charles, 91, 93, 94–95,
111
Coughlinites, 94, 129, 140, 172, 187, 230
Cummings, Homer, 73, 75
Czechoslovakia, German planning for
invasion of, 38, 44–47, 67–69, 71,
72, 105–6, 107

DAB. *See* German-American Vocational
League
Daily Worker, 53, 129, 287n
Daladier, Édouard, 71, 72
Danzig, *Anschluss* of, 107, 108, 115,
118–19
Dasch, George, 256
Day, Beth, 286n
Denmark, invasion of, 166, 178, 180
Dewey, Thomas E., 95
Dickstein, Samuel, 305–6n, 307–8n
Dieckhoff, Hans, 50, 74
Dies, Martin, 51–52, 73, 94
Dies Committee, 51–52, 72–73, 94, 209,
307n
Dix, George C., 79–80
DNB News Agency, 50, 107
Donegan, Thomas, 237
Donovan, William "Wild Bill," 223

326

INDEX

INDEX

INDEX

INDEX

INDEX

ABOUT THE AUTHOR

Peter Duffy is the author of *The Bielski Brothers* and *The Killing of Major Denis Mahon: A Mystery of Old Ireland*. He writes regularly for the *New York Times*, the *Wall Street Journal*, *New York*, the *New Republic*, *Slate*, and many other outlets. He lives in New York City with his wife and daughter.